Discipline Through Virtue

The Pilgrim Mother

"They brought up their families in sturdy virtue and a living faith in God without which nations perish."

Illustrations: Katherine Myers
Printing: Gilliland Printing, Inc.
          215 N. Summit
          Arkansas City, KS 67005

DEDICATION

To my wife and sweetheart, Valerie, who served as a wise counselor and kept our home together during the stressful times that accompanied the composition of this book. To my children for their patience. To Max and Bonnie Mortensen, who provided numerous contributions and encouragement throughout the project.

ACKNOWLEDGMENTS

I wish to acknowledge Lockheed-Martin Technologies who provided financial support when this book was no more than an idea.

I also acknowledge the following individuals who helped launch this project with their support and input: David Peck, Ed.D., Superintendent, Pocatello Schools; Al Blacklock, Principal, Cole Elementary; Michael T. Johnson, Director, Idaho Juvenile Corrections Department; Elwood Wilson, Superintendent, Rigby Schools; James L. DePaepe, Ph.D., Dean, Idaho State University, College of Education; Mike Friend, Ph.D., Executive Director of Idaho Association of School Administrators; Darrel Burbank, Principal, Garfield Elementary; Christine Donnell, Assistant Superintendent, Meridian Schools; Gerald Health, Teacher, Snake River Jr. High; Brent W. Orr, Superintendent, Madison Schools; Edward L. Davis, Ed.D., Assistant Superintendent, Boise Schools; Steven C. Norton, Ed., D., Superintendent, Blackfoot Schools, Michael B. Sessions, Principal, Central Elementary; Alan H. Smith, Executive Director, Idaho School Boards Association; Darrell Loosle, Deputy State Superintendent; and Richard Adair, Superintendent, Burns Oregon Schools.

Finally, I acknowledge the following educators and parents: Nanette Gee, Mary Louise Barney, Laurie Orduno, Helen Stewart, Gwen Kerbs, Carol Call, Cindy Romney, Scott Ferguson, Lance Lindley, Karalee Ricks, Toni Gee, and Mike Call, who reviewed the evolving manuscript and offered helpful and timely input.

TABLE OF CONTENTS

Discipline Through Virtue - The Process

Forging a Pathway to the Heart - Tag along on a teacher's journey to discover a means to touch young peoples' hearts and minds. Hopefully, you will identify with her mounting excitement as she clears away the underbrush obscuring her vision. Enjoy the companionships she cultivates and join them as they negotiate the streams, cliffs and ravines that block the path. This two-hour journey is time well spent because few destinations can be appreciated and understood without just experiencing the trail. You will value the insights and strategies that await you along the way. The means to build character in our young people is too important a journey to pass up.

Discipline Through Virtue - The Techniques

Twenty-six obstructions to learning are listed and defined. They range in severity from those which disrupt classrooms and entire schools to those which suffocate the individual learner.
An exhaustive cross-reference that matches appropriate entries from <u>The Book of Virtues</u> with the disciplinary dilemmas they are intended to address. Entries include brief descriptions, key points and questions to stimulate discussion.
Twenty-five follow-up activities are listed to assist in implanting the virtues as an integral part of the young person's character.

FREQUENTLY ASKED QUESTIONS CONCERNING
DISCIPLINE THROUGH VIRTUE

What is <u>Discipline Through Virtue</u>? It's a book that teaches a disciplinary approach that uses stories, discussions and follow-up activities and provides the means for timely and effective use of its techniques.

Is <u>Discipline Through Virtue</u> intended to replace existing disciplinary plans? No. It replaces the tendency to lecture or sermonize each time a teacher or parent wishes to make a point. Existing management disciplinary plans remain unaffected.

Is <u>Discipline Through Virtue</u> another curriculum? No. It is a disciplinary tool designed to improve the learning environment. Its use is limited to those occasions when a teacher or parent chooses to deal with a specific problem. It does emphasize character virtues as it treats the root causes of inappropriate behavior or ineffective learning..

Does <u>Discipline Through Virtue</u> impose values on young people? No, but it does expose the young people to virtues that society has accepted as keys to happy and productive lives. The approach is designed for self-discovery of these virtues after being exposed to the stories, discussions and follow-up activities.

Is <u>Discipline Through Virtue</u> based on research studies? No. The basis for the approach is grounded in common sense and experience. History provides numerous examples of great teachers who used stories and discussions to shape behavior. <u>Discipline Through Virtue</u> formalizes this time-tested approach and provides a practical means for its timely use.

Will <u>Discipline Through Virtue</u> work equally well for all teachers and parents? No. The best results will be accomplished by those who exercise the best judgment, creativity and commitment.

Will <u>Discipline Through Virtue</u> work for all young people? No, if success is measured in terms of observable behavior. Teachers and parents will still need to manage the more challenging of our young people. It will work for the great majority if success is measured on a long-term basis where time allows the subtle, internal changes to manifest themselves through improved behavior.

WHY THE NEED FOR <u>DISCIPLINE THROUGH VIRTUE</u>?

Disciplining through virtue is an alternative to the lectures and sermons that have served as the principal means to teach correct behavior in the schools. The technique gets at the root causes of a disciplinary dilemma. How? By instilling those virtues whose absence or lack of influence allows problems to surface and escalate. In essence, the technique will provide the young person with the personal resources (character virtues) needed to confront today's challenges and temptations.

Disciplining through virtue is not designed to replace the management considerations of discipline. However, if properly executed, this approach will greatly reduce the use of the myriad of management plans practiced in today's schools and homes.

<u>Discipline Through Virtue</u> will greatly reduce the amount of time teachers currently spend on discipline problems. *This increases the amount of time the teacher will have available for teaching the basic curriculum* required by the school and expected by parents and society.

This disciplinary approach is appropriate in both the school and home settings. It can be adapted to fit the circumstances and the maturity levels of those involved. The nature of the approach allows for easy adaptation in its choice of stories, discussion topics and follow-up activities.

Disciplining through virtue fosters the exchange of impressions and ideas between the adult and young person. This allows for the mutual understanding required to work out long-term solutions rather than short-term fixes.

<u>Disciplining Through Virtue</u> is intended to reduce the contention that arises when adults and young people engage their energies in adversarial relationships rather than cooperative learning exchanges. Reduction in contention results in increased learning which is the intent of both the school and home.

BRIEF OVERVIEW OF DISCIPLINING THROUGH VIRTUE

In **Phase One** the teacher (or parent) turns to page 78 in <u>Discipline Through Virtue</u> for a listing of the twenty-six disciplinary dilemmas treated in the book. Here the teacher determines which of the dilemmas most approximates the behavior she wishes to target by examining the descriptions that accompany each dilemma. Once the dilemma is determined, the teacher refers to the page numbers provided for quick access to the appropriate ready-reference section in <u>Discipline Through Virtue</u>. (Note to reader: The terms 'teacher and student' reflect school situations. The terms 'parent and child' can easily be substituted to reflect home considerations.)

In **Phase Two** the teacher locates her dilemma in the ready-reference section and scans the available options. These options are stories, poems, fables, etc. from William J. Bennett's <u>The Book of Virtues</u> that deal with the disciplinary dilemma. Each option contains a brief description of the plot, a recommended target audience, an estimation of the option's length, key points and suggested questioning strategies. The teacher selects the options that have the best likelihood of assisting her in her disciplining through virtue and then confirms her choices by reviewing the options in their entirety.

In **Phase Three** the teacher determines when and how the option should be introduced and discussed. Care should be taken that the option not be offered too close to the discipline dilemma, lest the students make the connection and resist the intended message. Choice should be made to read orally, silently read or have the option presented in the deliverer's own words.

In **Phase Four** the teacher reads the option from <u>The Book of Virtues</u> with the class. She then facilitates an analysis of the option with carefully chosen questions. The initial discussion should address the message of the option in its original setting (i.e.; King Alfred's time). This reduces the likelihood that the discussion will be taken as personal chastisement and provides a climate where students feel free to express their thoughts. The less direct involvement by the teacher, the better. It is hoped that the discussion will yield a shared understanding of the message of the story and a greater commitment to a particular virtue.

In **Phase Five** the teacher will shift the discussion from the story's original context to one that relates to the day-to-day circumstances the students live in. Teachers need to focus on a school context while parents focus on the home. The transfer from one context to the other may occur naturally or it may require the careful involvement of the teacher. This involvement should be restricted to questions posed to the class rather than direct connections offered by the teacher. Again, caution should be taken to reduce the likelihood that the discussion or conclusions be taken as personal chastisement or just another lecture from the teacher.

In **Phase Six** the teacher assists the students in determining follow-up activities. Such things as writing projects, skits, collection of real-life illustrations, etc. can be productive. The extent of student self-direction should be determined by the circumstances of the dilemma and the maturity levels of the young people. See page 229 - Considerations for Follow-up Activities.

In **Phase Seven** the teacher assesses the progress to date to determine what, if any, additional follow-up should occur. A second or a third selection from The Book of Virtues is a consideration as well as additional follow-up activities as described in Phase Six.

In **Phase Eight** the teacher determines or assists students in determining means for students to practice the desirable behavior (virtue) that has been the focus of the learning. Options would include simulations, new class expectations and practices, incentive programs, etc.

In **Phase Nine** the teacher employs whatever means she can to keep the desirable behavior in the conscious thought of the student. This requires imagination and creativity. The eventual goal of Discipline Through Virtue is to foster the means whereby the desirable virtues become habits. The longer the student's positive exposure to the virtue, the greater the likelihood that it becomes a personal resource, readily accessed when needed.

MODEL SYNTAX

PREPARATION	
Phase One	Determine the disciplinary dilemma to be targeted. See Disciplinary Dilemma's pages 78-81.
Phase Two	Locate appropriate dilemma in the ready-reference section of Discipline Through Virtue, select option(s) from The Book of Virtues that will assist in disciplining through virtue and review options
Phase Three	Determine when and how the option should be introduced and discussed
LESSON	
Phase Four	Read the option from The Book of Virtues with the class. Facilitate discussion on the message of the option using the actual context of the option
Phase Five	Shift discussion from the original context to one that relates to the day-to-day circumstances of the student
Phase Six	Assist students in determining follow-up activities. See Considerations for Follow-up Activities pages 229-231.
FOLLOW-UPS	
Phase Seven	Assess progress in solving the disciplinary dilemma and determine if additional follow-up is needed
Phase Eight	Determine or assist students in determining means to practice the desirable behavior (virtue)
Phase Nine	Employ whatever means available to keep the desirable behavior in the conscious thought of students

Discipline
Through
Virtue

The Process

Chapter One
Lost in the Forest

"Without courage there cannot be truth, and without truth there can be no other virtue."   Sir Walter Scott

CHAPTER ONE

Joan Walker glanced up at the clock. A slight wave of anxiety surfaced, but she quickly dismissed it. She resisted the question that recently had been plaguing her, "No, I'm not becoming a clock watcher." She smiled as a second thought materialized. "Now I'm talking to myself."

The clock read 3:30. Joan put aside the papers she was grading and glanced around her classroom. She took in the twenty-six desks that were symmetrically arranged and made a mental note to think about something new and different for the start of next week. It felt like Friday, only worse. Something was eating at her, and as of yet she couldn't place it in terms or images that would allow her to deal with it.

As her eyes continued to roam, she locked in on her teaching certificate. A second smile surfaced, only this one was spontaneous and genuine. She had worked hard for that piece of parchment, and the care she had taken with matting and framing demonstrated that pride. Her eye spotted a slight accumulation of dust, and this was never tolerated, even when she felt as tired as she did now. She was one who rarely missed a detail, and this talent had served her well in her eight years of teaching. As she reached for the dust rag conveniently placed in her left drawer, her thoughts leaped back three years to the day she first secured the certificate and frame to this particular wall. A momentary sense of comfort surfaced as the details of that day played through her mind. She had just learned of her sixth grade assignment in the new school and was hurriedly preparing for her students to arrive. Right or wrong she considered this new placement as a promotion for the successful years she had spent at Lincoln. Pam Phillips, her Lincoln colleague and close friend, had taken the time to assist her in her move. The new school hadn't been completed until one week into the start of the new school year, and Pam's kind assistance had transformed an otherwise arduous task into an enjoyable experience. Joan and Pam had been classroom neighbors for five years and had developed a close working relationship. There was little that one didn't know about the other. Joan thought of the hours the two had spent hashing over their school days, exchanging a good idea and, on occasion, crying on each other's shoulder.

Things had changed in the three years. Joan rarely had opportunity to see her friend, and the few times they did cross paths were usually at activities that permitted little time for visits. Again her eyes roved about the room, and each desk, display or teaching tool conjured up a memory. The smile quickly fled as the negative impressions began to gang up on the more pleasant recollections. Finally her thoughts focused on the two back seats in the third row, and she was dismayed to note that the all too familiar quickening of her pulse had returned. She had assigned Scott and Lance to these seats as a last

1

act of desperation. Every other placement had proven disastrous, and she had hoped that their relative isolation would curtail some of their more disruptive tactics.

Her feeling of despondency deepened as she felt a pit in her stomach gaining strength, and she knew the inevitable headache was soon to follow. Her thoughts on Scott and Lance soon moved to other students and other concerns until everything meshed into a confused blur of causes and effects. Joan felt somehow responsible for her recent classroom problems, but her hours and days of introspection had failed to come up with concrete explanations. She realized that she was on overload with no end in sight.

Her thoughts were interrupted by a tapping sound. Joan glanced up to see Mary Ashcraft gently closing the door behind her. Mrs. Ashcraft had been the building principal at Roosevelt since its inception. Mary had been handpicked by the district office to guide the school in its infancy, and she in turn had handpicked Joan Walker. The two had shared common philosophies, and over the course of their three-year relationship had developed some close ties.

Mrs. Ashcraft knew something was bothering Joan and had chosen this particular afternoon to see if she could help in some way. Mary was never one for small talk and came immediately to the point. "Joan, something is wrong, and I can't stand idly by and watch you suffer."

Joan managed a smile, "You mean to tell me that my feelings are that transparent." Her smile wasn't genuine, and she knew it. Worse still, she knew Mary knew it.

"I'm afraid so. I began to figure something was amiss when you would pass me in the hall and barely acknowledge me. At first I thought I had somehow offended you, but eventually I came to realize that you were so preoccupied with your thoughts that little else mattered."

"I apologize for my behavior, and no, it was nothing personal," Joan confessed. Her smile was little more than a slight upturn of the lips, but this time it was genuine.

"Well, are you going to confide in me or must I force the issue by doubling your recess duty?" Mrs. Ashcraft had the ability to put people at ease, and Joan responded as she had hoped.

Laughing, Joan answered, "Taken in that light, I'd be delighted to talk." The smile quickly disappeared as Joan added, "I really don't know if you can do any good. Maybe time will work things out or maybe . . ." Joan stopped herself abruptly as she realized what she was about to disclose.

Mary Ashcraft rarely missed anything, and this instance proved no exception. She confided gently, "I've had times in my career when a few cylinders were misfiring. Come to think of it," she continued, "there were times my starter was broken."

Joan knew enough about Mary Ashcraft and automobiles to grasp the fact that her principal had managed to figure out what was bothering her. This comforted Joan. She needed answers, and a faint glimmer of hope began to take root.

Mary used everything she had learned about counseling to convince her colleague that her tomorrows would be better times. She reminded Joan of her past successes, pointed out her best qualities, even offered to give her some time off to visit other schools.

Unfortunately, Joan anticipated every bit of counsel Mrs. Ashcraft offered, and this had the effect of diminishing its worth. Joan had already covered each of these points in her countless hours of introspection. The fact that Joan was hearing these points from someone other than herself failed to impress her. As the minutes passed, Joan felt the glimmer of hope fade until it extinguished itself completely.

None of this was lost on Mary. She knew when she was being tuned out, and it saddened her to see this wonderful teacher so determined to give up trying. Mary was about to give up herself when a thought struck her. She asked, "Would you give me a minute to retrieve something from my office?"

Joan simply nodded her head, choosing to say nothing that might offend her well-intentioned principal.

Mary soon returned grasping a small piece of paper with some scribbling on one side. She wasted no time getting to her point. "I first heard this at the graduation ceremony for my youngest daughter. I was so impressed that I jotted it down and added a few thoughts of my own. It's now in typed form for readability." Mary then handed Joan a second piece of paper whose contents were masked by a stapled fold. Pointing to the first paper she stated, "After first reading and pondering this, remove the staple to see what this second piece has to say." Mrs. Ashcraft surprised the teacher by excusing herself without another word.

Joan's interest was piqued, and she wasted no time getting to her task. She found herself viewing a short excerpt that included what appeared to be a list of accomplishments.

Some people find their road to accomplishment rocky at best. They know what they wish to accomplish but are met with opposition that seems unrelenting. Consider the hapless politician who amassed this record:

> *Failed in business*
> *Defeated for Legislature*
> *Second failure in business*
> *Suffered nervous breakdown*

Defeated for Speaker
Defeated for Elector
Defeated for Congress
Defeated for Senate
Defeated for Vice President
Defeated for Senate

Who would be foolish enough to keep trying in spite of so many failures? Who in his right mind would continue to expose himself to the anguish that accompanies each new defeat? Is it now reasonable to expect such an individual to back away from trying lest the hurt become too heavy a burden to bear?

It took Joan less than a minute to read the material, but her reaction was an altogether different matter. She leaped from one impression to another with little closure to her thoughts. She vacillated from thinking the man a hopeless dreamer, to admiring his tenacity, to determining that some people don't know when to quit. The one conclusion she held firm was her conviction that this track record must have caused a burden difficult to bear. Mrs. Walker even found herself pitying the man and feeling a conscious kinship.

Finally, she turned to the second piece of paper and removed the staple. It, too, was typed.

Some people keep going, even when they fail in their endeavors time and time again. TO SUCH PEOPLE BELONGS THE WORLD.

ABRAHAM LINCOLN:

Failed in business	*1831*
Defeated for Legislature	*1832*
Second failure in business	*1833*
Suffered nervous breakdown	*1836*
Defeated for Speaker	*1838*
Defeated for Elector	*1840*
Defeated for Congress	*1843*
Defeated for Senate	*1855*
Defeated for Vice President	*1856*
Defeated for Senate	*1858*
Elected President of the United States	**November 6, 1860**

Pam was visibly shaken by what she had just read. Many of the impressions that had surfaced from the first piece had now returned to haunt her. Her feelings moved from guilt to confusion to hope. She began to feel a quiet resolve begin to take shape as she thought of her obstacles in light of what this man had chosen to endure.

A second thought struck her with the impact one might liken to a brick striking a pane of glass. "I feel the resolve I have sought for months, but I'm not sure I understand why," she stammered to herself. "How could a simple story have this much power to redirect my thoughts?" Joan shook her head in wonderment as she recalled how Mary's well-intentioned words of counsel had failed to faze her in the least.

Chapter Two
Thunderstorms on the Horizon

"The virtue lies in the struggle, not in the prize."
Milnes

CHAPTER TWO

Joan's thoughts returned to her present circumstances, and the pit in her stomach began to take shape. Her determination to keep trying was a good beginning, but she still hadn't a clue as to how to proceed. She was facing some serious classroom problems, and everything she had tried had failed.

Her gaze again fixed on her certificate, and recollections of times past flooded her mind. Thoughts of Pam recurred, and the more she recalled, the more convinced she became that her former colleague was the one person who might help her find her answers. Joan spotted the district directory and paged to the section on Lincoln Elementary. As she dialed Lincoln, she hoped Pam was continuing her practice of using Friday afternoons for planning purposes. A sense of relief warmed her as she and Pam exchanged greetings. When chitchat of families, health and diets reached a logical stopping point, Pam moved the conversation to a more serious note. "I'm delighted you called. I've been thinking about you and realized how much I missed our Friday afternoon gab sessions. Something is wrong, isn't it. Remember how we could never mask those times when one or the other of us was struggling with a concern? Well, something is troubling you, and I sense a need to talk."

Joan laughed. "I guess things haven't really changed. You still read me like a book despite my best efforts at concealment. Could we talk soon?"

"How about now?" Pam offered. "Your place or mine?"

Joan thought a moment before answering. "Could we make it yours? Perhaps a return to Lincoln is the tonic I'm searching for."

"Sounds serious," Pam said gently. "Pick up some donuts at Saul's, and we'll have you good as new in a shake."

"Your confidence is admirable, but I suspect my difficulties might prove a greater challenge than you expect." Joan's voice sounded tired. "Anyway, I'll see you in about twenty minutes."

Pam eased the phone receiver down, bought two cans of diet pop and headed back to her classroom. Her thoughts returned to those days when she and Joan were close associates, but she hadn't a clue as to what might be wrong. Joan was a professional in every sense of the word and always had school matters in firm control. Pam remembered times when her friend needed a little advice or encouragement, but what teacher didn't on occasion. As Pam settled back at her desk, she made a mental note to slip back to her classroom on Saturday afternoon to prepare the history activity she had promised her students.

Joan arrived, donuts and all, and the two embraced as would be expected of two friends who hadn't seen each other for an extended period. As they stepped back to exchange smiles, Pam spotted a teardrop welling up in her friend's left eye. It moved her deeply, but she couldn't come up with an

6

appropriate thing to say. Joan, sensing the awkward tension, broke the ice with her best smile and an observation that each could do with a chocolate donut.

"So what's the problem?" Pam asked as she wiped her lap clean of crumbs. "I presume this runs deeper than a simple clash with a parent or a less than successful lesson activity."

Joan really didn't know where to start. Finally, she determined that the best course was to plow into the meat of the matter. "I've got a problem with a number of this year's students, and two in particular are causing me fits. I've always prided myself on the close relationship I develop with my students, but the past few years haven't been the same."

"How about giving me a 'for instance'?" Pam asked. "I can't imagine you having trouble relating to your students. You're going to have to convince me that something's wrong."

"Okay, I guess I could start with today's episode. Unfortunately it's pretty much a rerun of incidents that have seemed to plague me on a regular basis." Joan took a long swallow from her pop can and then started in.

> I have two boys who I've struggled with this entire school year. Their names are Scott and Lance. Things came to a head this afternoon following lunch. I could tell at a glance that there had been trouble during the lunch break. Sammy Hough, a large and awkward boy, looked on the verge of tears as he made his way straight to his desk. This was my first indication that something had happened. He and his few friends were usually first to the water fountain.
>
> Scott and Lance were the last to return to class, and despite the sound of the tardy bell, they still sauntered over to get a drink. All eyes followed the two as they slowly made their way back to their seats--that is, all eyes except Sammy's whose continued their focus downward. The room was unusually silent, but it was the kind of silence that was unsettling.

Joan stopped her narrative at this point to collect her thoughts. She fidgeted a moment with the tab on her pop can before directly addressing her friend. "Have you ever felt the sickening feeling that comes when you know you let someone down?"

Pam saw where this question was headed, and it upset her. She remembered an instance that was much like Joan's, and the memory of the episode still haunted her. "Yes," Pam stammered in what amounted to little more than a whisper.

Joan acknowledged this support with a slight softening of her expression and proceeded with her account.

7

I know the silence was directed at me. Everyone knew that this wasn't the first time Lance and Scott had humiliated Sammy. Everyone was also aware that I had taken a personal interest and had promised this poor boy that the bullying would stop. Now they were waiting to see how I was going to respond.

Glaring at the two boys, I noticed the hint of a sneer, and this was all it took to set me off. I felt that quickening of pulse that always develops when I sense an upcoming battle. I still had no idea what transpired, but I knew without hesitation that I had let Sammy down by failing to keep these two boys in check.

At this point Pam interrupted her friend by gesturing for an opportunity to speak. She asked, "How many times had you talked to Lance and Scott, and what did you say? I'm still not convinced that you were responsible for Sammy's misfortune!"

Joan was not to be put off in her self-incrimination. "I should have been able to protect that poor boy. I had talked to Lance and Scott no less than eight times. I took every approach I knew, but nothing sank in."

Pam raised her eyebrows as if to ask for examples. Her friend caught the gesture because she immediately proceeded to review all that she remembered about their exchanges. She ended by summing things up. "So you see I had tried appealing to their sense of justice, I tried having them walk in Sammy's shoes and I tried building them up as leaders who should set proper examples. Nothing worked because the incidents continued. Finally, I began telling them what behavior I expected of them and what I would do if they chose to ignore my guidelines."

"So you threatened them," Pam teased. This brought a smile to Joan's face as she nodded her head in agreement. Joan then added, "None of the punishments affected the two. If anything, they seemed to fuel their resolve. The whole thing became a game of how can we torment Sammy without leaving evidence of our guilt. Believe me Pam, these two play the game well." She concluded her point with the sad admission that all the while Sammy continued to suffer.

"Okay," Pam offered, "I have the picture up to this point. What had happened at recess and what did you do about it?"

Joan closed her eyes as if searching for an image and then continued her narrative.

I knew I had to act or I would lose all credibility with my class. The anger was beginning to build as I directed the class to read the first four pages of chapter twelve in their science text. I figured this would allow me the time I needed to deal with the boys. I then motioned to Scott and Lance to follow me out in the hall.

When we found ourselves alone, we glared at each other as a matador and bull might. Scott finally broke the eye contact by glancing down to the floor. This sort of response often identifies the guilty party, but in this case I wasn't sure. Scott's attention rarely focused on anything for more than a few moments. I wasn't surprised when he began fidgeting with his ballpoint pen.

My first impulse was to let them have it with both barrels, but I was still in control enough to recognize that I hadn't a clue to what they'd done. Looking Scott squarely in the eyes I asked, "Why was Sammy almost in tears?"

Lance assumed his customary role as spokesman and responded first. "We're not exactly sure, but don't blame it on us."

Scott broke in at this point. "He is probably going to tell you that I purposely tackled him in the soccer game. Well, I didn't, I was only going for the ball."

I was not convinced I was hearing the whole story, so I then asked, "Why did the entire class quiet down when you entered the room and then train their eyes on Sammy?" I was getting angrier, and I'm sure it showed.

Lance shrugged his shoulders and said, "Beats me. I only know that nothing really happened besides us defending ourselves. He started it."

"Started what!" I snapped. This unexpected disclosure was all that I needed to confirm my suspicions.

Lance immediately realized that he had already said too much. "Nothing," he muttered.

I then turned my attention back to Scott and asked him point blank, "Did either of you hurt him? What's Sammy going to say when I ask him the same question?"

Scott's gaze returned to the floor as he said, "I did nothing more to him than he did to me. He tried to push me, and I just pushed him back."

The two boys' attitudes were belligerent, and this had the effect of deepening my anger and frustration. I stared at the two of them and asked clearly, "Did either of you touch Sammy in a physical way that could not be considered as part of the game?"

They both nodded yes but not without Lance adding, "We hardly touched him, and we were only defending ourselves."

I then reminded them of one of the rules I had established and told them that they owed me their next two recesses. One of the two began to protest, and I immediately doubled their punishment. By this time we were all so angry that I ordered them to remain in the hall until I called for them. Just before I reentered the classroom I turned back, pointed my finger and threatened them with suspension if it happened again.

Pam, sensing her friend's tenseness, was about to suggest that they purchase a second pop when Joan lowered her head and confessed, "Then the day went from bad to disastrous."

The remark surprised her friend. Pam embarrassed herself by blurting out, "What could possibly have happened to make it any worse than it already was!" The slip caused them both to laugh, and much tension began to dissipate.

Joan continued her account but now in a more relaxed tone.

After dealing with the two boys, I marched back into the classroom. Don't ask me why, but my anger actually increased as I set my glare on the class. Thinking back on it, I suspect it was my pride telling me that the students should share in the fault. My mind quickly locked in on the numerous instances where Sammy's classmates failed to support their friend in his hours of need. I also recalled times when others aided Lance and Scott or acted out on their own.

"Pam, you know this isn't me, and yet at that moment I could see no other course than a frontal attack. The constant badgering from these two boys and the small but growing peer support was ruining the learning climate of my classroom. My heart was aching for Sammy and the dozen or so students who served as the unwilling victims. All their spark was gone, and they had ceased looking to me for help. You know that a student can't learn when his self-confidence and worth are lower than the baseboards in the classroom. Anyway, I then turned my indignation on the whole class. I covered how loyalty, friendship and kindness were essential for everyone's well-being. I explained about class unity and the need for courage when faced with adversity. I really got on the soapbox. What is so discouraging is that I quickly surmised that most of the students had tuned me out, yet I felt compelled to continue. You know how we always prided ourselves in fixing problems."

Pam nodded in acknowledgment, but said nothing.

"Well, I knew something was broken, and I was determined to fix it with the only things available at the time--the best words of counsel I could muster for the moment. Like with Lance and Scott, I concluded with a firm admonition that continued bullying from anyone would be met with stiff consequences. The rest of the afternoon was a complete waste. I had expended all my energies in what I had hoped was an appropriate fix to the problem. All it turned out to be was one more reason for the students to put further distance between themselves and their teacher. I'm at my wits end."

Silence followed for a period, and Pam took it as a cue that Joan was waiting for some response. Pam was identifying so acutely with her friend's situation that she had given no thought to how she might respond. She knew her friend too well to try to pass on simple platitudes or cheerleader encouragements. The two sat and stared at each other for what seemed like a lifetime before Pam finally broke the ice. "I think I have something to share that might prove helpful, but I need to first preface my comments with a caution. I don't share advice as I did in times past when the two of us took turns giving and receiving. Please be patient, and hopefully you will come to understand why I do what I do."

Joan looked up with a quizzical expression but did nothing but nod.

Pam stalled momentarily to gather her thoughts before starting in. She was going to deal with her friend as she had trained herself to deal with her students, and the thought both pleased and frightened her. She always felt this unnerving rush when she was about to chart new waters.

Chapter Three
Unforeseen Companionship

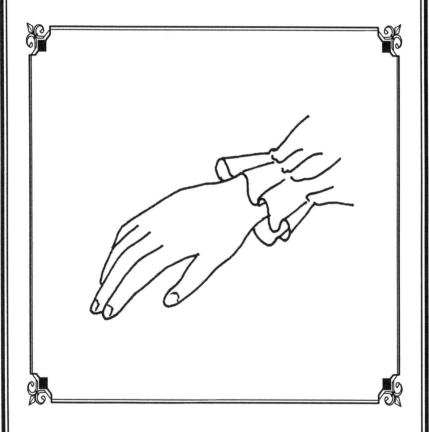

"In prosperity our friends know us; in adversity we know our friends." Churton Collins

CHAPTER THREE

"Joan," her friend began, "could I tell my own classroom story? Hopefully, it will serve as a helpful beginning. I'm sure you will have no trouble identifying with the situation." It was apparent that Joan's curiosity was piqued, and her anticipation appeared to have displaced a bit of the despondency she was feeling.

"I, too, had a classroom situation arise not that different from your own. It happened last October," Pam began. "Instead of Lance and Scott, I had Vicki and Janet. The two had been best friends since the first grade and frequently had difficulty distinguishing class time from free time. I'm the first to admit that I have little tolerance with disrespect, but you know that as well as I."

Joan smiled despite her determination to be miserable. She could still remember times when a student would touch just the right button, and Pam would lower the boom.

Pam noted her colleagues smile and continued on. "Anyway, these two always seemed to have something to say, particularly after first recess or lunch. You know how I allow for student interaction during class time, but I still insist that it not be conducted at a time or in a way that disrupts my learning environment. Well, on this particular morning, I had to caution the girls on three different occasions. The details aren't important, but suffice it to say that each instance caused a breach in my classroom momentum. I handled the first two episodes with my usual glance." Pam laughed and continued, "You remember the look! It's the one I practiced in the mirror. Apparently the girls refused to heed the warnings because the third disturbance fell close on the heels of incidence number two, and I felt my heart begin the pounding you so aptly described."

Joan's thoughts crept back to her own afternoon, and the pit in her stomach began to return. She silently resolved to put her disastrous afternoon on the back burner and returned her attention to her companion's account.

Pam closed her eyes as she scanned her memory for details. Continuing she said, "You have to understand that this problem had been building for weeks. Like you, I had numerous chats with the girls, and little change had occurred. I guess my own ego began to cloud my judgment because I began to react to incidents in a stronger fashion than circumstances normally called for. There is little doubt that the two girls were determined to have their way and were willing to match wits if required to do so."

It was Joan's turn to fish for details, and she was anxious to learn more of Vicki and her friend. "Give me an instance where you matched wits," she asked.

"Fair request," Pam conceded. "I'll tell you of a confrontation we had a couple of weeks prior to this particular day. Let me see if I can restrict myself to the important details." Pam closed her eyes in much the same way her friend had done and began.

We were working on a science unit that covered such things as conservation and protection of the environment. I had invited a representative from Fish and Game to cover the precautions that must be taken to preserve our nature trails. The class was especially involved in the discussion because we had planned a nature hike for the next day.

Joan gave her friend a look that urged her to cut out the background stuff and get right to the point. Apparently, the look was lost on Pam because she rattled on for two additional minutes before first mentioning the two girls. Finally she stated:

Here is where the problem began. The field agent was responding to questions when Suzy Roberts launched one of her off-the-wall questions. The class had gotten used to Suzy's whoppers except for my two young ladies. In this particular instance, Suzy asked if it was true that traps were set to punish hikers who refused to stay on the trails. Vicki and Janet saw this question as their opportunity to stir up the class. Vicki made some comment that I missed that got most of the class laughing. She then raised her hand in jest and announced that Suzy should be put in charge of keeping everyone on the path. This stirred the class all the more.

Janet removed what little was left of my classroom control by asking if those ensnared by the traps were then turned over to the police. Most of the students erupted into spontaneous laughter, and dozens of little conversations consumed the class. The poor field agent looked shocked, and Suzy was reduced to tears. I, needless to say, was embarrassed to death.

"What did you do?" Joan's question came out so sternly that it bordered on rudeness. Catching herself, she softened her response by adding quietly, "It must have been an unsettling experience."

"It was," Pam replied matter-of-factly. "I can laugh about it now, but at the time I was awfully mad."

Joan gave an empathetic look and again urged her friend to continue.

I responded pretty much as you had done with your two boys. I left the class to the poor man from Fish and Game and motioned for Janet and Vicki to follow me into the hall. As I lit into them, it dawned on me that the two were shocked that I would single them out for a lecture. They seemed to have little understanding that their comments had caused Suzy hurt, nor did they have any remorse over their disruption of the activity. Their anger mounted in direct proportion to my own. Frankly, I was appalled at what I perceived as a lack of feeling and told them as much.

Like you, I could see the wall going up, but I wasn't going to let a little thing like that get in my way. I was determined to have my say--to fix the problem as you so aptly described. It was at this point where my relationship with the girls really took a nose dive.

Joan said nothing for a few moments as she considered all that she had heard. She noticed the predictable quickening of her pulse as she broke the silence. "Thank you, that gives me a clearer picture. I apologize for the interruption," she then volunteered, "I know it's hard to switch from story to story. You were saying before the interruption that the two girls had just acted up for the third time in a single day, and you were preparing for a matching of wits."

Pam nodded in acknowledgment before continuing her account.

You also must understand that there was a second reason for my added concern. Vicki and Janet were popular young ladies, and their actions often served as catalysts. I picked up that other students were beginning to push this rule, and I began spending undue class time and energy in maintaining classroom control. Things came to a head the last period of the day as I was conducting a discussion on the Roman's tendency to allow a small measure of self-rule in their conquered territories. By their actions it was apparent that my two young ladies had more important items to discuss than Roman politics, and their antics were clearly disrupting the flow of my discussion.

Pam locked her eyes on Joan and declared, "I know exactly how you felt about Lance and Scott because that's where I was at the moment." Joan sensed that this was the critical juncture in her friend's story and anxiously awaited for details.

Chapter Four
North Star Appears

"The moral education of the young is the greatest need in our nation." *William J.Bennet*

CHAPTER FOUR

Pam reached over for a book entitled <u>Discipline Through Virtue</u> and turned to the last chapter. While paging forward she commented.

> I wanted desperately to deal with this disrespect immediately, and I don't mean that in a management way. No, I wanted to fix the problem permanently and leave no question in anyone's mind. Civilized behavior requires little more than simple respect, and these two were long overdue for a piece of my mind.
> I said nothing. Instead I walked quietly to the back of the room and beckoned each of the girls to follow me. When we reached the hallway I reminded them of the class rules and asked them to remain in the hall until we finished with our discussion. I suggested that we discuss the incident at the school day's end and returned to my class. I did not sermonize the girls nor did I comment to the class. That's not to say I didn't want to say something but I had an alternative in mind, and I was determined to put it to the test.

Pam glanced at her friend's posture and knew that she had captured Joan's undivided attention.

"So what did you do?" blurted out Joan. "You just can't tiptoe around the topic indefinitely. Someone has to teach them right from wrong." Pausing, Joan asked, "Does this have something to do with calming down before talking to the students?"

Pam flashed a smile and quickly responded, "Yes it does, but that's only a small part of what I'm suggesting you consider. Calming down is important because we both know that words in the heat of emotion are rarely constructive. Neither of us can count the number of times we met a crisis head-on only to find that our passion of the moment led to further worsening of the problem."

Joan nodded in a agreement. "I have only to think back a few hours to substantiate the wisdom of that counsel. It's been the same way with my three children. If I could take back a fourth of the threats spoken in haste, I would have avoided considerable stress and disruption."

"I agree," Pam replied. "Immediate action has its place, but often it changes a bad situation to a terrible situation. However, as I said previously, the timing of a response is only a small part of disciplining through virtue!"

"Say what?" Joan interrupted.

"Disciplining through virtue," came the reply. "It's a disciplinary approach that I have recently been introduced to. Hold your questions for a moment, and let me continue on with my story."

15

Joan smiled and nodded, and Pam began again. "Well as I previously stated, I avoided the topic and finished my discussion on Roman politics as planned. At day's end I visited with Janet and Vicki and gave what I hoped was an appropriate punishment. As soon as I was alone, I opened this book to this page and followed down until I came to the section entitled Disrespect." Pam turned the contents of the book to face her friend and placed her finger on that particular section.

Joan focused on the print before her, and after a brief scan blurted out, "Okay, you've got my interest. What is all this supposed to accomplish?"

Pam seemed in little hurry to answer her companion's inquiries. "Let me read you an entry from Bennett's The Book of Virtues. Then we will talk." Pam reached across her desk and grasped a hardbound book in a buff-colored jacket.

Joan gazed intently at the thick book. She had heard good things about Bennett's work, and a few friends had even encouraged her to pick up a copy for her family. She watched as Pam quickly turned to a specific story and began to read.

REBECCA,
WHO SLAMMED DOORS FOR FUN AND PERISHED MISERABLY.
By Hilaire Belloc

A trick that everyone abhors
In Little Girls is slamming Doors.
A Wealthy Banker's Little Daughter
Who lived in Palace Green, Bayswater
(By name Rebecca Offendort),
Was given to this Furious Sport.
She would deliberately go
And Slam the door like Billy-Ho!
To make her Uncle Jacob start.
She was not really bad at heart,
But only rather rude and wild:
She was an aggravating child. . . .
It happened that a Marble Bust
of Abraham was standing just
Above the Door this little Lamb
Had carefully prepared to Slam,
And Down it came! It knocked her flat!
It laid her out! She looked like that.
Her Funeral Sermon (which was long
And followed by a Sacred Song)
Mentioned her Virtues, it is true,

16

But dwelt upon her Vices too,
And showed the Dreadful End of One
Who goes and slams the Door for Fun.

The children who were brought to hear
The awful Tale from far and near
Were much impressed, and inly swore
They never more would slam the Door.
---As often they had done before.

"Okay, so what's the point. Talk!" Joan managed a smile to take the hard edges off her pointed request. She wasn't wishing to be rude, but her impatience was getting the best of her, and she wanted to get to the bottom line. "So may I presume you read this to your class?"

"Yes and no," Pam replied. It was clear that Pam was enjoying this interplay. It reminded her of old times when the two of them would do battle in good nature. "I first had them read the selection silently, then I read it orally in my best voice."

Joan couldn't hide her disappointment. "Are you telling me that this is how you now handle your discipline? Aren't you still teaching the sixth grade? Surely this is a bit childish for this age."

Pam took no offense at her friend's abrupt response. She remembered how anxiety often brought out the worst in Joan. Patience was never one of her friend's strong suits. Pam was almost cheerful in her reply. "Not in the least. It was the poem's simplicity that made it work. This was my first attempt at this approach, and I must admit that I shared your skepticism."

"So what happened?" Joan wasn't going to let Pam tiptoe around the main point for too long.

"The students were hesitant at first," Pam began. "They wanted to first gauge the reaction of their classmates. It only took one person to chuckle before the whole class seemed to loosen up. I took this as an encouraging sign, so I moved to the next step."

"What was that?" Joan obviously had softened in her skepticism and again began her search for solutions.

"I asked the class if this had ever happened to any of them. They laughed; my ludicrous question seemed to have opened things up. I asked if anyone could think of a rude habit they had observed in a little brother or perhaps had seen in a movie or cartoon. One student shared how his little sister would throw her cereal bowl when she tired of eating. Apparently, it didn't matter if any cereal was left. The students laughed, and one student asked what the boy's mom did to stop it. He explained how his dad had screwed a cereal bowl into the tray of the high chair. When he further described how awkward it was to wash this particular cereal bowl, the class howled with amusement. Two additional students had 'little brother' stories to recount before I moved my students to a new question."

Pam could see that Joan's mind was turning something over, and she wasn't surprised at her friend's unsolicited observation, "The students had no idea that this story was about disrespect, did they?"

Pam only smiled and went on. "I asked them how they thought their parents felt about the rude behaviors they had just laughed over. The first boy who had responded didn't hesitate to reply. 'They hated it,' he exclaimed. 'The first time it happened a half bowl of cereal splashed on mom's best cookbook. The second time it was soup, and it landed on the new carpet. My parents were pretty steamed.'"

"I asked the class if the young child should have been punished. The class leaned slightly in favor of punishment, but the show of hands indicated a close decision." Pam chuckled as she continued. "I then asked the students to explain why they answered as they did. They seemed to relish the opportunity, so eventually I took my seat and let them conduct their own discussion. It worked reasonably well. A few students got off track, but eventually the question of punishment was resolved to everyone's satisfaction."

Joan was taking in each of Pam's words and applying them to what she had learned about sixth graders' behavior. "May I predict their final resolution?" she stated. It really wasn't a question because she went ahead with her opinion before Pam had a chance to grant her request. "They discovered that punishment was only fair if the little one understood that what he was doing was bad."

Pam gave her friend a knowing glance and confirmed her guess. "You are almost right on. The only thing you missed was the students' insistence that in addition to the child's understanding, the punishment also had to hinge on whether or not the thrown cereal caused someone some harm."

"I don't know if I can agree with that," volunteered Joan. "But it sounds like they made some progress."

"I felt the same way and decided that I would take my victories a step at a time."

"Did you bring up the subject of disrespect at any time in the discussion?" Joan now seemed hungry for all pertinent details. Some things were falling into place, and this had a tendency to fire up her motors.

"No," answered Pam. "I didn't want to push my luck. Interestingly enough Vicki participated in the discussion. Apparently she hadn't a clue that her actions were an integral part of the discussion."

"I take it that the two girls took no offense at the subject nor the timing of your little poem." Again, Joan was making an observation more than posing a question. "This is beginning to make some sense, but there are still some large gaps in my understanding."

Pam appeared delighted with the comment. "I hope you haven't figured it all out this quickly. I've been experimenting with this approach for five months, and I know there's much more to learn."

Joan glanced at the clock and surprised her friend by undergoing a complete change of demeanor. After what appeared to be a private, internal debate, Mrs. Walker appeared to have gathered her courage for a difficult pronouncement, "Here I go again--clock watching. I've been told that it's the first sign of burn out."

The mere mention of the term had an immediate impact. Both recalled conversations they had over colleagues who were struggling--teachers who had once provided a quality education for their students but had now lost much of their former enthusiasm and commitment.

Joan fidgeted a moment before finishing what she had committed herself to disclose. "I am almost too ashamed to admit this, but I have to share this with someone because it has chastised my conscience for months!"

Joan lowered her eyes as she confessed, "I guess I have finally come to the realization that I don't enjoy my students, and teaching has lost much of its luster. There are days I can hardly drag myself to school. Then the guilt sets in, and my sense of worth takes a nose dive. I've been riding this roller coaster for more time than I'd care to admit. Pretty sad, huh?"

Smiling Joan then confided, "In fact, I'd all but given up trying to do something about my predicament when a simple story changed my attitude. It's what encouraged me to seek you out."

Pam could empathize with her friend. She too had experienced similar feelings but had found them to pass away with time. Joan's wasn't a terminal illness, but she couldn't find the words to comfort her friend. Then a thought hit her, and she walked to the back of the room where she kept a personal file. After a minute or two of foraging, she was rewarded with the object of her intentions. She pulled out a folded piece of paper and handed it to Joan. "Here, read this when you have a few quiet moments. We can visit on it the next time we get together. Besides, we haven't spent enough time on disciplining through virtue. How does next Friday sound. Same place, same time and same donuts!"

"Yes, I'd like that very much," Joan responded, "and thank you for this time together. It brings back wonderful memories."

Pam pointed to the paper she had given her friend and said, "After you've allowed the message of that poem to sink in, I'd like you to think about why a story such as this can be such an effective tool in a classroom setting. You are the best idea person I know, and I'd like to hear what you come up with."

19

Joan's countenance brightened. "Thanks for the compliment. I think I needed it! I must admit that you have provided me much to think about. My intuition tells me that you are on to something significant. I'm anxious for next Friday." Pausing at the door, she smiled and stated, "I'll be sure to read this poem at my next free moment."

It was late, and Pam needed to scurry home. "I hope Joan finds the quiet moments needed to read what I've offered and then think it through. I hate to see her this despondent. She's too good a teacher and too caring an adult to do this to herself." With that thought, Pam grabbed a few test papers, turned out her lights and gently eased her door shut.

Chapter Five
Resolve to Get Started

"Only a virtuous people are capable of freedom."
Benjamin Franklin

CHAPTER FIVE

It turned out to be Tuesday afternoon before Joan found the time to pull out Pam's story. She had not intended to wait this long, but school and home concerns had commanded all her time and attention. The sight of the paper caused her to recall snatches of her conversation with her old teaching buddy. The notion of stories resurfaced, and Joan was pleased to note the small sliver of hope gaining a foothold in her outlook. "After all," she noted, "Mrs. Ashcraft's little story on Lincoln had performed wonders on me!"

Her thoughts then swept back to the past two school days, particularly with respect to the behavior of her two bullies. She shook her head slowly as she concluded that not much had changed. It suddenly occurred to her that she had given as much thought to Pam's two young ladies as she had to Lance and Scott. "That's odd," she thought. After pursuing this for a moment she finally concluded that she had unconsciously connected Pam's challenge with that of her own, and her colleague's success would somehow insure a comparable success on her part.

She laughed silently to herself as she returned her attention to Pam's story. "The Touch of the Master's Hand" by Myra Brooks Welch was printed in bold type across the top of the page. Just as she was about to begin reading, the thought again diverted her attention that Pam had purposely withheld the final resolution of her disciplinary dilemma. Her confrontation with the two girls had occurred months ago, and it stood to reason that something had changed by now. It was so unlike Pam to keep things from her, but it was apparent that this had been her intention from the beginning.

She glanced again at the paper in her hand. "And why this story?" she continued. "The Pam I know would have taken the two minutes required to read me the story." Again Joan found herself quietly verbalizing her thoughts.

"I must be cracking up," was her final thought before launching in to her reading.

THE TOUCH OF THE MASTER'S HAND
By Myra Brooks Welch

'Twas battered and scarred, and the auctioneer
Thought it scarcely worth his while
To waste much time on the old violin,
But held it up with a smile:
"What am I bidden, good folks," he cried,
"Who'll start the bidding for me?"
"A dollar, a dollar"; then, "Two!" "Only two?
Two dollars, and who'll make it three?

21

Three dollars, once; three dollars, twice;
Going for three--" But no,
From the room, far back, a gray-haired man
Came forward and picked up the bow;
Then, wiping the dust from the old violin,
And tightening the loose strings,
He played a melody pure and sweet
As a caroling angel sings.

The music ceased, and the auctioneer,
With a voice that was quiet and low,
Said: "What am I bid for the old violin?"
And he held it up with the bow.
"A thousand dollars, and who'll make it two?
Two thousand! And who'll make it three?
Three thousand, once, three thousand, twice,
And going, and gone," said he.
The people cheered, but some of them cried,
"We do not quite understand
What changed its worth." Swift came the reply:
"The touch of a master's hand."

And many a man with life out of tune,
And battered and scarred with sin,
Is auctioned cheap to the thoughtless crowd,
Much like the old violin.
A "mess of pottage," a glass of wine;
A game--and he travels on.
He is "going" once, and "going" twice,
He's "going" and almost "gone."
But the Master comes, and the foolish crowd
Never can quite understand
The worth of a soul and the change that's wrought
By the touch of the Master's hand.

As she neatly folded the page, an overwhelming emotion swept over her. It took some effort to limit her tears to a gentle stream. Joan shook her head in disbelief. She rarely cried, and this was by design. Tears were almost always followed by a headache, and she could ill afford another migraine. So why the tears? What had this poem expressed that would cause such a reaction in herself? Tears again welled up as she visualized the gray-haired man slowly walking up to retrieve the violin. Then the image changed to his loving execution of the melody. She thought of who the gray-haired man might be and then to the violin itself. Perhaps it was a genuine Stradivarius, spurned for its scarred and battered appearance. She shuddered as she thought of the injustice that would have transpired had it not been for the gray-haired man. A Stradivarius unloved and ill-used was a staggering thought. What a waste of true worth.

A flash of inspiration hit her all at once, and the tears now flowed in an unbroken stream. "This story wasn't about an auction," she stammered to herself, "nor was it a tribute to a caring man. The violin was the whole point, and it had nothing to do with music." Joan suddenly realized that she had been entrusted with twenty-six violins, some polished but many tattered and dusty -- twenty-six Stradivariuses that depended on her for polish, fine tuning and opportunities to shine. She had always believed that teachers could make a difference, but all the lectures and textbooks never conveyed what she was now feeling. Lance and Scott might shine like the scarred violin if only she could develop the love and skill described so poignantly in this poem. Joan's thoughts returned to Pam's response after hearing her heartfelt confession. There were no words of advice, sympathy or encouragement--only the gift of a simple poem. The tears returned, but Joan didn't seem to mind.

Chapter Six
An Obscure but
Promising Path

"America has the best stories to tell...if America has a task now it is, I believe, to restore some of the fundamental beliefs and values that made your country great." *Margaret Thatcher*

CHAPTER SIX

Thursday afternoon was an early dismissal day for the students, so the teachers could be freed up for purposes of collaboration. Joan usually teamed up with Fred Jones, a colleague in the sixth grade hall. Fred and she were as different as night and day, but they had developed a level of mutual respect. Each acknowledged the other's strengths, and each accepted the other's weaknesses. Fred was not one to get involved in the personal lives of his students. He treated teaching as a science and did his best to prepare and deliver clear and precise lessons. He was a popular teacher with those parents who insisted on a no-nonsense curriculum, plenty of homework and challenging tests. His temperament fit his teaching style, rarely excitable but always consistent and firm. Joan admired these traits but wisely followed her own natural inclinations.

As the two spread out their materials, Joan noticed a copy of The Book of Virtues on his bookshelf. She walked over and lifted it out. She then returned to her chair and placed the book in front of Mr. Jones. "Why is this here? Do you use this as part of your instruction?"

Fred was taken back by the intensity in Joan's voice. Her words and body language were almost confrontational. "Why do you ask?" was the only response Fred could come up with.

Joan's excitement calmed as she explained her recent introduction to the book. She provided few details choosing instead to further interrogate her hallmate. "Have you used the book in any teaching situations?"

"Actually, no." he confided. "I received this copy from a patron who asked if I might consider its use in the classroom. Naturally, I couldn't turn her down, but I have some misgivings about teaching values. Besides, I have little enough time to teach my core subjects with everything else crammed into the curriculum. I tried to put off the patron by citing our responsibility to cover drug and sex education as well as suicide and multi-cultural education. The patron wasn't impressed and insisted that I at least give the book a few moments of my attention. This all happened a month ago, and I don't look forward to having to report that I have yet to lift its cover."

Joan thought a moment and then asked, "Do you know much about the book? Have you ever heard it used as a disciplinary tool?"

"No to both questions." was Fred's reply. "I fail to see its value if what little I know is accurate. I'm not comfortable teaching my students about honesty or faith. I'm paid to teach academics, and the rest I leave to the homes and churches." Fred's answer sounded much like that of a judge rendering his final verdict. He meant it as his concluding remarks and left little doubt that as far as he was concerned, the matter was closed.

Notwithstanding her colleagues finality, Joan wasn't to be put off so easily. She decided on a different tact. "Do you see any value in using stories as teaching tools? Can you picture how a story or poem could replace a teacher's verbal handling of a disciplinary problem?"

"Frankly, no." he replied. "When I have something to say, I get on to it. I haven't the time to fish around for a story that may or may not get the point across. I'd rather handle it in my own words. That way I'm sure I've made my point!"

Joan knew that Fred held strong opinions and wasn't surprised nor offended by his response. She wasn't prepared to back away yet and asked if he minded listening to a short story and then responding to a few questions. She assured him that his participation would be most helpful in her preparation for tomorrow's lessons. She wasn't sure what she hoped to accomplish but felt a need to continue to pursue some loose ends of Pam's approach. "What do you remember about the story of Pinocchio?"

"Very little," Fred admitted.

"Good, then let me first provide you with basic components of the story. It starts with a woodcutter by the name of Geppetto, kindly old Geppetto!"

Fred knew when it was useless to resist further. He had spent enough time with this colleague to know that she wasn't easily put off when she had a head of steam. He settled back in his chair and nodded to Joan to begin her story.

Geppetto the woodcarver created a masterful puppet who he named Pinocchio. Geppetto's last utterance before retiring for the evening was to wish that his little Pinocchio might become a real boy. The beautiful Blue Fairy, upon hearing the wish, chose to grant it but with conditions attached. She warned Pinocchio that to become a real boy he first must prove himself brave, truthful and unselfish. In addition, he must learn to choose between right and wrong.

His first days proved disastrous. Presented with choices, Pinocchio always took the pleasurable but unwise option. He shunned school for puppet theater, then avoided home for the enticements of Pleasure Island. In each case his poor judgment brought on calamity, remorse and regret. Finally a wiser Pinocchio reached home only to find that his father had been swallowed by a monstrous whale during his search for his boy. The little puppet boy resolved that he would risk everything, even his own life, to save his father. The story resolves itself nicely with Pinocchio showing unselfish courage in his daring rescue. True to her word, the Blue Fairy kept her promise by turning Pinocchio into a real boy.

"So what do you think? Is it a story worth sharing with your class?"

Fred was taken back by the question and for the first time in weeks was unable to think of a quick rejoinder. Finally after an awkward pause, he responded in a subdued and careful manner. "I'm sure the story has its place in the primary grades, but I can see little value using it with a class of sixth graders. Besides, I'm sure they have seen the video."

Joan still wasn't through with Fred. "Fair enough answer. Now I'd like you to consider this next question. What do you think is the author's intended message? I hope you will agree that the story does generate some interesting conclusions."

"Okay, I can concede that much." Fred thought a few moments and then slowly and cautiously offered his opinion. "I would guess that it has something to do with conscience. Isn't there a song in the movie that mentions something about letting your conscience be your guide?"

"Would it interest you to know that I shared this same story with my class this very morning and heard of no less than eleven messages? You should be pleased to know that your choice was expressed by a few of the students." Joan could see that she was stirring some interest in Fred, and this was no small feat. "Want to hear the remaining ten answers?"

"Sure, why not." The veteran teacher's attention was increasing by the minute, and Joan took this as reason enough to move ahead.

"The other choices were 'You should never tell a lie!', 'Be careful with the company you keep!' and 'If you wish for something hard enough, it just might come true!'"

"Here's a couple of interesting ones. 'Don't trust anyone who has anything to do with the theater!' and 'Don't mess with whales or sharks!'"

Recalling how Lance brazenly offered the message concerning the sharks caused her to pause momentarily.

Fred took advantage of this lapse to interject, "I can think of a few students who might have come up with those last two!" He laughed as his mind searched for the two students who would be likely to offer those conclusions. Oddly he then visibly shifted his attention to another matter.

Joan could see that something was eating at Fred. She suspected that he was waiting for a specific answer. Her observation was confirmed when Fred interrupted her efforts. "So how many students opted for conscience. Surely, sixth graders have some judgment." Fred masked his question as a modest attempt at humor, but Joan wasn't fooled in the least.

"Patience," she teased. "Let me finish the list. The remaining five are actually quite profound. 'Parents should never give up on wayward kids!', 'Children must be a real pain to raise!', 'School is probably the best place to be when you're still a kid!', 'Those who persevere will often be rewarded in the end!' and 'People are better off if they set goals and stick to them.'" Joan paused to provide Fred with the time to ponder her list.

Just as she was about to continue, she again was interrupted. "You say the students came up with these messages?"

"Yes, I had little to do with the discussion after a certain point," Joan confided.

"Did the students come up with the actual wording?" Fred inquired hastily.

"Kind of," she laughed. "I cleaned the language up a bit. A few of their terms were a little off center!"

"So how about my question? What was the top choice?" Fred was tenacious if nothing else.

"Well, I'm sorry to inform you that I didn't take a final tally." This was beginning to get fun for Joan. She always enjoyed a good discussion, and it was so unlike Fred to allow her this pleasure. "Now try this one on for size: Which message is the most correct?"

Fred still wasn't sure where this discussion was heading, but he could sense an entrapment on the horizon, and the thought didn't please him in the least. He decided on a safe approach. "I guess I would need more time to analyze the story before committing to a single best choice."

"Come on, Fred. Surely you can commit to a single choice!" Joan knew she was pushing her colleague, but she was having too much fun to stop. Besides she thought this discussion might prove helpful to him despite his hesitancies.

"Okay, I'm still comfortable with my original choice," Fred confided, "but I must admit that you've given me a good question to ponder. Some of the other responses have a lot of merit in their own right."

Joan was sympathetic to Fred's uneasiness. She knew she was proceeding cautiously and remembered her own impatience with Pam when her questions were not answered immediately. "Be patient with me for another moment. I do have a point to this inquiry, but I must admit that I'm using your input to help me make sense of an intriguing but still unfamiliar concept. Will you hang in there for a few more questions?"

Fred couldn't say no. He sensed that Joan had a more profound agenda than a discussion on Pinocchio, and she needed to work it through. He also realized that his own curiosity was deepening. "Sure, ask away."

Joan worded her question carefully, "When you want to hammer home a point, do you have a technique that ensures that your students get it?"

"I'm not completely following you. Are we talking academics?" he asked.

"Well... yes, I guess that's a good place to start. How do you ensure to your complete satisfaction that your students understand the concept you are teaching? For example, what if your teaching outcome is an understanding that economics played a major role in the outbreak of World War II?"

"I'd prepare a lesson that is clear and concise and try to supplement the information with whatever aids are available. Then I would test for

27

understanding. If the test results were discouraging, I would spend some time reviewing the original material." Fred's words lacked their usual conviction. He knew that Joan had something else in mind, and this exchange was still a bit unsettling. He also suspected that they were just beginning to address the real issue.

"Why do you teach this particular concept?" Joan inquired. "Obviously you or someone somewhere considers this a valuable piece of information, crucial to a thorough education." Joan was beginning to see where she needed to go with this discussion, and this self-discovery invigorated her.

Again Fred took the cautious approach. "I'd need to think about this a few moments for a thorough response. Off-the-cuff, I'd say that I teach this material because it's a lesson from the past that should never be repeated. The German people were so stripped of their pride and worldly goods that the perfect environment was created for a Hitler to emerge."

Joan dreaded to take her colleague's point a step further. "Can you agree that this same message is applicable in this generation and that we, as a world community, need to be mindful of the economic conditions of each and every sovereign country?"

"Certainly, I'll buy that!" Fred was grateful for a question that required little mental taxation.

Joan surprised her colleague with her next point. "You say that you check for understanding. How do you know that the students have internalized this concept? Does your test go beyond the students responding to facts that align themselves with the concept?"

Fred revealed a slight defensiveness in his follow-up comment. "Well, I usually spend class time discussing the key points; but no, my tests can't tell me if the students have internalized the concept. However, I would hope that some of them picked up on it."

Joan moved quickly to the next question. "I agree that surely some students would not only be equipped to repeat the main points but would actually feel and understand the essence of the message. Why would some students internalize and others not? Is it a simple matter of intelligence and maturity?"

Fred was clearly fascinated by the question. He was finally feeling more the participant than the unwitting target of the discussion. In fact he was beginning to consider questions of his own. "I'm sure intelligence and maturity played a part, but I suspect their influence was minor. As I think it through, I'm sure the key factor is a student's readiness and willingness to learn. They would have to be looking for something as a necessary first step before positioning themselves to receive their answers!"

"That makes sense!" Joan added. "A student of German ancestry, embarrassed over certain events during the war, might be looking for answers.

A descendant of a holocaust victim might have a similar personal interest. What about those with no significant ties to the subject matter?"

"Good question. I guess that's where we come in as professionals. We somehow have to create a need for the students to plug in to what's being offered." Fred wasn't finished. He then added, "I must admit that there are times I am passionate about a certain subject and almost go overboard in my presentation, only to find a handful of students interested enough to give it more than a moment's thought. In fact, I find that many students turn me off when I get too aggressive in stating my points!"

"I know exactly what you are saying," Joan acknowledged. "Let's return to the story of Pinocchio. What if you were attempting to teach your class about the dangers of succumbing to peer pressure? What if this particular problem was growing on a daily basis and you feared its effects could prove disastrous to many of your students? What if the influence of negative peer pressure was creeping into your classroom affairs and affecting the learning."

"I would have no choice but to deal with it immediately." Fred replied. "I'd sit the class down and point out why it had to stop."

"How many students do you think would internalize your message?" Joan's question hit home if Fred's expression was any indication of what he was thinking.

"Probably only these students who hadn't a problem with it. The rest would probably fail to recognize its connection in their own lives and dismiss my comments as irrelevant. I guess I have seen the blank stares often enough to recognize the many times I'm tuned out."

Joan couldn't help but be sympathetic. Tuning out was a frequent occurrence in her classroom. Only she could take it a step further. "Unfortunately, I can identify with your concern. I hope you aren't at the stage I'm at, where my sermons seem to aggravate the problem. I usually deal with a situation as it occurs, and I can't help but point fingers at the guilty. Oh, I never use names and do my best to speak in general terms, but everyone knows who I'm talking about."

"You're right," Fred agreed, "it's hard to avoid hurt feelings or the perception that you are picking on a particular student or group of students. I've been fortunate this year, and the students haven't seemed to take things too personally, but I must admit that I don't know what they are feeling inside." Fred laughed, "You know I'm not known as Mr. Warm and Fuzzy, and I rarely provide opportunities for my students to express how they truly feel. I guess I have always acted on the premise that no news is good news. I have addressed a number of disciplinary concerns and could easily have alienated some of the students."

"Think again about two of my first questions. Do you see any value in using stories as teaching tools? And can you picture how a story or poem could replace a teacher's verbal handling of a disciplinary problem?" Joan scored. She knew it, and Fred knew it.

"The clouds are dissipating, and the light of wisdom is descending," he quipped. "Can I change my answer? Pinocchio or a similar story might work rather well. I can see your point in the need to avoid direct assaults. Pinocchio, with its varied message, could be read and discussed with no obvious tie into the peer pressure problem." Fred paused for a moment, and a smile creased his face. "I hate to reveal my ignorance, but I'm still unclear about the issue you made over students internalizing what they choose."

Joan confessed, "I wasn't exactly sure where I was heading myself. Remember that this is something I've only begun to think about. I'll tell you my present thoughts and hopefully you can help me make sense."

"Fair enough." Fred's body language confirmed his support.

"I'm thinking that a story or similar medium would greatly enhance the prospects of constructive learning. The learning may not relate to your primary focus but be equally valuable. For some students, the story of Pinocchio may illustrate the folly of succumbing to unwise peer pressure, and these students might profit by this particular message. But a portion of your class may be struggling with why they must attend school. Why shouldn't they be spending their time having fun. Pinocchio provides an answer if someone has enough interest in the subject to give it some thought."

"You have a point." Fred's mind began turning over a number of possibilities. "Then, there are those students who might be discouraged with the slow progress they are making in an area important to them. Pinocchio's struggles might help them understand how easily it is to make mistakes, but success can still be obtainable. Our examples are illustrating the versatility of a story. Interesting."

"I agree," Joan replied. Joan looked up at the clock and then surprised her colleague by laughing heartily.

"Have I missed something?" Fred asked.

"No, and please excuse my odd reaction," she laughed. "My glancing at the clock just reminded me of something I'm trying to forget. It's late, and I've taken up much of your time. Thanks for your willingness to bear with me. You have been a great help."

Joan's appreciation was sincere, and Fred found a new sense of respect for his colleague. "Let me return the thanks. You have given me much to think about. I'm still not sure where you are heading, but I would love to be kept abreast."

Joan answered with a smile and headed back to her classroom. Gathering up her take-home materials, she hustled out to her car. It was getting late, and she had a number of issues to deal with at home.

Chapter Seven
Another Path to Consider

"Virtue is not hereditary."   Thomas Jefferson

CHAPTER SEVEN

She made a willful effort to switch gears from classroom teacher to mother of three as she sped her way home. Her oldest was pressuring her and her husband about having her own car. Marie was building her case on the fact that every one of her friends drove their own cars. Marie's strongest point to date was the horror that would result should her ride let her down and she be seen riding a yellow school bus. Joan and her husband were trying their best to empathize with this horror, but they were having a difficult time of it. Undoubtedly, round six would occur soon.

Joan swerved her car to miss a beer can lying in her path and then was compelled to repeat the action to avoid what appeared to be a mangled hubcap. The littered street refocused her attention to her youngest son's bedroom. Billy was bright, loving and brimming with confidence. That is good she thought. His bedroom was a different matter. It was bright, loving and brimming with junk. That is bad. She thought of the many times had she reminded Billy of the advantages in maintaining some semblance of bedroom order. He constantly was searching for something or other in the various piles of stuff that decorated his room. This issue had become a testing point in an otherwise good relationship. Lately her reminders had evolved to lectures and threats, and neither party seemed inclined to give in.

Joan's thought turned to Pete and their most recent argument. She could almost remember the entire conversation, word for word, and the mere recollection of the event triggered much of the same emotion that shrouded the original exchange. Pete was sandwiched in age between Marie and Billy, and his persona did nothing to dispel the commonly accepted characteristics of a middle child. Pete viewed the world as a tribunal where everything must first pass the fairness test. Their most recent court drama was over use of their Sega video controls. Pete was convinced that his little brother had been given easier access than he and was determined to argue the point until the wrong was corrected. As Joan continued her drive home, she found herself lecturing her son on the pitfalls in viewing his life in terms of how it compares with his siblings.

Joan rambled on for two or three minutes before she realized what she was doing to herself. Her imaginary lectures, discussions or warnings were occurring more frequently now, and they always produced little more than a headache and an increase in pulse rate. She knew this rehashing was a senseless waste of energy, but each real encounter had to be replayed again and again until she found a proper resolution. That was the problem--she was finding it increasingly difficult to find proper resolutions.

Joan expertly dodged Billy's skateboard left unlovingly in the middle of the driveway and brought her car to a neat stop just to the left of Billy's box of basketball cards. Her irritation quickened as she recalled her recent counsel and warning about this very thing. "Well, I suppose I will need to deny him use of these two items if he's going to continue to ignore me." She and her husband, Lorin, had worked out various natural consequences for various infractions. Thinking back she realized that this was the sixth time in three weeks she had used this particular consequence, and it had not even slowed her youngest down.

Stepping into her kitchen, Joan was seized by two distinct thoughts. One impression pleased her immensely; the other raised her level of concern. The first thought was a logical extension of her afternoon's discussion with Fred-- Why couldn't she apply her new school approaches in the disciplining of her own children? The second thought was more a question than a deduction-- What does it take to change behavior and not simply manage it? Joan placed her books and papers in their appropriate spot and headed for Billy's bedroom.

Chapter Eight
Second Bearing on
the North Star

*"Ideals can take a mob of appetites and organize
them into an army of purpose and principle."*
George B. Shaw

CHAPTER EIGHT

Lorin Walker worked as a sales representative for a pharmaceutical company which compensated him well but required more of his time than he would have preferred. It was not unusual for him to arrive home late in the evening or to be on the road for days at a time. Joan had come to grips with this negative side of her husband's employment and made the necessary adjustments. The first adjustment was to rarely build dinner times around her husband's schedule. A second and more difficult adjustment was to accept the reality that Lorin would often be absent when a parenting problem cropped up. During the seventeen years of their marriage, the two had worked out a fairly effective system. Joan handled most of the day-to-day problems. The big decisions or major changes in approach were held in abeyance until the two had time to sit down together and come to a common understanding.

As Joan prepared the evening meal, she played with some disciplinary options that might first seem radical to her husband and children. The more she played with the options, the more hopeful she became. Luckily, Lorin was due home at a decent hour she recalled, and the two would have some quality time together before the hour got too late. They would need the private time together she confided in herself because she was about to take a risk that would surprise Lorin as much as the kids. As she reviewed her tentative plans, she found herself trying to anticipate the response she might receive. Her thoughts were interrupted as her husband's car rattled as it came to a stop next to her Sunbird. Joan smiled to herself as she rehearsed her forthcoming announcement.

Finally, with plates and utensils cleared, Joan knew it was time to put her plan to action. She cleared her throat and said, "I've been struggling with a school problem for days, and I could really use help from the four of you. I know you are busy, but I'm really at a loss, and you're my last hope."

"This sounds serious," quipped Lorin, "and my consultation fees always double when matters are serious."

Pete, always quick to see a good thing, added, "Yea, serious discussions run time and a half pay. I'll take my pay in Sega time. I figure an extra hour on Friday ought to be about right."

"Pete, grow up. Mom's serious, and you bring up that stupid video argument again," Marie complained. "Besides, I think both of you boys waste too much time on that childish machine. You notice how I'm not going to bring up the car at this point. That would be taking advantage!" Marie's eyes twinkled, a point that didn't escape her two parents.

"Can I assume then that the answer is yes." Joan resumed. "Besides, you should enjoy the challenge."

Billy was still sulking over the loss of his skateboard and was slow to warm up to anything that required cooperation. However, he wasn't about to get Dad on his case, so he nodded his head in agreement along with everyone else.

"Thank you. I know I could count on each of you. It should only take a few minutes." Joan picked up the copy of The Book of Virtues that she had purchased the evening before. I'd like to read you a short story and then hear your comments and observations. I'm seriously considering using this collection of stories as a teaching tool."

Pete was instantly captivated. He loved to offer an opinion, and here was an open invitation to say whatever he thought without any chance of admonishment. "Mom, I can tell you already that you're doomed to fail. I paged through the book last night and saw a bunch of poetry. That will never fly with sixth graders. Trust me. I'm an expert on sixth grade. It was my best year!"

Billy finally spoke up. "Does it have pictures and stuff?"

"No, honey. But how about holding your judgments until I have a chance to explain what I intend to do with the book." Joan found herself enjoying this exchange. It dawned on her that the entire family hadn't had a talk such as this for months.

Joan's patience was obvious, and it pleased her husband. Lorin had noticed the strain on his wife these past couple of months and was delighted to see her so relaxed. "Go ahead, Joan. We promise no further interruptions." Father gave Pete the look!

"Sorry, Mom," Pete conceded. "I'll shut it for a while."

Marie chuckled quietly to herself. She was anxious to see what Pete considered 'a while.' She could hardly remember an instance where he held off on a comment or question for more than a few moments. Pete had to express every notion that popped into his head. Her all-time favorite was when her brother had asked if today was tomorrow. Marie jokingly referred to Pete's talent as diarrhea of the mouth.

Joan opened the book to page 196 and announced that she was going to read them a short story about King Alfred the Great. "Before beginning," she added, "I've found that there are times in any school day when circumstances leave me with time to spare. I have often used these times for silent, sustained reading or free time. Lately, I have found many of my students abusing these free moments, and their disruption is hurting everyone's opportunity to learn. An old colleague of mine convinced me to fill these time gaps with good stories and poems." Joan glanced at Pete and smiled.

Marie quickly recognized that Mom's playful challenge would surely be too great an opportunity for Pete to resist. She was surprised and slightly disappointed when Pete let the invitation slide by without comment. She knew that her mother was testing Pete's resolve, and he somehow managed to pull it off.

Pointing again to the book Joan continued, "The entries from <u>The Book of Virtues</u> are considered classic examples of virtue or," concluding her thought, "the lack of virtue. In addition, they are valuable illustrations of our culture, and I begrudgingly admit that my students aren't being exposed to this information to the extent that I would like."

"So where does our help come in?" Lorin interjected. "This looks like an open and shut case. I'd say just do it." He had beaten Pete to the punch, and the room's smiling eyes pinned him to his chair. It took a moment before he realized that he had spurned the advice he had just cautioned his family on. Blushing slightly, Lorin whispered, "Sorry, dear, for the interruption. I'm sure there's more to this than what you have related thus far."

"Well yes, there is. I'll try to get quickly to the point," Joan confided. "I am wondering if the students would profit more if we moved beyond the literary and historical value of the pieces to the virtues illuminated in the stories. I'm not sure it can be done in a classroom without offending someone's family values. Hopefully, the messages from the different entries are generally accepted expressions of the various character virtues. In addition to this concern, I'm not convinced I can successfully teach something as elusive as a virtue. Could I experiment on the four of you and then get your honest opinion?"

"Sure Mom," Billy shouted out. From the nods around the room, it was obvious that Joan had won both their attention and support.

"Okay, here goes." Joan read through the story and didn't pause or offer comment until the entire piece was completed.

KING ALFRED AND THE CAKES
Adapted from James Baldwin

In England many years ago there ruled a king named Alfred. A wise and just man, Alfred was one of the best kings England ever had. Even today, centuries later, he is known as Alfred the Great.

The days of Alfred's rule were not easy ones in England. The country was invaded by the fierce Danes, who had come from across the sea. There were so many Danish invaders, and they were so strong and bold, that for a long time they won almost every battle. If they kept on winning, they would soon be masters of the whole country.

At last, after so many struggles, King Alfred's English army was broken and scattered. Every man had to save himself in the best way he could, including King Alfred. He disguised himself as a shepherd and fled alone through the woods and swamps.

After several days of wandering, he came to the hut of a woodcutter. Tired and hungry, he knocked on the door and begged the woodcutter's wife to give him something to eat and a place to sleep.

The woman looked with pity at the ragged fellow. She had no idea who he really was. "Come in," she said. "I will give you some supper if you will watch these cakes I am baking on the hearth. I want to go out and milk the cow. Watch them carefully, and make sure they don't burn while I'm gone."

Alfred thanked her politely and sat down beside the fire. He tried to pay attention to the cakes, but soon all his troubles filled his mind. How was he going to get his army together again? And even if he did, how was he going to prepare it to face the Danes? How could he possibly drive such fierce invaders out of England? The more he thought, the more hopeless the future seemed, and he began to believe there was no use in continuing to fight. Alfred saw only his problems. He forgot he was in the woodcutter's hut, he forgot about his hunger, and he forgot all about the cakes.

In a little while, the woman came back. She found her hut full of smoke and her cakes burned to a crisp. And there was Alfred sitting beside the hearth, gazing into the flames. He had never even noticed the cakes were burning.

"You lazy, good-for-nothing fellow!" the woman cried. "Look what you've done! You want something to eat, but you don't want to work for it! Now none of us will have any supper!" Alfred only hung his head in shame.

Just then the woodcutter came home. As soon as he walked through the door, he recognized the stranger sitting at his hearth. "Be quiet!" he told his wife. "Do you realize who you are scolding? This is our noble ruler, King Alfred himself."

The woman was horrified. She ran to the king's side and fell to her knees. She begged him to forgive her for speaking so harshly.

But the wise King Alfred asked her to rise. "You were right to scold me," he said. "I told you I would watch the cakes, and then I let them burn. I deserved what you said. Anyone who accepts a duty, whether it be large or small, should perform it faithfully. I have failed this time, but it will not happen again. My duties as king await me."

The story does not tell us if King Alfred had anything to eat that night. But it was not many days before he had gathered his men together again, and soon he drove the Danes out of England.

"Neat story," Billy exclaimed. "They're lucky the king didn't get ticked off."

"What do you mean?" his mother asked. Joan carefully chose this story and wasn't surprised by Billy's reaction. She now had to capitalize on her youngest son's opening. "Do you think King Alfred should have punished the woodcutter's wife?"

"Of course," Billy answered. "He was king and could do whatever he wanted!"

"That's true. He could do anything he wanted," acknowledged Joan, "but he didn't choose that particular course."

"I don't think he had the right to punish the woman." Pete was obviously ticked that his little brother would come up with such a preposterous point of view. "It wouldn't be fair."

"Hold it, hold it," Lorin broke in. "Say what you like, but do it in a way that respects each person's opinion."

Pete, sufficiently chastised, toned down his follow-up comment. "It doesn't seem right for a person to play by a different set of rules than everyone else. So what if he is a king."

"I agree with Pete." This was the first indication that Marie had been listening to the discussion. She had spent much of the time gazing at the ceiling. "The king agreed to watch the cakes and then went ahead and did his own thing. He didn't deserve to be fed."

"Each of you is making good points. Thank you." Joan tried to conceal her growing excitement. Things were going better than she had hoped. "Billy gave us something to think about. Would the king have been justified in punishing the woodcutter's wife? After all, he was king."

Lorin had been weighing various perspectives and was still unsure of where he stood. "You know, we are talking about a different time and culture, and many of the rules were different. I suppose that we must concede that the king had the right to punish the women for disrespect."

"But she didn't know who he actually was," responded Pete. "Doesn't that count for something?"

Marie took this opportunity to express a consideration that had not as yet surfaced. "Don't you think the wife was kind of rude? Didn't she accuse him of being lazy and good for nothing? She didn't take the time to hear what the stranger had to say. There had to be a reason why a hungry person would allow his own meal to go up in smoke. It seems to me that she could have been more understanding."

Lorin was impressed and frankly surprised with his daughter's insight. He couldn't recall a past instance where she displayed this level of maturity. He made a mental note to spend a little more time with Marie. He obviously didn't know his daughter as well as he thought. "This is a good point that Marie makes. I wouldn't be surprised if this woman didn't have a problem with jumping to conclusions and allowing her temper to guide her actions."

Much of this was passing over Billy's head, but he could see a little of what his sister was getting at, and it only served as a reinforcement of his original opinion. "Yeah, I still think the king should have thrown her in jail or something like that. You shouldn't mess with a king."

Pete was only waiting for Billy to take a breath to seize his opportunity to speak. "Rudeness is rudeness whether it happens to a king or a regular guy like me. I guess I'm not sure now if the king had the right to do something to the woman. It wasn't fair for her to yell without first learning all the facts."

"It must have been difficult being a king," Joan found herself saying. She realized she had stopped being the teacher and was now as interested in the story as her family. "Just think, he had the power to react as he saw fit. He literally had the power to do as he chose. He showed a lot of courage in conceding his fault in the situation."

Marie was struck with a new insight that she had never before thought about. "You know I can see what Mom is talking about. It really took courage on the king's part to admit to blame. I know how hard it is for me to admit to a mistake when friends and family are concerned," she shot a glance at Pete, "especially a brother who will remain unnamed." The whole family laughed when Pete put on his well-rehearsed facial expression of innocence.

The discussion continued for the better part of an hour before mother brought it to a halt by announcing that tomorrow was a school day, and she was sure there was unfinished chores and homework to be done. The children begrudgingly filed to their respective bedrooms and appointed tasks. Both Joan and her husband followed their departure with keen interest. Each noted that the children had enjoyed the activity, and the sad expressions were more a result of an end to the discussion than a disdain for the work that awaited them.

It took an additional twenty minutes of tidying and such before the two parents found themselves ready to talk. These discussions were usually reserved for the master bedroom where privacy was virtually assured. This instance proved no exception.

"I was impressed. This was a good experience for each of us. I learned a great deal more about the children, and I enjoyed the opportunity to think about respect, law and courage." Lorin usually was the one to break the ice.

Joan smiled and added, "Don't forget fairness. I think Pete used the term at least fifteen times." They both laughed. They weren't exactly sure how this meeting affected each of the children, but they were confident that some good had occurred.

"I presume this story and discussion goes deeper than what you confided to the children. Well you captured my undying admiration and keen interest, so the floor is now yours!" Lorin placed his feet on the ottoman which was a sure sign that he was ready to talk.

"Well there really isn't that much to say," Joan began. "I have been feeling estranged with our children and knew the status quo was no longer acceptable. Do you know that Billy left his skateboard in the middle of the driveway, and I almost ran over it. This, after a fifteen minute lecture on Tuesday about putting things away. I'm convinced that my children are tuning me out, and its frightening me terribly. What's going to happen when the issues change from sloppiness and cars to experimentation with drugs or choice of friends. I'm afraid I'll have no chance to offer them needed counsel because they have long since written me off as uninformed and unfeeling."

Lorin was surprised at the tears welling up in his wife's eyes. He marveled at how deeply she loved her children and how seriously she took her responsibilities as a mother. He hadn't given her last point a moment's thought, but he now found himself searching his own heart and fears. Where did he stand with his children? How well did he actually know them? He had been surprised with Marie's depth of maturity and was now conceding his failures in keeping up with the changes in the children. This matter of parental influence was also unsettling. It dawned on him that he hadn't a clue as to where he stood. Most of the discipline had fallen on Joan, but he could remember the frequent instances when he stepped in to lay down the law. No question that they were one-sided lectures despite how he may have labeled them at the moment. He acknowledged to himself that he rarely listened to what the children had to offer. It pained him suddenly to realize that he often acted as the woodcutter's wife, quick to react without first grasping the full picture. "So what should we do?"

Joan managed a smile. "What about this evening? What about making this activity a regular part of our lives? Do you realize that we didn't once get on our soapboxes and sermonize?"

"You're right," he responded. "I can't ever remember a time I didn't preach something or other. There was something about the story that discouraged sermonizing, and I think I know why. The lectures usually come when something has gone wrong. You and I see it as a crisis, and the children don't. So what happens if we dominate the exchange because we are the only ones really interested in the problem? The children are only interested in minimizing the damage to themselves, and all their comments are geared toward this end. You know how we like to fix problems, and we are going to act whether they choose to participate or not. The lecture approach wins out by default!" Lorin sat back, obviously pleased with his insightful discovery.

"Honey, sometimes you amaze me," Joan teased. The smile vanished as she asked, "What do you think about holding these discussions on a weekly or a bimonthly basis. Reacting to a story provides us a perfect opportunity to listen to what our children are telling us while at the same time learning more about a particular virtue."

"Well, based on tonight's experience, I think it's a great idea. You mentioned learning about a particular virtue. Virtues is probably the more appropriate term. Each of us hit on insights and perspectives that held personal meaning," added Lorin. "For Pete it was often a matter of fairness. Remember how Marie latched on to the king's humility. She somehow linked this up with courage, and to her this made the king pretty special."

"I had to laugh when she stated that there weren't many King Alfreds available today. Actually, I laughed, then cried when I realized how hard it is to find suitable role models for our own children," Joan continued. "I know how few of my school children have someone close who can teach by example."

"I'm sure your comment is accurate. I suspect that many young people reinvent who they are on a monthly basis. All it takes is the right movie, rock concert or playground encounter to reshape who or what they intend to be when they grow up." Lorin wasn't usually this philosophical, and it surprised his wife. "In fact, I've almost come to terms with the notion that all of America reinvents itself from year to year. It's as if we're riding a runaway train with different groups manning the switches, and the direction we take is purely a factor of who's in control at the critical time. You only have to note who's filling the magazines and endorsing the products to predict our newest American persona."

"My, this is getting depressing," his wife admitted. "Let's get back to what we can do for our three children. I'll leave my classroom and societal concerns till this Friday when I get back together with Pam."

"Pam?" Lorin questioned. "I haven't heard you talk about her in years. I should have known that the two of you had gotten together. You were always bringing home something interesting during your years at Lincoln."

"Yes, guilty as accused! Seriously though, she is the one that started me in on the value in teaching through stories. Since then I have bounced some of my ideas off colleagues, and our successes this evening only confirmed what I was coming to accept. I don't know why it has taken me this long to figure it out. Think about history's greatest shapers of human thought. The most powerful teaching tool has often been some form of a story. Jesus used the parable. We studied about the Good Samaritan in a recent Sunday School class. He didn't preach a long and flowery sermon to make his point that true charity suffereth long and never faileth. In fact he provided a simple yet sublime example of how kindness is defined in actual practice. And then there's the widow's mite. He left little doubt how generosity should be measured. Then there's..., well you get my point!"

"And it's a good point," Lorin replied. "We could add Confucius, Buddha, Ben Franklin, Solomon, Ronald Reagan..."

"Ronald Reagan?" Joan was amused and couldn't resist the dig. "Weren't you the very person speaking critically of President Reagan just a short week ago?"

"Well, yes, that is true," Lorin admitted, "but I think he earned his label as the great communicator. He had a real knack for making his point through simple stories and witticisms, and the public appreciated this unique ability. They appreciated it because they could grasp his point without having to rummage through a lot of unnecessary and often misleading verbiage."

"Touche, I concede the point," she acknowledged with the same smile brightening her face. "Let me share a concern that still has me baffled."

Joan continued, "When does a concept or virtue sink in to the point where it becomes a part of the person and a resource to draw upon? Or taken from a different perspective, how does one adapt a good story to insure that the listener internalizes its meaning? It's not enough to inject platitudes into someone's head, equipping them to do little more than pass the platitudes on to someone else."

The full import of Joan's words finally hit home as her husband grasped the full meaning of her concern. He asked, "How can we avoid raising young people who have little to hold on to when circumstances test their true mettle?"

"Exactly. I have many students who will acknowledge the risks in abusing drugs. They can cite the statistics and even back their arguments with true life examples. But their understanding is all in their heads and not in their hearts. Given the right circumstances, they succumb to the temptation time and time again. Using stories to discipline through virtue is a wonderful idea, but it's only part of the solution I'm searching for. We're missing something, and I'm determined to get to the bottom of the matter."

Lorin gazed at his wife in admiration. He believed her when she announced her intention to tie down all the loose ends. He had seen her in action too many times to harbor any doubts. She would discover what she needed to make full use of this disciplinary approach. "So you plan to meet with Pam on Friday? Wish I could be there; it should be an interesting exchange." He smiled to assure her of his full support.

The smile obviously pleased her. "Interesting? That's too passive a term. How about challenging and combative. I can't wait to get a second shot at Pam. She tantalized me the entire two hours and forced me to dig for everything I sought. Well, her strategy worked because I've continued to dig for the past five days. I know exactly where I wish our dialogue to begin, and I predict more of the same from her. She kept referring to her new approach as disciplining through virtue. I'm hoping that the answers to my questions are found here."

41

Chapter Nine
Obstructions Block
the Way

"I have learned that the head does not hear anything until the heart has listened, and that what the heart knows today the head will understand tomorrow."
James Stephens

CHAPTER NINE

Friday afternoon finally arrived, and Joan quickly made her way to Lincoln Elementary. As she passed the main office and headed down A Corridor, she glanced up at the south wall. It must have been an unconscious movement born of long habit. This wall had been reserved for sixth grade displays, and she had spent many an hour adorning the brick facade. Her eye caught the teacher's name whose students' efforts were now on display. It was Pam's class, and it appeared that she had elected to post short stories written by her students. She stopped and read the heading that had been constructed in large block letters-- Courtesy In Action. Each selection was near a full page in length and identified by the signature of the author. Jean randomly chose two stories, read through them carefully and then hurried on to her friend's classroom.

Pam was visiting with two students and was unaware of Joan's arrival. Joan was intrigued by the scene before her. It was obvious at first glance that her colleague and the two students were the best of friends. One of the students, a pretty round-eyed young lady, was teasing her teacher about her mismatched blouse and slacks, and Pam was returning the teasing barb for barb. The other student, a lanky, athletic looking young lady, was giggling in obvious pleasure. Joan reflected back a number of years when she had enjoyed close relationships much like this. A slight wave of remorse came and went before Joan made her presence known by stepping forward.

"Joan, it's good to see you again. Did you bring the donuts?" Pam laughed as she peeked in Joan's paper sack. "Oh good, you've got extras. Could we spare a couple of donuts for these two characters? They've earned it after the ribbing I've given. Besides they're responsible for that bulletin board on the back wall. Look's pretty good, huh?" The two girls were obviously pleased by the compliment but remained respectfully silent.

Pam gestured to each student as she made her introductions. "This is Vicki Meyers, and this is Janet Godfrey--without question two of my all-time favorites. Students, this is Joan Walker, an old teaching buddy of mine."

Joan was taken back momentarily at the sound of the names but recovered before any hint of her surprise could be picked up by the two students. "It's a pleasure to meet you, and I agree with your teacher that your bulletin board is a work of art." Composing a business-like expression, Joan joked, "Are you available for hire? Or better yet, would you consider transferring to my school?"

The questions brought on more laughter. Both teachers noticed how the jelly donuts didn't even survive the girls' passage through the doorway.

Pam waited until the two students were out of hearing range before apologizing. "I hope you didn't mind my offering the donuts." She smiled,

"Besides, I can ill afford to pig out as I did in our last visit. I was so guilt ridden that I starved myself the entire weekend."

Mrs. Walker gave her friend the eye before announcing, "Those were your talkers, weren't they? Did you purposely assign them the bulletin board to allow me to meet them?"

"Guilty as charged," Pam confessed. Smiling she added, "I thought it would provide you with some hope for the future!"

"I dare say I'm impressed," Joan disclosed. "They seemed delightful and apparently you have established a wonderful relationship with the two girls. Disciplining through virtue?"

Pam nodded her head. "Without a doubt, it has played the key role in turning around these two students. Much of the change is the natural consequence to my calling a halt to past practice of lectures, sermons and threats. However, I'm beginning to see evidence that the students are gaining a greater appreciation of how the exercise of respect is a win-win situation."

"Pam, could we wait on our discussion about "The Touch of the Master's Hand" and stories in general? I first need you to explain how you use the stories to change hearts and behavior," she announced. "This question has been driving me nuts, and I know you have some answers." Joan could detect a carefully concealed enthusiasm in her friend as Pam reached for The Book of Virtues.

Pam confided, "I had this very question when I began to play around with the use of stories. One of Bennett's entries demonstrated this concern very well. I came across this insight while reading through a story listed under Loyalty. I recognized how this particular entry could fit under Friendship and Loyalty, but the story provided a far different message to me. Have you had chance to read "The Devoted Friend" by Oscar Wilde? It's found on page 674 in The Book of Virtues."

"No, I have not," was Joan's reply.

"Good," laughed her friend. "This is one of my favorite stories, and I rarely pass up the opportunity to share it. It's one of the more lengthy selections, so I will restrict myself to a few excerpts from the book while using my own words to fill you in on the essential details."

"Let me kick my shoes off and settle in," Joan teased. "Your buildup is impressive, and I don't want to miss a word."

Pam glanced through the book, noted a few paragraphs with a yellow outliner and then began, "A water rat makes the claim he knows of nothing in the world that is either nobler or rarer than a devoted friendship. When challenged by a linnet to describe the duties of a devoted friend, the water rat unhesitantly responds that a devoted friend should be devoted to him. Yet the rat is at a loss when the linnet asks the water rat what he would be expected to do in return. This prompts the linnet to tell a story about two men, a prosperous

43

miller and a humble gardener, who shared an unusual relationship. The linnet relates how the miller continually asks for and receives gifts and favors from Hans, the gardener, but never returns the favor. We will first pick up the story where the two's relationship is first explained.

> "Little Hans had a great many friends, but the most devoted friend of all was big Hugh the Miller. Indeed, so devoted was the rich Miller to little Hans, that he would never go by his garden without leaning over the wall and plucking a large nosegay, or a handful of sweet herbs, or filling his pockets with plums and cherries if it was the fruit season.
>
> "'Real friends should have everything in common,' the Miller used to say, and little Hans nodded and smiled, and felt very proud of having a friend with such noble ideas.
>
> "Sometimes, indeed, the neighbors thought it strange that the rich Miller never gave little Hans anything in return, though he had a hundred sacks of flour stored away in his mill, and six milk cows, and a large flock of woolly sheep; but Hans never troubled his head about these things, and nothing gave him greater pleasure than to listen to all the wonderful things the Miller used to say about the unselfishness of true friendship.
>
> "So little Hans worked away in his garden. During the spring, the summer, and the autumn he was very happy, but when the winter came, and he had no fruit or flowers to bring to the market, he suffered a good deal from cold and hunger, and often had to go to bed without any supper but a few dried pears or some hard nuts. In the winter, also, he was extremely lonely, as the Miller never came to see him then.
>
> "'There is no good in my going to see little Hans as long as the snow lasts,' the Miller used to say to his Wife, 'for when people are in trouble they should be left alone, and not be bothered by visitors. That at least is my idea about friendship, and I am sure I am right. So I shall wait till the spring comes, and then I shall pay him a visit, and he will be able to give me a large basket of primroses, and that will make him so happy.'"

We again pick up the tale as the impoverished gardener confides to the miller how he was forced to sell many of his possessions including his wheelbarrow just to keep from starving. Hans concluded his tall tale on an optimistic note. He confided how all would be set right when money from the sale of his flowers would buy back the items he had sold. The miller snatched this opportunity to show Hans how generous he was.

44

"Hans," said the Miller, "I will give you my wheelbarrow. It is not in very good repair. Indeed, one side is gone, and there is something wrong with the wheel spokes. But in spite of that I will give it to you. I know it is very generous of me, and a great many people would think me extremely foolish for parting with it, but I am not like the rest of the world. I think that generosity is the essence of friendship, and, besides, I have got a new wheelbarrow for myself. Yes, You may set your mind at ease. I will give you my wheelbarrow."

Pam looked up from the book and added, "The miller now felt that his promise of generosity should place little Hans forever in his debt. This next excerpt describes just one of many favors asked of the impoverished gardener."

"And now, as I have given you my wheelbarrow, I am sure you would like to give me some flowers in return. Here is the basket, and mind you fill it quite full."

"Quite full?" said little Hans, rather sorrowfully, for it was really a very big basket, and he knew that if he filled it he would have no flowers left for the market, and he was very anxious to get his silver buttons back.

"Well, really," answered the Miller, "as I have given you my wheelbarrow, I don't think that it is much to ask you for a few flowers. I may be wrong, but I should have thought that friendship, true friendship, was quite free from selfishness of any kind."

"My dear friend, my best friend," cried little Hans, "you are welcome to all the flowers in my garden. I would much sooner have your good opinion than my silver buttons, any day." And he ran and plucked all his pretty primroses, and filled the Miller's basket.

Again, Pam stopped her reading to provide her friend the details necessary in following the story line. "Eventually little Hans died while performing yet another service for the rich miller. Now we pick up the story immediately following the funeral procession which not surprisingly was headed by his best friend, the miller."

"Little Hans is certainly a great loss to everyone," said the Blacksmith, when the funeral was over, and they were all seated comfortably in the inn, drinking spiced wine and eating sweet cakes.

"A great loss to me at any rate," answered the Miller. "Why, I had as good as given him my wheelbarrow, and now I really don't know what to do with it. It is very much in my way at home, and it is

in such bad repair that I could not get anything for it if I sold it. I will certainly take care not to give away anything again. One always suffers for being generous."

Pam shot a glance at her friend, and Joan picked up a slight edge to her manner. "Is something wrong?" asked Joan. "May I presume this concludes the linnet's story?"

"Very good," Pam responded as she lightened up her manner. "No matter how many times I read this story, it always hits me as a tragic situation that shouldn't ever happen. It's silly of me to react this way. Let me finish up by reading how the water rat responded to this well meaning attempt to teach him how true friendship should work."

> *"Well?" said the Water Rat, after a long pause.*
> *"Well, that is the end," said the Linnet.*
> *"But what became of the Miller?" asked the Water Rat.*
> *"Oh! I really don't know," replied the Linnet. "And I am sure that I don't care."*
> *"It is quite evident then that you have no sympathy in your nature," said the Water Rat.*
> *"I am afraid you don't quite see the moral of the story," remarked the Linnet.*
> *"The what?" screamed the Water Rat.*
> *"The moral."*
> *"Do you mean to say that the story has a moral?"*
> *"Certainly," said the Linnet.*
> *"Well, really," said the Water Rat, in a very angry manner, "I think you should have told me that before you began."*

Joan waited patiently to hear what Pam had to say, all the while turning images through her mind. She made a mental note to read the entire story. Pam chose wisely because this particular piece clearly expressed her chief concern. Despite the powerful message drawn by the story, the water rat seemed completely unmoved.

Joan made an eye contact that conveyed her readiness to proceed with the discussion.

It appeared that Pam was waiting for a signal because she spoke up immediately. "There is no assurance that a person will grasp the significance of a message as it relates to his own affairs. The water rat never caught on that the character of the miller was a mere image of himself. Worse still, the rat hadn't a clue that the miller's view of friendship left much to be desired."

"Yes," interrupted Joan, "that is what's still bothering me about the use of stories to change behavior. Some students will miss the point even when the story's message hits them right between the eyes."

"I can see that you have arrived at the point I did a short three months ago. May I also presume that I need no longer convince you of the power in using stories to discipline and instruct others?" Pam inquired.

Joan nodded. "I've been consumed with the topic these past seven days and have even gone so far as to share my thoughts with a colleague at the school."

Pam raised her eyebrows as if to ask for the identity of the colleague.

Her friend immediately picked up the cue. "Fred Jones."

"You're kidding," Pam joked. "From what you have told me about Mr. Jones, you must have been desperate for a sounding board."

Joan acknowledge the gentle jab with a smile of her own before adding, "Actually, Fred was really helpful. His initial posture was to play the unconvinced cynic. The more we talked, the more interested he became." Joan let a smile slip out before continuing. "I used a few of your recent tactics and kept him dodging by an ongoing barrage of questions. I don't think the poor man knew what hit him."

The two shared a laugh before Joan concluded her point. "You may find this surprising, but Fred began to offer some helpful insights before we drew our discussion to a close. I was duly impressed as well as rewarded by his contributions."

"I know you well enough to predict that you didn't stop with Fred. Who else did you wear out with your incessant questioning?" Pam knew her guess hit the bull's-eye as she observed her friend's slowly widening smile.

"Okay, so I pestered my family a little. They indulged me by listening as I read a story and then joined me in a lively discussion. It turned out wonderfully!" Joan announced. "Even Lorin agreed. We have even decided to incorporate disciplining through virtue into our parenting approach," she paused for effect before adding, "as soon as you feel inclined to tell us what it is."

Chapter Ten
Familiar Landmark Is
Sighted

"The foundations of our national policy will be laid on the pure and immutable principles of private morality."
George Washington

CHAPTER TEN

Pam loved her friend's pause and showed her appreciation by throwing a paper clip at Joan's head. "Are you suggesting that I purposely evaded your questions? You know me better than that!"

"I do know you, and that has been the most perplexing thing about the whole situation. I can never remember a time you passed up an opportunity to give me advice!" Joan watched her colleague's reaction and knew her observation pleased Pam.

"It's the new me," Pam confessed, "and it is one of the keystones in disciplining by virtue. This approach is meant to eliminate our need to offer unsolicited advice. But I can tell that you have already figured that out. I'm right aren't I?" Pam searched for confirmation.

Joan's grin widened as she nodded her head in agreement. "I have managed to pick up a thing or two. But I confess that I still have more questions than answers."

Pam Phillips offered an encouraging observation, "It is my guess that you have already grasped the basics of the approach and are ready to extend your understanding to the
all-important subtleties. This is where disciplining through virtue moves from the science to the art form."

"Now I suppose you are going to insist that I share what I have discovered about using stories as a disciplinary tool," Joan challenged.

"That would be nice," Pam quipped. "Consider it a test to determine what you have learned in your seven days of discovery."

Joan Walker unabashedly admitted, "Actually, I was hoping for the chance to share what I've learned."

"Knowing you as well as I do, I suspected that might be the case," Pam teased.

Joan then proceeded to review in some detail her eventful week. She related how she discovered the versatility in a story and how a story often has multiple messages that serve personal needs. She expressed her frustration over the mismatch that often occurs when a teacher counsels on matters that have little meaning for many of the students and how a story with discussion greatly increases the likelihood that each student will gain something valuable from the process.

She shared her appreciation for a story's gentle approach to discipline and how it enables a teacher or parent to deal with a troubling dilemma without personal attack or boring and repetitive sermonizing. Joan shared how she and Lorin were delighted to find that the discussion following "King Alfred and the Cakes" provided wonderful insights into the thoughts of their children. Joan confided that she and her husband were encouraged that they had at last found a forum that nurtured meaningful discussion with their children. She confessed that she expected to gain many of the same insights on how her students were thinking.

Pam interrupted her friend at this point. "You say you tried this on your own family. I'm intrigued. That needs to be the topic of a future discussion."

Joan continued by describing her fears over being tuned out by both her children and her students. After citing four examples, she confided her hope that <u>Discipline Through Virtue</u> would be the means to build back the relationships as they should be. Joan concluded with a statement of resolve, "I'm determined to make this approach work, and I'll continue to hound everyone, including myself, until I've discovered and mastered the subtleties you made reference to."

Pam listened without further comment until Joan's expression indicated that she had said her piece, and it was Pam's move. Pam began with a heartfelt compliment. "I'm impressed as usual. You've hit on some notions that I've not entertained, and this has given me something to think about." Pam took a visible departure from the earnest nature of their discussion by warmly stating, "It's so refreshing to share your company once again. Don't you think we make a great team?"

Joan nodded, attuned to what her friend was trying to express.

"We've been down this road before," Pam continued, "and I owe much of my success and personal fulfillment to your willingness to exchange ideas and concerns."

Joan felt the same way. "Remember how we discovered that we were practicing synergism. Leave it to a university professor to attach a term to something we had been practicing on our own for years. Do you remember how we laughed when we first learned that there was a term to describe our antics? It does feel good to work through these ideas with a colleague whose judgment I trust. Let's not let another three years pass before we get together again."

Pam blushed slightly before returning the conversation back to business. "You know, I believe you have stumbled on one of the subtleties. The wise teacher needs to match up with a trusted colleague to bring out the best in both. When we brainstorm ideas, share successes or confess to failures, we can't help but gain the insights required of this disciplinary approach. It's no small task to touch the hearts and minds of thirty sixth graders."

Apparently Joan didn't see the need to verbalize her agreement. She merely smiled.

Pam knew it was time to talk about the subtleties. She moved the discussion forward with a question that she intended to answer herself, "So why didn't the water rat gain from the linnet's story? When I first asked myself this very question, I had difficulty pinning it down. I finally concluded

49

that the water rat had never felt the need to examine friendship as an object worthy of study. Without occasion for concern, the matter held little interest. It would be much like my asking you to give me your thoughts on what it's like to grow up with two noses adorning your face."

Joan laughed at the analogy. "That makes logical sense. But, how would a teacher assure herself that an individual or class was first brought to the point where a story would have meaning to them. I am presuming that we can have some control over this. Surely you're not going to tell me that a student's readiness to learn is purely a matter of chance."

"No, we as teachers have some influence. We can nurture the learning environment to improve the odds that our stories and discussions are properly valued," Pam responded.

"Okay, so how does a teacher increase the likelihood that a story will be properly perceived?" Joan asked.

"To answer your question, let me begin by asking something of you. Can you devise a situation that would provide a plausible reason for the water rat's indifference to the story's message?"

"My best guess would have to be that the water rat had never had a true friend," Joan answered. "He missed the linnet's point because he didn't know enough about friendship to pay it any mind."

"A decent answer," Pam conceded. "Would you agree that a second reason might be that the rat had lost a dear friend and consequently had chosen to downgrade a friendship to nothing more than exchanging of pleasantries?"

"Perhaps, but I'm failing to follow your point," Joan confessed.

"My point is that the reasons for a student blocking out a message can be varied, and this requires a learning situation equally varied."

Pam gazed intently at her friend to try to determine if her point was understood. Joan did get the message, but was too deep in thought to provide her friend with the feedback she desired. Finally, Joan responded, "The discussions that follow a story have got to be a key factor in creating the readiness. Perhaps a student will express a perspective in a context that suddenly reaches a classmate. All that classmate needed was to hear the issue in terms he could relate to. We know that students are often more effective than their teacher in explaining a concept to a classmate. I suspect it has something to do with their frame of reference."

"You've hit on a good point," Pam acknowledged. "Some students will respond when things are presented in terms and images they understand."

"Joan was back in thought again, and after a considerable pause she spoke again. "You know," she began, "I am hesitant to discuss an issue when the topic is personally sensitive. Worse still, I will shun conversation that might reveal something about myself I'd rather not have known. If you first treat the issue as it relates to the actual story, you've provided a safe environment for discussion. Students that are part of the problem will still participate if they fail to see the discussion as a personal attack. For example, it's easy for a student to take a position on whether or not the woodcutter's wife was showing disrespect to King Alfred. The circumstances surrounding this story are so different from the world the students are living in that much of the threat must be gone."

"Joan, that's a key point," Pam confirmed. "I agree completely, and I must confess that your explanation has added some depth and breadth to my understanding--synergism at work."

Joan, obviously pleased, added, "I noticed this in my three children during our discussion. No one appeared to be threatened in the least. In fact, it was very much to the contrary."

"I found that to be the case when our class read and discussed "The Golden Touch" from The Book of Virtues. My reason in choosing this particular entry centered in a classroom problem that had been developing. A number of students were wanting me to hand them everything on a silver platter, and I found myself giving in to their constant pleas. Finally, I realized that life doesn't work that way, and I was providing my students a great disservice. Well, as I began to back off, the students' complaints increased."

"Anyway, the story of King Midas was a wonderful forum to talk about the worth in meeting challenges and the pitfalls to having everything come too easily. Most of the students didn't make the connection between their insistence to be spoon-fed and the king's desire to amass gold as quickly and as easily as possible. Consequently, everyone seemed at ease in participating in the discussion, and we unearthed a barrel-full of insights on the matter. But I must add that as the discussion progressed, the students' comments moved from the time of King Midas to the circumstances of today. Here is where a second subtlety occurs. It's essential to move the issue to a context that allows a student to examine his own standing with respect to the dilemma. This is the first step to meaningful change. We have little hope to change behavior if the issue remains obscured in a fairy-tale setting."

"I suspect that by session's end, a number of the students made the connection to our present classroom dilemma. So the initial story and discussion created an awareness in a certain percentage of the class. That's a good start," Joan conceded. "Is a second story and discussion the logical second step?"

Pam Phillips thought a moment before responding. "Sometimes a second round is the wisest course to pursue, but not always," she added. "Let's hold up on this question for a few more moments."

"Fair enough," Joan answered. "How about a follow-up question before we leave this particular subject." Without waiting for the go ahead she queried,

"What other outcomes do you hope to achieve after your first classroom exchange?"

"You should have been a trial lawyer," Pam responded. "Your questions are unrelenting!" Joan merely ignored the remark and waited on her friend's response.

Pam stalled, trying to pull her thoughts together. This was a good question, but one she had not anticipated. Her friend came to her rescue by offering to share what she had determined. Pam didn't hesitate here. "By all means," she joked. "I'm delighted to hear what you have to say!"

Joan was too engrossed in thought to notice her colleague's relief. She began, "I would hope that a number of valid observations would surface in the discussion. Can you see the value in the class agreeing that certain behaviors are okay while others are not okay? This removes the need for the teacher to preach these points. We just talked about students personally relating to the dilemma, but I see this as a completely different outcome."

"Wonderful insight," Pam conceded." "I might add that a third outcome should be the bonding that occurs when a group of individuals share a common interest. That's why it's important to have as many students participate as possible. I have found that it sometimes helps to set up ground rules for the discussion."

"That makes sense," her friend volunteered. "That bonding can work magic. We have both seen how a learning environment improves when the little cliques, petty arguments and social stratums are eliminated. Forgive me," Joan insisted, "but I have another question. You mentioned your use of "The Golden Touch." I don't believe you just stumbled onto this particular story. Surely this choice came as a result of considerable research and thought."

"No, I arrived at this decision in a matter of minutes," Pam replied. "You may find it hard to believe, but within this same time span I had also determined the two additional stories I would use if follow-ups seemed the prudent course of action."

"Okay," Joan announced, "you've got my curiosity stirred. How did you manage this feat?"

Pam was tempted to tantalize her friend for a few more moments but decided against this option. She smiled inwardly as she pictured Joan aiming an eraser at her head. Instead, she promptly responded by handing her friend her copy of <u>Discipline Through Virtue</u>. "Turn to the section entitled Disciplinary Dilemmas. It's organized alphabetically. I then had to figure out which dilemma described the problem I was having with my students. After scanning the list, I chose "Indulgent" pages 159 to 168. This guided me to the appropriate pages in the Ready-Reference. The story on King Midas was one of the options that was listed under Indulgent. After reading the story's description and key points, I decided "The Golden Touch" would get the job done. I then used the same process to select two additional options that I could use if needed."

Joan turned to the Ready-Reference and found the section entitled Indulgent. It took but a moment to locate "The Golden Touch," and she quickly read through the different pieces of information. Joan looked up and nodded her head. "This answers my question, and I'm impressed with the ease in which a teacher can position herself to move ahead on her problem. I'm provided a description of the entry as well as key points and questions to aid in my follow-up discussions."

Pam glanced at the clock and decided to move the discussion back to Joan's question about follow-up stories. "You asked if a second story and discussion is the next step in increasing the likelihood that more students identify personally with the message you are hoping to convey. I think we both agree that it's not enough for a mere handful of students to profit from the experiences. We want to reach the entire class."

Joan acknowledged the insight with a slight nod of her head.

Pam took this as the okay to proceed with her point. "There is a process that provides the means to address our concern, and we have only discussed a few examples of its application. It's called apperception and is defined as the process of understanding something perceived in terms of previous experience. Once the students have defined the virtue in relationship to the story's characters, setting and circumstances, apperception is the process required to transfer these insights to the world our students understand. It's a difficult task, but not impossible. I mentioned that our classroom discussions often evolve naturally to how the virtue should be applied in our classrooms, playgrounds, homes, etc. I rarely have had to instigate the transfer, but occasionally I trigger the change with a question. I have found the questions provided in <u>Discipline Through Virtue</u> helpful."

"I see what you are driving at," interrupted Joan. Pointing to a section in "The Golden Touch" she read, Can anyone think of something where it is okay to never be satisfied with what you have?

"You've got it," Pam exclaimed. "Now the art is in shaping the questions to get the students thinking about their own lives. Done properly, the students will offer their own examples and provide their own illustrations of what's right or wrong about a particular behavior. The teacher's biggest challenge is to be patient and allow the students to make the discoveries. This may take more than a single discussion, and here's where your second and third stories fit in."

Joan offered, "I can see that the second story or perhaps the third story may prove the catalyst to tune in a particular student. It may boil down to a specific aspect included in the story that triggers the connection."

"Right again," Pam commented. "Now I don't wish to discourage you, but getting the students to tune in is only the first step. I've found that while it is essential for a student to understand, even internalize a new perspective, it is still not enough. We will have failed if our students leave our classrooms with invaluable insights but with no experience in their application."

"I'm not with you yet," Joan pleaded, "but I understand enough of what you've said to beg for your patience and ask that you try once more to penetrate my thick skull."

"Sorry," Pam teased, "let me try a different slant. I'm convinced that virtues first need to be viewed concretely. It's too easy to lose your grasp of an abstraction. Loyalty is a concept easily confused, even forgotten, if not grounded in concrete examples of application. All the better if the applications are personal experiences. This is especially true for young people whose set of beliefs are in constant flux."

Joan thought back to her husband's comments about the lack of suitable role models and how our young people reinvent themselves on a monthly basis. She acknowledged her agreement by stating, "I'm now following you, and it makes a lot of sense."

Pam continued, "I suppose the best way to explain this is to frame it in the context of developing a new habit. You've got to create a learning environment where a student can combine knowledge, desire and application in repeated situations."

"Habits, you're kidding me. Must it be that involved?" Joan asked.

"I'm afraid so," replied her friend. "I don't stop with the story and discussion, or for that matter three stories and three discussions. I search out ways to keep the virtue in the forefront of the students' minds."

Mrs. Walker thought back to the essays posted in the hallway and couldn't resist having fun with Pam. "I hope you wouldn't suggest something as mundane as an essay."

Pam was too startled to immediately reply. As she grappled for the right words she was stopped abruptly by Joan's laughter. "Okay, what have I missed?" Pam growled.

"Nothing, and I'm ashamed of myself," Joan giggled. "I noticed the essays when I just entered the school, and in truth I think they're a marvelous idea. I even read two of them."

Back in control Pam quipped, "Laugh all you want. I always get even. Anyway, as I was saying, I look for opportunities to highlight some aspect of the virtue. The essays have worked well as have haiku assignments and similar poetry endeavors. I particularly look for opportunities to applaud the practical application of the virtue. I've asked the students to look for good and bad examples of the virtue in action. I tried a bulletin board on honesty that the students filled with articles and clippings from magazines and newspapers. On one occasion I had the students divide up into groups of four. They were instructed to develop a four-minute skit and then put it on for their classmates. You might be interested to know that this activity afforded me the opportunity to turn things around with Janet and Vicki."

Chapter Eleven
A Trail Sign at Last

"Injustice anywhere is a threat to justice everywhere." *Martin Luther King, Jr.*

CHAPTER ELEVEN

Joan's interest quickened with the mention of Vicki and Janet. She was hungry for details on the girls' developments and wasn't going to permit this opportunity to pass her by. "Could I talk you into indulging my preoccupation with these two girls? My curiosity is all but driving me crazy."

Joan's confession got them both laughing, and Pam used this interlude to suggest that they wander down to the faculty room for a second can of pop.

"Only if you promise to satisfy my curiosity," Joan conceded as the two headed down the corridor.

Joan got things going again by teasing, "You were saying..."

"Okay, okay, I'll give in and tell you what happened." Pam seemed almost embarrassed, and it struck Joan as rather odd.

Continuing, Pam said, "I've been purposely avoiding the incident because the whole activity turned out to be something of a disaster. I know how good you are with these sorts of things, and I hate to admit to my ineptness."

Joan laughed as she quipped, "What a lame excuse for holding out on me! Now get on with it."

"Okay, let me give you a snapshot of what occurred over the course of three days." Pam began her account by reaching for her personal copy of The Book of Virtues. "This all happened about a week after reading and discussing "Rebecca." I had a few minutes of dead time prior to lunch, so I grabbed my copy of Discipline Through Virtue and spotted this little selection."

Pam turned to page 109 in The Book of Virtues and pointed to a poem entitled "Kindness to Animals."

Compassion may be first learned through kindness
to all creatures great and small.

Little children, never give
Pain to things that feel and live;
Let the gentle robin come
For the crumbs you save at home;
As his meat you throw along
He'll repay you with a song.
Never hurt the timid hare
Peeping from her green grass lair,
Let her come and sport and play
On the lawn at close of day.
The little lark goes soaring high
To the bright windows of the sky,
Singing as if 'twere always spring,

And fluttering on an untired wing--
Oh! let him sing his happy song,
Nor do these gentle creatures wrong.

"I wasn't convinced the students would respond as I'd hoped, but I was coming to believe that meaning could be drawn from the simplest of poems. Anyway, I figured what could I lose? I chose to read the poem myself but had the students follow along in their own copies. There was little discussion at first. I asked if anyone had a personal experience they might share that involved something from the wild. This is what happened."

Trudy Jordan described an incident that happened while her family was vacationing at the New Jersey shore. She related how her brother was throwing rocks at seagulls to pass the time away. Apparently he took aim at a bird swimming off shore. She described how the stone curved slightly to the left before striking the gull in the wing. She confessed to sharing in her brother's excitement over hitting a target that far away. Then she told how the gull began to struggle and shake each time it attempted to fly. Before long a crowd of children had gathered to watch the plight of the bird. Trudy admitted that the struggling gull made a pathetic picture. Finally, a young boy asked another how it was that the seagull was in such an awful state. Trudy and her brother were in earshot of the conversation and heard the older boy's reply. Apparently, the older boy hadn't seen Trudy's brother throw the rock because he stated, "I don't know. I can't imagine anyone cruel enough to want to hurt a harmless bird. Maybe a passing boat struck the gull." Trudy then described how awful her brother felt that his target practice would be described as cruel. It had never dawned on him that his having fun was actually an act of cruelty.

Pam stopped her account at this time as if lost in thought. It appeared that she was reliving the moment in her mind because a warm, funny look took hold in her expression. This only served to heighten Joan's curiosity.

I looked for the reaction of the class. It was subdued and silent except for one notable exception. Janet was sobbing quietly at her desk. Fortunately the lunch bell rang at that moment, and I was able to dismiss the class. Janet hesitated to take her place in the line, and I quietly motioned to her that it was alright to remain where she was. After the classroom was cleared of students, I sat down beside Janet

57

and asked if there was anything I could do. I had no idea why she was crying, but her pathetic appearance tore at my heart.

After a conscious effort to control her tears, she managed to confide that she was too embarrassed to be seen like this. She asked if she might stay a few more minutes, and I quickly consented.

Finally I broke the silence by asking, "Would you like to talk about it?" I no sooner finished the question before her words and tears literally flowed. Janet recounted how she had an experience similar to Trudy's brother and how she had kept it a secret these past few months. I could see that she needed to talk and promised her that I wouldn't repeat it to the class.

Apparently the incident happened in August at the pond in Carney Park. Janet described how she was bored and chose to amuse herself by throwing little stones at some mallard ducks. Eventually, she hit one of the younger ducks, and the bird began to struggle in the water. She described how her remorse was heightened when the other mallards began to attack their helpless companion. The activity in the water attracted a bunch of kids, and soon she found herself surrounded by others watching the same spectacle. Like Trudy's brother, she heard the other children discussing the incident. Janet cried again when she related how the duck's eventual death brought sobs from everyone around her. The children were pointing blame at the attacking ducks, but Janet confided that her actions were the true cause of the tragedy. I gave her a hug, thanked her for her trust in me and sent her off to the lunch room.

Joan was clearly touched by Pam's account. She gently asked, "You mentioned the skits. How did they come into play?"

Pam smiled before admitting, "I guess you won't stop until you have the entire story, so I might as well get on with it!" She then took a drink from her can and continued.

Following lunch, I took a few minutes to ask if they had any ideas on how they might express their thoughts on this particular poem. I expected to hear someone suggest a writing activity and was completely caught off guard when Trudy suggested that the class do skits. Before I could slow them down, the class had broken themselves into groups of four and were busily discussing what they were going to perform. Janet and Vicki had teamed up with two other girls, and I paid particular attention to their progress. Janet still appeared subdued. After about fifteen minutes, I called a halt to the

58

their chatter and suggested they have their skits ready to go by the last period tomorrow. Just before turning my attention to math, I suggested they invite their parents.

Only three parents showed up the following afternoon, and one turned out to be Suzy's mother.

Joan caught the significance of this statement and motioned Pam to continue.

The skits turned out awful from a director's point of view. Most of the skits missed the message of the poem, and it was clear that the majority of students hadn't mastered their parts. I'll assume the major portion of blame because I realize now that I failed to provide the needed direction and time.

The turning point for Janet was during Suzy's skit. This particular group had decided to show the cruelty of hunting squirrels for sport. Two boys played the role of the hunters, and Suzy and a classmate served as the squirrels. The squirrels were discussing friends and movies as the two hunters crept up on them. The plot called for the squirrels to be shot as they ascended what was intended to serve as a tree. Suzy attempted to fall down as planned but managed to catch her foot on the corner of a desk. She banged her head on the side of the desk as she fell to the floor. Her mother cried out in alarm, and half the class began to scream. There was blood everywhere, and this only added to the bedlam.

Joan looked concerned, and Pam reassured her with a smile. She continued.

It turned out to be nothing more than a flesh wound, and Suzy was up and going within minutes. Eventually the class settled down. That is except for Janet. Her sobs continued beyond the dismissal bell though she managed to conceal it from the majority of her classmates. I was aware of the crying and so was her friend, Vicki.

The following morning, the two girls showed up fifteen minutes before class and asked if they could speak with me. I was surprised when they produced a note and asked if it was wise to give it to Suzy. As I read the note, I could quickly see that it was a letter of apology. I had trouble holding back my tears as I saw the remorse that engulfed the girls. They managed to tell me how they hadn't really understood how their actions might affect others. Janet confided that the poem, her experience with the ducks and Suzy's accident somehow caused her to come to her senses.

I hugged each of the girls, and we've been the best of friends ever since. Now when they talk out of turn, I need only to smile to gain their immediate compliance. All the anger and defiance is long forgotten.

Joan loved how things worked out and felt a growing hope that she would somehow find the means to reach Lance and Scott. A thought struck Joan and a question followed close on its heels. "What about parents? How do they fit in?"

"Good question, and one I'm still working on." Pam assured. "Schools don't operate in a vacuum, nor should they. Ultimately, it is the home that shapes a young person's character. I'm trying to work on disciplinary problems that are impeding learning. I've chosen to concentrate on the root causes and here is where my disciplinary approach ties in with the teaching of character. But my chief concern is how the virtue should work in a school setting. How it works in the home is really the home's responsibility. Does that make sense?"

Joan nodded in agreement. "I concede the point, but I'm still unclear as to how the parents fit in. Are they active participants in your school-based emphasis?"

"Now be patient for a moment. I'm getting to that part." Pam paused as if searching for just the right words. "I recognize that the school and home environment are closely intertwined. Accordingly, I've tried to keep the parents up to speed on our activities without making too big a deal."

"I'm lost again. What's wrong with making too big a deal about the development of self-discipline?" Jean asked.

"That's simple enough to answer," Joan's friend replied. "Too big a deal has nothing to do with parent awareness of what we are working on. It has everything to do with the student's perception of the process. The power in disciplining through virtue is in the nature of how the learning takes place. Too much structure and too high a profile can reduce this approach to just another example of the same old thing. I choose the selections from The Book of Virtues and, as such, determine much of the content of our discussion. I also take a shadow leadership approach as the process of discovery unfolds. But hopefully, my involvement will not extend much beyond these actions." Pam quieted for a moment to determine if her friend was following her point.

"I believe I'm catching your drift," Joan entreated, "but I'm afraid you'll need to pursue this a bit further."

Pam Phillips leaned forward as if to shorten the gulf hindering her words. "Our chances for meaningful change are greatly reduced if it is perceived that

Mrs. Phillips is in full control. I'm continually looking for opportunities for the students to take charge of the discovery process. The greater their ownership, the better they will involve themselves in the learning."

Joan decided to play devil's advocate. "Aren't you running some risks with this approach? First, you may go nowhere with the disciplinary dilemma because the students choose not to pursue the issue. Then, aren't you worried that the students might arrive at perspectives that are inappropriate?"

"True there are risks, but they are not as great as you might think. Shadow leadership is not without some influence."

"For example?" Joan asked.

"You're not making this easy are you?" Pam teased. "Okay, I first state that we are about due for an art lesson. Rather than announce how we will proceed, I might mention that it would be interesting to incorporate some aspect of our recent discussion with our art. Often a student will come up with an idea that meets reasonable art standards while continuing focus on our virtue."

"What if the students fail to provide a workable activity?" Joan was tenacious if anything.

"Then on that occasion we don't use art class as a means to internalize our virtue. If the process breaks down, I may choose an additional story selection or try another school subject to return focus to the dilemma."

Joan seemed satisfied with her friend's explanations. She backed off the pressure by admitting, "Here again, we are talking about the subtleties, and the art in teaching will always be our greatest challenge. I can see the value in the teacher maintaining a low profile, especially with the upper grades."

Pam appeared pleased that her colleague had backed off her critical posture. "Naturally the age of the students must first be factored in. Primary children would accept and profit from greater teacher control. The older students, particularly those in the secondary grades, need more opportunities for self-discovery."

Pam shot a curious look to her companion. "We have really taken a bird walk from your initial question. Getting back to the parents, I keep them posted on our special activities and maintain portfolios to share student work." Pam chuckled as she added, "I invited the parents to view the skits on respect. As I said before, only three attended. I'm going to try it again, and this time I'm going to work harder at involving the parents." She smiled as she added, "I've even toyed with the idea of suggesting that the students consider using their parents in the skits."

"So all these activities are expressions of apperception," Joan announced, "and you do your best to keep the tone relaxed and supportive."

"Right on both counts," was Pam's reply. "You've now met Vicki and Janet. How do you think it's working?"

"I'd say it must be working well." Joan looked up at the clock and then laughed with her friend. "Thanks for the story about the old violin. You have no idea how deeply that touched me. I'm convinced I can make a difference with the Lances and Scotts of the world. In fact, I'm rather anxious to get moving. I need to get a copy of <u>Discipline Through Virtue</u>, and then I'll hit the ground running!"

"Knowing what I know about you, I would be surprised if you took any other approach." Pam spotted a mischievous glint in her friend's eyes. "Okay, what are you up to now?"

"Nothing really," was the quiet reply. "I just thought of something that we've failed to consider. I need time to think it through, but I suspect it will prove the icing on the cake."

"Care to share this thought?" Pam urged. "It's not fair to hold out on me."

"I'll tell you what," Joan paused, obviously relishing the moment. "I'll send you a copy of a story I once heard. It might take me a few days to track it down, but I'm sure I can get it located." Joan smiled as she concluded the visit. "I'm sure you'll manage to figure it out on your own!"

Chapter Twelve
Pause for Bearing

"What is the best government? That which teaches us to govern ourselves." Goethe

CHAPTER TWELVE

Two days had passed since Joan's latest visit with Pam. The issue of parental involvement had yet to be resolved in her mind. Lorin was due home later in the evening, and she was anxious to visit with him on the matter.

With her husband away on business, Joan chose to spend the majority of the weekend with her children. This fact may have continued to foster her preoccupation with the parental role. She had long since become adept in changing roles at a moment's notice, and her mother's hat had displaced the teacher's hat the moment she walked through her kitchen door, and it still remained securely on her head.

The weekend's activities had impressed on Joan the affection she felt for each of her children. She thought often of how much they needed her in their early years. Now with Marie approaching young womanhood and Billy and Pete independent in so many ways, Joan knew she was experiencing the anxiety and frustration that accompanies a changing in roles. Her greatest frustration came when she caught herself viewing her children as opposing combatants. She shuddered as she recalled instances where pride and ego displaced love, and her energies were dedicated to proving some silly point or winning a meaningless argument. And this was the way she was behaving with her own flesh and blood. It's no wonder she was struggling with the virtual strangers she was employed to teach.

Joan's thoughts drifted to her classroom, and she found herself visualizing the frequent clashes she had with Lance and Scott. This in turn cast her mind back to other incidents with other students, and soon she found herself wallowing in self-remorse. Catching herself, she thought again about "The Touch of the Master's Hand," and a calm settled in again. "How easy it is to lose sight of the importance of another human soul," she thought.

Joan thought back to Pam's comments about a teacher's responsibility to insure a suitable environment for learning. The textbooks often labeled this responsibility as the ability to manage a classroom for learning. What had gone awry with her old and time-tested classroom management techniques? Why weren't they working as they once had? Had the students changed or had she? What did disciplining through virtue have to offer that separated it from her present methods? Would it truly make a difference?

Joan knew she was on overload but felt compelled to continue her probing. Her mind touched on many of the disciplinary dilemmas cross-referenced in Pam's book. There were those grouped as severe, and it was easy to see why they earned a placement on the list. But some of the moderate and individual learner dilemmas seemed oddly out of place on a list of disciplinary problems. After all, they caused little disruption to a classroom environment.

Joan picked up a pencil and jotted a few of these minor concerns on the back of a magazine cover. Timidity, defeatist attitude, victim, distrust, impulsive were the first five to come to mind. As she read through her list, an impression calmly nestled in. "This is all about self-discipline through virtue," she thought. "These minor dilemmas can be just as devastating to learning as cheating, lying, substance abuse and temper displays. We are not ensuring a suitable environment for learning if we are restricting our efforts to managing the big ticket concerns. Those dilemmas that often go unnoticed and left untreated can suffocate an individual's capacity to learn just as significantly as the high profile disruptions."

The thought bounced around for a few more moments before a second bit of inspiration settled in. "I can never be a successful disciplinarian and teacher if my focus remains on the class or even a particular group. The attention must focus on each individual student. Then the classroom will take care of itself. So this is the essence of disciplining through virtue," she exclaimed to no one in particular. Recalling Lorin's tool box left unceremoniously on the kitchen step, Joan made an instant connection. "The virtues we hope to instill are nothing more than personal tools. When properly mastered, each will be positioned to assist with life's great challenges." The profundity of the thought sent chills down her back.

Joan's thoughts returned to her husband. "Where is he when I need him," she spoke to no on in particular. "He knows my need to share what I've discovered."

She looked at the clock and noted that he could return within the hour. This triggered a thought that caused Joan to laugh out loud. "Unlucky Lorin, I've had two days to recover from my visit with Pam. Two days to calm my excitement, and now I'm as pumped up as I've ever been. The poor man, I'm going to hound him mercilessly with a never-ending stream of comments and question. Well, he knew what he was getting when he married me." This slick piece of rationalization amused her the more.

The two days had produced another positive outcome. She had promised to share a story with Pam, and it had taken her two days and eight phone calls to locate a copy. Her hand felt down in her pocket for reassurance that the story remained in its secure resting place. Her thoughts were interrupted by the sound of a car motor. Lorin soon appeared, obviously tired, but appearing generally relaxed. This pleased Joan and served as all the encouragement she needed to move ahead with her comments and concerns.

"Hi, honey. What's in the fridge?" Lorin asked. He dropped the materials he was carrying and hugged his wife. "Did you miss me?"

"Yes," she replied a split second before punching him sharply in the side.

"Hey, what was that for?" he inquired with a startled look on his face. "What did I forget?"

"Nothing," Joan insisted. "But you weren't here when I needed to talk with you. Now you're going to pay for your absence." She smiled and pulled out her story. "In last Thursday's discussion, you had mentioned Solomon and that had reminded me of a story I'd recently heard in church. Please, could you read this, and tell me what you think."

Lorin grasped the outstretched sheet and glanced at the title, "The Actor." He was delighted to note it's brevity. Smiling he replied, "Sure, I'll give it a shot if you fix me a sandwich."

Joan got immediately to work preparing a tuna sandwich but found herself stealing occasional glances at her husband. She was pleased to note the attention he was giving the story. He had a tendency to counteract her more serious passions with lighthearted jostling, and she was delighted that on this occasion he remained attentive and thoughtful as he read.

THE ACTOR

One time there was a very prominent actor in New York City. He possessed a special oratorical gift which enabled him to completely captivate any audience. One night after his recitation, he was applauded tremendously, and as he came back on stage to take his bows, a lady in the crowd called for him to recite the 23rd Psalm. This request startled the actor, but being familiar with the scripture he consented to do so. As he delivered the recitation, he endeavored to mold and beautify it with all the color, emotion, and personality that the long hard years of work had taught him. His delivery was excellent. Nothing had been forgotten or omitted. The crowd burst into a thunderous applause and praised him for his noble talent. As the applause subsided, the actor called an old gentleman from the front row to the stage and asked him to also recite the psalm. The old man appeared nervous, but consented. As he turned to the crowd he closed his eyes and bowed his head. He spoke the words:

> *The Lord is my shepherd, I shall not want.*
> *He maketh me to lie down in green pastures;*
> *He leadeth me beside the still waters.*
> *He restoreth my soul; He leadeth me in the paths*
> *of righteousness for his name's sake.*
> *Yea, though I walk through the valley of the shadow*
> *of death, I will fear no evil; for Thou art with me;*
> *thy rod and thy staff they comfort me.*
> *Thou preparest a table before me in the presence of*
> *mine enemies; Thou annointest my head with oil,*

My cup runneth over.
Surely goodness and mercy shall follow me all the days
Of my life and I will dwell in the house of the Lord
forever.

When the old gentleman finished, there was no thunderous
applause; there were no cries of praise; but there was also not a dry
eye in the crowd.

The young prominent actor faced the crowd and said, "Ladies
and gentlemen, I know the words to the 23rd Psalm, but this man
knows the shepherd."

Lorin's first reading took but a few moments. Joan was pleased to see his reaction. It appeared that the story affected him in much the same way it had touched her. He continued deep in thought, perusing it for the second time. Finally he looked up. "Wonderful story, and very well written. It almost seemed as if I was part of the audience."

"What message did it convey to you?" Joan was anxious to hear her husband's reply. "Do you want a hint?" she coyly whispered.

The humor was not lost on Lorin who quickly countered, "Nothing doing. I'll think for myself, thank you! Just give me a minute, and I'll figure it out."

Joan showed her impatience in her usual way. She first twisted her auburn hair around her right index finger and then commenced to twirl it around in a slow, continuous stroke. This was all lost on her husband who was still mired, deep in thought. Had he looked up he would have spotted the signs in a moment and taken his cue to get on with it.

Perhaps a full three minutes lapsed before Lorin finally spoke. "This has something to do with the genuine article, doesn't it?"

Joan beamed and couldn't hold in her enthusiasm a moment longer. "Yes, that's exactly what it's about," she blurted out. "This story hits the nail on the head. Can't you see how the actor was adept, even brilliant in going through the motions? But it was all an act. He was reciting a prayer, not offering a prayer, and there's an immense difference between the two. When the chips were down, he would have been ill-prepared to draw on the prayer for assistance. The audience may have been amused, even entertained by the young actor, but few if any would have relied on him for spiritual guidance."

Lorin continued in thought for a moment before saying, "This has something to do with disciplining through virtue, but I admit to a stupor of thought. Perhaps some of the fog I encountered in Dallas has lodged itself in my head."

"You're excused, considering it's 10 p.m. on Sunday night," Joan laughed.

"Say, I just had a thought," her husband interjected. "Let me retrieve one of Stephen R. Covey's books I've recently read. There's a part that I've underlined that fits in nicely with this story." He returned shortly and pointed out a particular passage.

We see the world, not as it is but as we are or as we are conditioned to see it. When we open our mouths to describe what we see, we in effect describe ourselves, our perceptions, our paradigms.

"I believe I see what you are trying to express," Joan confided.

Lorin continued, "Your actor was the first to recite the 23rd Psalm. The audience, expressing its appreciation, burst into thunderous applause. The actor was followed by the old gentleman who repeated the same verses. While the spoken words were identical, the audience reaction was not. The older gentleman's rendition brought heartfelt tears. What made the difference? Upon opening his mouth the actor revealed himself for who he was. The audience saw in him an accomplished actor and applauded him for his effort. Then the old man opened his mouth and who he was became apparent. His relationship with his God transcended his words, and the audience responded in the only way it could. The old gentleman was the genuine article, and the actor was merely going through the motions. You can't fake sincerity."

"Very good," Joan admitted. "How about letting me take this notion a step further? I'd like to ask you a personal question."

Lorin feigned apprehension before smiling his consent.

Joan looked at her husband in earnest and asked, "How do you feel when you are counseling your youngest son about tidying up his room?"

"You know I leave that up to you," Lorin replied.

"And why do you leave it up to me?" his wife countered.

Lorin laughed and pointed his finger at his wife. "You've just made your point, haven't you? I don't call Billy to task because I often leave my own tools laying about. Rather than be a hypocrite, I quietly make myself scarce when you go on one of your crusades."

"Crusades?" Joan teased.

Lorin conceded, "Sorry dear, poor choice of terms."

Lorin's apology fell on deaf ears because Joan was already voicing another question. "Can you see the connection between yourself and the actor?"

Lorin nodded, choosing to maintain a low profile on this particular subject.

"Now extend this connection to the classroom teacher." Joan paused a moment to find the appropriate words. "How effectively will a teacher perform if her behavior is inconsistent with the message of her story?"

"Go on," Lorin encouraged, "I'm beginning to grasp your point."

"Take the teacher who wishes to encourage a more respectful class," Joan began. "She's going to have a problem if she has a tendency to be overly sarcastic or judgmental. Don't you think her students will view her in much the same way the audience viewed the actor--good for what he does, but don't expect us to follow his spiritual lead?"

"You're placing a great responsibility on the teacher aren't you? In fact you're placing a great deal of pressure on yourself. You, like everyone else, isn't perfect," her husband stated.

Joan wasn't to be deterred on this point. "I recognize my failings, but this needn't act as a deterrent. What is wrong with my honest involvement in the learning experience? We are back to role models aren't we? Think of the value in allowing the students opportunities to observe me in my struggles to discipline myself."

Lorin was intrigued by the thought and allowed it to show in his demeanor. "Oh no, I see where this is leading. This works the same way in the home, doesn't it?"

Joan sweetly smiled. She didn't have to say a word; Lorin had already figured it out. She broke the silence with a comment of obvious gratitude and sincerity. "This is the missing part I've been searching for!"

Lorin laughed, "Does this mean I can now eat my sandwich?"

Halfway to the bedroom he turned to his wife and confided, "All kidding aside, I'm impressed with what we've been discussing. I enjoyed our chat about King Alfred and the woodcutter's wife, and I know the children felt the same. From what little I have picked up, I have every confidence that your story approach will do good things for our family. He smiled before adding, "And I've no doubt of your willingness to fill me in on all the missing details." With that fitting close, he continued his way down the hallway.

Joan smiled at her husband's retreating figure. Her thoughts then returned to Pam and the memorable journey they shared in discovering some of the subtleties. The name passed through her mind, Discipline Through Virtue. "A fitting name," she thought.

Joan was about to follow her husband when she recalled her promise to Pam. She made a mental note to get the story out in tomorrow's mail. "I think I'll let her stew over the story a bit before we visit again. It will be good for her." Joan allowed a last smile to surface before heading down the hall.

Chapter Thirteen
New Sense of Direction

"The truest friend to the liberty of his country is he who tries to promote its virtue."   *Samuel Adams*

CHAPTER THIRTEEN

Four days had passed since Joan had sent her husband off to bed with his sandwich. The days had not been without event, and Joan was taking the well-deserved break she had promised herself. Fred Jones was expected to join her at 4 p.m. which left her with the better part of thirty minutes to enjoy her peace and quiet. She glanced around and spotted her new classroom additions.

Her crowning possession was the classroom set of The Book of Virtues resting comfortably on a library cart. It had taken her four attempts over a two-day span to convince Mrs. Ashcraft that they were a bargain at any price. The argument that settled the issue boiled down to Mary's inability to deny the impact of a carefully selected story. Of course, Joan was persistent in pointing out that it was Mary's own story that had made such a difference in her life and how the students deserved this same opportunity. By Wednesday afternoon it was a done deal, and Joan had her books.

She laughed to herself as she recalled Fred's reaction to her books. "You got what?" were his exact words she recalled. He had calmed down when Joan had promised to share her prize.

Her eyes continued until they focused on her bookcase. There, nestled in with her other professional books was Discipline Through Virtue. Not wishing to wait, Joan had purchased it on Monday with her own money. A second smile surfaced as she thought of how she might approach Mary for a reimbursement.

Finally, she looked at the bulletin board she had just prepared. The border and matts were in place, but it still lacked the students' efforts that would fill its empty spaces. She complimented herself on the quality of her work.

The bulletin board returned her thoughts to Lincoln Elementary and Pam Phillips. She had gotten "The Actor" out in Monday's mail, and Pam had confirmed its safe arrival with a Tuesday phone call.

Joan felt a warmth inside as she recalled Pam's excited chatter. Yes, she enjoyed the story; yes, she figured out Joan's point; and yes, she could see the importance of learning and growing side by side with her students. They had arranged a third meeting this Friday and had even agreed to invite Fred.

The mention of Mr. Jones brought her thoughts back to the present. As Joan glanced at her watch, she became aware of someone approaching her desk. Surprised, she found it to be Mary Ashcraft.

"Was our money well spent?" Mary asked with her usual directness.

"Based on today's results, I would have to respond yes," the teacher replied.

Mary smiled and left without further comment. The abruptness of the exchange amused Joan, and Fred found her still chuckling when he made his appearance.

Fred was carrying two pops, a sure sign that he was after a favor. Placing Joan's can before her, he opened up the discussion by stating, "I couldn't help but notice the excitement in your students as they filed past my room. Sounds like you pulled it off. Any chance I can borrow this <u>Discipline Through Virtue</u>?"

Joan accepted this as Fred's best attempt at a compliment and felt obligated to agree to his request. Gesturing to her diet drink she replied, "Considering you chose the right flavor, you may use the book for the evening. Besides, I've already selected a follow-up story!"

Taking this as his opening cue, Fred announced, "Well, I'm here as arranged to hear all the gory details. How about taking it from the top?"

Joan described how she had first asked the class if they had any interest in reading a few accounts of heroes. She reported how the class readily agreed.

At this point Fred interrupted. "Why heroes?" he inquired. "I thought you were concerned about bullying?"

"I was, and that's why I chose two stories on heroes," she responded. "Now be patient, and you soon will see my reasoning."

Joan then described how she had deliberated on a number of selections before settling on two. The first was "An Appeal from the Alamo." Joan turned to page 484 in <u>The Book of Virtues</u> and suggested that Fred read it silently to himself.

Mr. Jones rested the opened book on his lap and proceeded as directed.

Commandancy of the Alamo, Texas
February 24, 1836

To the People of Texas and All Americans in the World.
Fellow Citizens and Compatriots:

> *I am besieged by a thousand or more of the Mexicans under Santa Anna. I have sustained a continual bombardment and cannonade for twenty-four hours and have not lost a man. The enemy has demanded a surrender at discretion; otherwise the garrison are to be put to the sword if the fort is taken. I have answered the demand with a cannon shot, and our flag still waves proudly from the walls. I shall never surrender nor retreat. Then, I call on you in the name of Liberty, of patriotism, and of everything dear to the American character, to come to our aid with all dispatch. The enemy is receiving reinforcements daily and will no doubt increase to three or four thousand in four or five days. If this call is neglected, I am determined to sustain myself as long as possible and die like a soldier*

who never forgets what is due to his own honor and that of his country.

VICTORY OR DEATH

William Barret Travis
Lieutenant Colonel, Commandant

When Fred completed his reading, Joan continued. "I first asked the students what they knew about the Alamo. I was pleasantly surprised to learn that a few of the students had actually visited the site. It took less than five minutes to get everyone up to speed on circumstances surrounding the appeal. I might note that this was an instance where the students knew more than their teacher."

Fred smiled to acknowledge her point. Showing his first signs of impatience Fred prodded, "How soon did you get to your message?"

Joan was having too much fun to be rushed. "I'll get to that in a moment," she calmly announced. After first taking a deliberate pause she continued on with her account. "Once I was satisfied that I had everyone's interest, I asked why Travis was considered a hero."

She then described how the students produced a lengthy list of reasons for this esteemed distinction. Joan mentioned how Lance and Scott were enthused with the topic and how they showed a particular admiration for Commander Travis's courage.

"I then asked the students to write down a short definition for courage and then list three or four people who were known for their courage."

Fred asked Joan if she had collected the students' responses, and she answered his question by dropping a stack of papers on his lap. He acknowledged her response with a smile and proceeded to peruse the selections. Joan amused herself during this interlude by trying to guess what Fred was thinking as he passed from paper to paper.

"The responses are pretty much as I expected," he announced as he returned the stack to his colleague. "Most of the students made reference to fighting in their definitions, and their lists heavily favored the warrior-type." He paused in thought a moment before commenting, "You set them up, didn't you?"

Mrs. Walker was impressed, and it showed in the smile that brightened her face.

Fred noted the smile but didn't treat it as a compliment. He was trying to make sense of Joan's approach, and her smile served as nothing more than his confirmation that he was beginning to follow her thinking. He broke the silence by confiding, "Lance made it clear how he views a hero."

71

Joan nodded, recalling how Lance had chosen Davy Crockett, Wyatt Earp and Butch Cassidy to top off his list.

"You mentioned a second selection," Fred began. "May I presume you introduced it after the definitions?"

"Right again," she laughed. "I didn't want them too stuck on their original assumptions, so I moved to the second selection."

Joan then reached for the <u>Book of Virtues</u> and turned to page 533, a selection from the chapter on perseverance. Again, she handed the book to Fred and asked that he read the story.

Fred noted that she had chosen "The Little Hero of Holland" and began to play with the possibilities that presented themselves. After a full two minutes he began to read. He skimmed the beginning paragraphs until he came to the meat of the story. Then his attention fixed on the material before him.

> *Suddenly he noticed that the sun was setting, and that it was growing dark. "Mother will be watching for me," he thought, and he began to run toward home.*
>
> *Just then he heard a noise. It was the sound of trickling water! He stopped and looked down. There was a small hole in the dike, through which a tiny stream was flowing.*
>
> *Any child in Holland is frightened at the thought of a leak in the dike.*
>
> *Peter understood the danger at once. If the water ran through a little hole it would soon make a larger one, and the whole country would be flooded. In a moment he saw what he must do. Throwing away his flowers, he climbed down the side of the dike and thrust his finger into the tiny hole.*
>
> *The flowing of the water was stopped!*
>
> *"Oho!" he said to himself. "The angry waters must stay back now. I can keep them back with my finger. Holland shall not be drowned while I am here."*
>
> *This was all very well at first, but it soon grew dark and cold. The little fellow shouted and screamed. "Come here; come here," he called. But no one heard him; no one came to help him.*
>
> *It grew still colder, and his arm ached, and began to grow stiff and numb. He shouted again, "Will no one come? Mother! Mother!"*
>
> *But his mother had looked anxiously along the dike road many times since sunset for her little boy, and now she had closed and locked the cottage door, thinking that Peter was spending the night with his blind friend, and that she would scold him in the morning for staying away from home without her permission.*

Peter tried to whistle, but his teeth chattered with the cold. He thought of his brother and sister in their warm beds, and of his dear father and mother. "I must not let them be drowned," he thought. "I must stay here until someone comes, if I have to stay all night."

The moon and stars looked down on the child crouching on a stone on the side of the dike. His head was bent, and his eyes were closed, but he was not asleep, for every now and then he rubbed the hand that was holding back the angry sea.

"I'll stand it somehow," he thought. So he stayed there all night keeping the water out.

Early the next morning a man going to work thought he heard a groan as he walked along the top of the dike. Looking over the edge, he saw a child clinging to the side of the great wall.

"What's the matter?" he called. "Are you hurt?"

"I'm keeping the water back!" Peter yelled. "Tell them to come quickly!"

The alarm was spread. People came running with shovels, and the hole was soon mended.

They carried Peter home to his parents, and before long the whole town knew how he had saved their lives that night. To this day, they have never forgotten the brave little hero of Holland.

As Fred finished the story, a wry smile began to form. "You must have shaken up Lance with this example," he quipped.

"I'm afraid you're right," Joan offered. "A little eight year old without uniform or weapon surely didn't fit their image. I noticed how little they had to say when we discussed this second situation."

Fred pursued this point. "Did you make any progress with either of the boys?"

"I suspect not. But they were not the intended targets when I chose this selection."

Chapter Fourteen
Pathway to the Heart

"Virtue is that perfect good which is the complement of a happy life; the only immortal thing that belongs to mortality." Seneca

CHAPTER FOURTEEN

"Now you have lost me," Mr. Jones conceded. "I thought this was about bullying. Correct me if I'm wrong, but aren't these two boys your prime culprits?" Joan had hoped for an opportunity to explain why she handled things as she did. She picked up <u>Discipline Through Virtue</u> and confessed, "I spent a few minutes over the possible selections before choosing these two. I had decided to focus on the class rather than the two boys. My reasoning was twofold. First, I didn't want to single out Lance and Scott in any way. It was never my intention to embarrass them or to give them special attention. Second, I felt that the two boys were reacting to their environment. If I could alter the environment, I might change their behavior."

Fred was obviously thinking this matter through. Joan could tell that he was making headway when he allowed her to continue without interruption. "I determined that the two boys were feeding off their classmates' attention. The privileges they enjoyed as class hooligans provided all the incentive they needed. If I could change how the class viewed courage, it might help. But if I could change how the class demonstrated courage, the bullying would stop because the class wouldn't tolerate it. I have tougher kids than Lance and Scott, but they had chosen to keep their distance. I also have the group that sustains the intimidation by their smiles and laughter. Finally, I have the victims themselves who view themselves·as cowards and accept the afflictions as their just due. Sammy is the type of boy who would persevere through a long and difficult night if it would save a friend from harm. He simply doesn't see this as a manifestation of courage." Joan paused as if to catch her breath.

Fred was impressed as he followed his colleague's account and was already formulating how he would proceed if this was his class. He didn't want Joan to continue before he had his say. When this opportunity presented itself, he jumped in, "I take it you spent some time analyzing why the little boy was called the hero of Holland. Did you then ask the class for other instances of courage that didn't follow the usual pattern?"

Joan smiled to herself at Fred's personal involvement in her class affairs. This was so unlike him she noted. Despite her bewilderment, she was flattered with his interest. She finally replied, "Yes, I almost used those exact words."

"What did the students come up with?" Fred followed up.

"We got off to a rocky start when Ted reminded us how John had the guts to walk into the girls' restroom during lunch break," confessed Joan.

"John may have been quiet, but I'll wager the girls weren't," Fred jested. "Anything else?"

"Let me see," Joan continued. "One student brought up a friend who didn't cry when he broke his arm. Another spoke of her sister who showed up her boyfriend by riding a roller coaster he would have no part of." That brought laughter from the girls and comments from the boys. "Come to think of it, this was the only time I heard from Scott!" She chuckled as she pictured Scott challenging the girls to a contest.

"Anything profound?" Fred pursued.

"Actually there was one excellent answer that surprised the class," Joan admitted. "Sammy described how his mother had spent three days without sleep when his little sister was in critical condition following an accident. I allowed the class a few moments to digest that one before I dared discuss it."

"And..." Fred pushed.

"It proved a wonderful forum for discussion. Eventually we decided to spend the next five days looking for quiet expressions of courage."

Joan then motioned to her bulletin board and said, "That's where we are going to display our findings. We've combined it with art. Students are working in pairs. One student is responsible for an article that gives an account of quiet courage, and the other must mount the article in a way that illustrates the message. It was the students' idea." Joan raised her eyebrows as if to plead that the activity might pull itself off.

At this point Fred returned to his skeptic mode. Smiling slightly he commented, "I'm not sure this activity will be worth the hassle. I can see the students arguing over who finds the article and who does the follow-up."

"Perhaps, but I'm hoping for at least one or two articles that provide worthwhile examples. Think of the discussions this would foster," Joan maintained. "I can iron out the difficulties you mentioned. Perhaps I'll insist they switch roles the next time we perform the activity."

Fred seemed pacified for the moment. His next question was insightful. "Have you thought of using a story that illustrates moral courage?"

"Are you reading my mind?" Joan teased good-naturedly. "The Book of Virtues has selections on Susan B. Anthony, Rosa Parks and Harriet Tubman among others. I'll see when the time is right to introduce one or more of these illustrations. I have even thought of using the entry on Lou Gehrig."

"Oh?" Fred questioned.

"Lance and Scott are avid baseball fans, and it might surprise them why this athlete is as popular as he is. I clipped out an article from last night's sports page that I'll add to the excerpt from the book. Take a look." Joan offered the clipping to Mr. Jones who quickly devoured its contents.

IRON HORSE

Joe DiMaggio, talking recently about his early New York Yankee years and playing with Lou Gehrig:

"I was placed alongside Lou in the locker room. We dressed together and talked. You know, we were a quiet pair to the press and

75

the public. But alone we talked mostly about the game, the opposing pitchers, injuries and maybe about our families."

In 1939, at the end of his career, DiMaggio recalled, Gehrig was barely able to stand.

"He'd lean into me trying to get up," DiMaggio said.

"The man had an iron will... He dressed so slowly. He'd get up and go out and try. It was so sad. We knew he was sick, but we didn't know why."

Two years later, at 37, Gehrig was dead.

"That man was one of a kind," DiMaggio said.

"This is wonderful. I like where you are headed and can see no reason why your approach shouldn't work. Permit me one final question before I let you go." Fred held off his question for a moment, as if trying to determine a delicate wording. "Now, I'm not trying to sound critical, because I truly am impressed with what you are doing. But I'm the kind of guy who needs to ground my thoughts in a realistic context. Surely, we can't be expected to reach everyone with this approach. Can we discipline everyone through virtue?"

"I have given this same question much thought, and I can only share what I have determined to this point," Joan confessed. "A good portion of our students, perhaps as high as fifty percent, needs little management. Our task is to provide these students the opportunities to direct themselves and enjoy an unrestricted access to learning. This group has suffered in times past when we have included them in our classroom sermonizing or denied them privileges simply because of their membership in the class. I'm sure you can recall times you canceled field trips or halted a fun activity because of the actions of a few. Disciplining through virtue should further develop their personal virtues curtailing instances when these mannered students must pay the price for the actions of those few."

Joan thought a moment before continuing. "The next group of students are those who sit on the bubble. Their numbers differ from class to class and school to school, but we can spot them in a matter of weeks. These are they who are easily led, lack the convictions we would hope for and are just as likely to follow the bad as follow the good. Many of these students have never been taught right from wrong and have picked up what they've learned from movies or friends. It is this group that will profit the most from <u>Discipline Through Virtue</u>. These are the ones who often act improperly out of ignorance, who have a tendency to side with their friends despite the circumstances and who can easily be turned off when a teacher cracks down too hard."

Joan sobered as she confessed, "I know I have assisted some of these students in their choice to misbehave because I have reacted rather than acted on the situation. This new approach is going to allow me to act on the roots of the problem rather than lose my composure and assail the symptoms."

Fred nodded in agreement. Joan's insights were making sense, and he was anxious to hear her thoughts on the Scotts and Lances of the world. He decided to move things along by asking, "Are there some who simply won't respond to this approach?"

Joan carefully chose her words of reply. "I'm convinced that every child is capable of wholesome growth. Whether or not the growth manifests itself in the classrooms and playgrounds is a different matter. My goal will be to have all my students gain at least one new insight before they leave me." Joan's eyes moistened as she thought again of the old man tenderly playing the tattered violin. Catching herself she managed to whisper, "I hope to never lose sight of the worth of each individual. I've been entrusted with the care of twenty-six young people for six hours of their waking day, and I'm not going to give up on a one of them."

Fred felt Joan's sincerity, and his own reaction was puzzling. He found himself wanting to give her a hug. She had unlocked emotions he hadn't felt in years. Hard as he tried, he couldn't find the words to express how he felt. All that he managed was a slight, but heartfelt, smile.

Joan realized that she had somehow touched Fred's heart and decided to risk a final thought. "I hope you don't find this preachy, but I consider this the essence of disciplining through virtue." Joan silently prayed that Fred might feel her message even if she failed in her choice of words. "I've reduced the whole issue of discipline down to a simple thought. It's our responsibility as teachers to eliminate the contention that besets our classrooms just as it's our job as parents to eliminate it from our homes. My own learning has suffered whenever contention persists, and I suspect that I'm no different from anyone else. The management of behavior has its place, but the essence of our duty is to teach the principles of good behavior. This character virtue equips our students to govern themselves. So much of our discipline has evolved to the confrontational level where we all but challenge the students to step out of line. Both educators and parents are investing boundless quantities of energy trying to outwit each other. Disciplining through virtue is the opportunity to step off this self-destructing treadmill before its momentum proves too strong a force to halt."

Joan made her point. She knew it, and Fred knew it. The two exchanged smiles before Fred quietly returned to his own classroom and his own thoughts, but not before first securing Joan's copy of <u>Discipline Through Virtue</u>.

Discipline
Through
Virtue

The Techniques

DISCIPLINARY DILEMMAS

COMMENTARY

It is critical that each disciplinary dilemma be viewed only as it relates to learning. Discipline Through Virtue is not designed to impose specific values. It is designed to remove obstacles that impede learning by teaching character virtues that should increase the likelihood that a young person is in full readiness to learn. Hence, only those expressions of a particular dilemma that disrupt learning should be dealt with.

You will find that the Disciplinary Dilemmas include examples that range from severely disruptive to what could be viewed as inconsequential. The more severe dilemmas usually receive the most attention due to their tendency to disrupt entire schools, classrooms and homes. Those problems restricted to a single individual's ability to learn often are ignored. We urge teachers and parents to pay heed to each of the dilemmas.

1. **Antisocial** (Discipline Through Virtue   pages 78-90)
    Young people who find extreme difficulty in relating to peers - Often they carry a chip on their shoulders and overreact to provocation. These have difficulty working in group activities in both classrooms and playground. They might also act and react in a callous fashion, showing little empathy toward themselves and others.

2. **Cliques** (Discipline Through Virtue   pages 91-99)
    Young people who purposely exclude others from full association with their group - The exclusions tend to undermine class cohesion and add undue tension to the learning environment. These cliques range from informal social groups and playground selections to organized gangs.

3. **Defeatist Attitude** (Discipline Through Virtue   pages 100-107)
    Young people who expect failure and pattern their actions accordingly - Often these will give up before trying or influence others not to try. These include those who see themselves as victims, with little control of their destiny.

4. **Defiance** (Discipline Through Virtue   pages 108-112)
    Young people who refuse to comply with a rule or directive even though they are clearly aware of the expectation - The defiance can be expressed openly or through more subtle means.

5. **Dishonesty** (<u>Discipline Through Virtue</u> pages 113-118)
Young people who employ dishonest means to achieve their goals - The goals include tests, competitions, impressing friends, avoiding consequences, saving face, etc.

6. **Disorganized** (<u>Discipline Through Virtue</u> pages 119-120)
Young people whose disorganization affects their ability to function properly - Often these can't locate what they need or lose the concept of time or fail to see the proper sequencing of objectives or events.

7. **Disrespect** (<u>Discipline Through Virtue</u> pages 121-129)
Young people whose actions or manners cause undeserved irritation or outright harm to others - Expressions of disrespect include inappropriate interruptions, unsolicited or unappreciated comments, poor manners, uncalled for familiarity, putdowns, etc.

8. **Distrust** (<u>Discipline Through Virtue</u> pages 130-136)
Young people who act or think on the belief that others are out to take advantage of them - These have a tendency to block out counsel or pay scant heed to directions because they have little trust in others' good intentions.

9. **Fighting** (<u>Discipline Through Virtue</u> pages 137-142)
Young people who engage in such things as heated arguments, name calling, push and shove matches and outright fisticuffs

10. **Guilt Denial** (<u>Discipline Through Virtue</u> pages 143-147)
Young people who refuse to accept blame for their actions - These often rationalize away responsibility for their behavior.

11. **Impulsive** (<u>Discipline Through Virtue</u> pages 148-154)
Young people who act and speak spontaneously without regard for circumstances or consequences - These are often remorseful after an incident but whose lack of control has them repeating the undesirable action time and time again.

12. **Inattentiveness** (<u>Discipline Through Virtue</u> pages 155-158)
Young people who fail to keep focus on the designated objective - Expressions of inattentiveness range from simple daydreaming to willful alternative pursuits.

13. **Indulgent** (<u>Discipline Through Virtue</u> pages 159-167)
Young people who are never satisfied that they have enough - These often feel little gratitude because of their compulsion for more.

14. **Intimidation** (<u>Discipline Through Virtue</u> pages 168-169)
Young people who use subtle or overt means to exercise power over others - The manifestations of the intimidation include threats, physical acts, extreme instances of ridicule.

15. **Judgmental** (<u>Discipline Through Virtue</u> pages 170-175)
Young people who chronically have concerns over such things as homework, scheduling class topics, etc. - These complain that there's too much of this or too little of that. They often have a preoccupation with issues of fairness and relevance.

16. **Laziness** (<u>Discipline Through Virtue</u> pages 176-183)
Young people who choose not to complete what is required of them - These often take the path of least resistance because it would be inconvenient to do otherwise. Manifestations include uncompleted assignments, willful failure to show up, halfhearted efforts, demands to be spoon-fed, etc.

17. **Peer Pressures** (<u>Discipline Through Virtue</u> pages 184-190)
Young people who are unduly influenced by their peers - Manifestations of the pressure include conformity of dress, language, recreation, standards and attitudes. This becomes a disciplinary dilemma only when the influence is destructive, particularly with respect to learning.

18. **Show-Off** (<u>Discipline Through Virtue</u> pages 191-197)
Young people who express themselves in ways to gain others' attention - Expressions of this dilemma range from innocuous classroom comments or outrageous grooming to outright boasting.

19. **Sloppy** (<u>Discipline Through Virtue</u> pages 198-200)
Young people who take little pride in appearance - Expressions of this attitude can be seen in assignments, homework, attire, grooming, etc.

20. **Stealing** (<u>Discipline Through Virtue</u> pages 201-204)
Young people who take things without authorization - Actions range from pilfering lockers and desks to walking off with another's possession with no intention to return it.

21. **Substance Abuse** (<u>Discipline Through Virtue</u> pages 205-210)
Young people who use illegal substances or who abuse substances in ways that provide harmful stimulation - The abuse can range from overeating or too many sweets to dependence on mind-altering drugs. Abuse might best be defined as any substance intake that tends to impede learning.

22. **Tardiness** (<u>Discipline Through Virtue</u> pages 211-212)
Young people who are chronically late on assignments or attendance

23. **Temper Displays** (<u>Discipline Through Virtue</u> pages 213-217)
Young people whose uncontrolled anger or frustration causes them a temporary loss of perspective and judgment - Manifestations of the temper include instances where young people barricade themselves in, refusing to deal with anyone as well as the outward explosions where words and actions occur without prior thought.

24. **Timidity** (<u>Discipline Through Virtue</u> pages 218-222)
Young people who lack confidence to proceed without unreasonable assistance - These demand constant reassurances from adults and peers or rarely participate or fail to extend themselves socially. In essence these fail to take constructive risks.

25. **Vandalism** (<u>Discipline Through Virtue</u> pages 227-228)
Young people who purposely damage the possessions of others - Acts of vandalism range in severity from the defacing of desks, bathroom stalls and textbooks to such things as arson, and other major acts of destruction.

26. **Vulgarity** (<u>Discipline Through Virtue</u> pages 218-219)
Young people who use language, gestures or other means to express sentiments or messages that are generally considered offensive to society - These expressions range from derogatory slurs against a particular culture or race to use of vulgar language.

READY-REFERENCE
A CROSS-REFERENCE TO THE BOOK OF VIRTUES

A Brief Word About Stories And Their Effective Use: Only a percentage of the stories, poems, etc. will be positioned to teach those specific aspects of a virtue that are of concern. What the recommended stories will provide are springboards for meaningful discussion and reflection. For example, the concern may be vulgarity, but the story will not treat this subject directly. Instead, the story provides an example of sublime language, and the discussion following the reading points out the power and respect that accompanies sublime expression. This is then contrasted with the impressions conveyed when vulgarity or slang is used. The story merely provides the opportunity to move the follow-up discussion in the desired direction.

```
┌─────────────────────────────────────────────────┐
│                      KEY                          │
│          The Book of Virtues - BofV               │
│   The Book of Virtues for Young People - YP       │
└─────────────────────────────────────────────────┘
```

ANTISOCIAL

1. **"The Kids Can't Take It If We Don't Give It"**
   Pages: 778-781 BofV
   Grade Levels: 4-12
   Description: Story - Babe Ruth describes his early youth and the training he received about right and wrong. He confesses how difficult it was for him to remember and live the principles he had learned but conceded that they still had their influence during his years of rough living. He pulled things together in his late years.
   Key Points: Ruth described how he resented all authority until he realized that one only had to be accountable to God. This helped him relieve himself of bitterness, rancor and the desire to get even.
   Questions: Why do you think Babe Ruth had such a distrust for authority? What perspective did he come to understand that helped him to remove his bitterness and desire to always get even? Who can remember times when they resented authority and didn't trust what was promised or said? What feelings accompanied these instances? Did these feelings bring you peace of mind or happiness?

2. **"Little Boy Blue"**
   Pages: 667-668 BofV
   Grade Levels: K-9
   Description: Poem - Describes toys that become faithful friends to the little boy who owns them.
   Key Points: We should learn to be steadfast and loyal as demonstrated by Little Boy Blue's companions.
   Questions: What "things" have been your most faithful friends? Who are some of the people that have been your faithful friends? In addition to those near your age, can you make parents, teachers, leaders, etc. some of your loyal friends? How? Why are faithful friends a helpful thing?

3. **"The Bundle of Sticks"**
   Pages: 388 BofV
   Grade Levels: K-9
   Description: Fable - Describes how a bundle of sticks is hard to break, but once separated, individual sticks easily fall prey. This example is then applied to people and our need to stick together.
   Key Points: Those who try to live life alone will soon find themselves prey to life's onslaughts. We need others for both comfort and strength.
   Questions: How did the wise father use the sticks to make his point about working together? What might befall someone who refuses the association of others and tries to live life completely on their own?

4. **"The Kingdom of the Bees"**
   Pages: 387-388 BofV
   Grade Levels: 4-9

   Description: Poem - Shakespeare describes how the bees serve as the perfect example of a well-ordered kingdom--each with his responsibilities, each contributing to the common good.
   Key Points: One can accomplish very little when existing alone. Safety and success usually come to those who have learned to work cooperatively with others.
   Questions: What would be the problem of one bee setting off on his own to live his life? How does this fable relate to our day-to-day lives? What are some examples of why we need to learn to live and work with others?

5. "The Pasture"

Pages: 271 BofV

Grade Levels: K-6

Description: Poem - Cites one expression of friendship where friends experience activities together including doing the chores.

Key Points: Life is enriched through friendships. These friendships can enrich a variety of activities including the mundane task of daily chores.

Questions: What two chores are mentioned in the poem? Why would someone want to ask a friend to join them in their chores? When is this a good idea and when might this be inappropriate? Who can think of activities or instances when inviting a friend has worked out well? Who can describe an incident when it didn't work out? Why? Why are friends valuable?

6. "Mending Wall"

Pages: 338-339 BofV

Grade Levels: 7-12

Description: Poem - Argues that the use of walls to keep things in or out has validity. However, the poem cautions against the use of walls where no compelling need exists.

Key Points: The wall described in the poem can be likened to personal barriers we erect that keep others from drawing too close to us. Sometimes the barriers are justified, and sometimes they are not. The unwise soul erects personal barriers that aren't necessary.

Questions: What did the wall separate? Did the author believe the wall was a useful thing? Why not? What personal walls do people build to keep out things? Who can think of an instance when a personal wall might be a good thing? What things does a person risk when he chooses to block out associations with others?

7. "The Influence of Democracy"

Pages: 180-183 BofV

Grade Levels: 7-12

Description: Lecture - Describes the author's reasoning that equality and compassion are directly related. He argues that men free of social strata and its inequalities are more inclined to pay attention to the misfortunes of others rather than focus all their energies on their own troubles.

Key Points: We have a greater capacity for mutual compassion when inequalities are minimized within a group. It stands to reason that those excluded will show less compassion because their reduced status keeps them focused on themselves rather than those around them.

Questions: What did the author cite as the chief reason for an American's tendency to come to the aid of his countrymen? Do you agree with this assertion? Why? What are some reasons why certain individuals will spurn the association of others? How might this tendency of disassociation relate to the author's position on equality? How might the phenomenon manifest itself in our schools and homes? How can we combat its pernicious affects?

8. "Aristotle on Pity"
     Pages: 171-172 BofV
     Grade Levels: 10-12
Description: Treatise - Aristotle argues his case for those who are most likely to pity the misfortune of others. He lists examples and rationales for why one group might and another group might not find pity for others.

Key Points: Provides stimulating thought on reasons why certain groups have varying capacities for pitying others. Allows opportunity to discuss empathy, sympathy and the like and why they are worthwhile things to experience.

Questions: What examples of people did the author offer as those most likely to pity the misfortune of others? Which groups did the author offer as those least likely to pity others? Do you agree? What do you think is needed to develop a capacity for heartfelt pity? Why is this a needed virtue in today's world?

9. "Where Love Is, God Is"
     Pages: 158-165 BofV, 71-81 YP
     Grade Levels: 4-12
Description: Story - Describes the story of a man who finds that by serving his neighbors, he is serving God.

Key Points: Man finds happiness in offering help to those in distress. He gains his reward in feelings of accomplishment and sacrifice. Often our actions and rewards seem insignificant, but when totaled together determine who we become.

What caused the man to look out his window on one particular day? What did he discover in his searches? How did he react to what he saw? Do you think he had a clue as to what was actually happening? What are acts of service or compassion that occur on a daily basis but often go unnoticed? Why should one strive to help others irrespective of who might be watching?

10. "Marley's Ghost"
Pages: 154-158 BofV
Grade Levels: 4-12
Description: Story - Describes the events in a miser's life that change his perspectives about how he should treat others. A deceased business partner and three ghosts expose the man to past, present and future occurrences that cause the change of heart.
Key Points: Illustrates how certain pursuits have little meaning if acted upon alone. The business of mankind is most important, and this demands that we interact with others in a positive way.
Questions: What was Scrooge like before the nightly visits? What was the significance of the chains? What did Marley mean when he stated that mankind was his business? Who can think of instances when we might be tempted to act without regard for others? When is it wise to work with people and not despite them?

11. "If I Can Stop One Heart From Breaking"
Pages: 147 BofV, 54-55 YP
Grade Levels: 4-9
Description: Poem - Describes a vision of life where compassion toward others is paramount.
Key Points: Life's purpose is serving others. Those who focus solely on themselves will miss much of life's opportunities and rewards.
Questions: What does the author consider as life's purpose? What examples does she use to make her point? Do you agree? What do the advertisements of today focus on? How do they differ from the message of the poem? Why does it make sense to look for opportunities to forget yourself in the service of others? What are some ways you can extend yourself in serving others?

12. "Old Mr. Rabbit's Thanksgiving Dinner"
Pages: 114-117 BofV
Grade Levels: K-9

Description: Tale - After gathering vast stores of food, Old Man Rabbit decides to share his bounty with his neighbors rather than keep it all for himself. He seemed to find great satisfaction in performing the service.

Key Points: The rabbit discovered that one can gain great satisfaction in associating with and serving others. Had he stayed home and kept to himself, he would have lost the sense of accomplishment and association. Note: He might have thought himself justified in keeping all his food because he did the work of gathering.

Questions: What purpose did Mr. Rabbit have in his early morning trip? What are some of the things he gathered? What do you think was his original intent for the food? What brand new idea did he discover? How did it make him feel in the end? What could he have done rather than involve himself with those around him? Which was the wiser course? What are some ways you can share what you have with others? Why is it wise to seek the association of everyone even if you are the only one with something to offer?

13. "A Child's Prayer"
Pages: 112 BofV
Grade Levels: K-6
Description: Poem - A plea for opportunities in life to bless mankind through acts of service.

Key Points: The point of this poem drives home our need to be involved in the lives of others. Those who purposely chart life's course on their own miss life's greatest opportunities for a rewarding life.

Questions: What are the opportunities this child is praying for? Why not ask for bikes, toys or vacations? Why do you think each of these requests involve others? What are ways we can involve ourselves with others in a way that makes us feel good? What is wrong about purposely avoiding the association of others?

14. "The Good Bishop"
Pages: 644-646 BofV, 266-269 YP
Grade Levels: 3-12
Description: Story - Describes how "The Good Bishop" helped Jean Valjean (who served 19 years in prison for stealing a single loaf of bread) rid himself of hate and replace it with love.

Key Points: There are those who choose to disassociate themselves from everyone else. Often, all they lack are opportunities to feel and experience the benefits of companionship and mutual support.

Questions: What events embittered Jean? What was his initial response to the Bishop's kindness? How do you think he felt toward the Bishop by the end of the story? What happened to change his attitude? Why do some people carry a "chip on their shoulder?" What is the danger in holding on to this attitude? What are ways to regain trust and affection toward others?

15. "The Children's Hour"
Pages: 242-243 BofV
Grade Levels: K-9
Description: Poem - Describes a point in the author's day when his children disrupt his activities in order to be with him. He points out the joy those occasions produce.
Key Points: Our associations with our loved ones are worth the disruptions they often produce. There is much good in taking advantage of the opportunities to associate with others.
Questions: What does the author mean by children's hour? What are some of the things that happen? Why doesn't the father mind the disruption? Who can think of instances when it is a good thing to be interrupted by family or friends? What are the benefits to these associations? What can happen to those who remove themselves from the company of others, particularly family members?

16. "The Perfect Dinner Table"
Pages: 241 BofV
Grade Levels: K-12
Description: Poem - Describes the joys of interacting with family at dinner time.
Key Points: Few, if any, pleasures in life can equal "the perfect dinner table." Some of our greatest pleasures come from association with others. Those who shun company miss out on many of life's simple but sublime joys.
Questions: What are some of the activities that are going on? Why do you think the author feels these activities are worthwhile and fun? How would this differ from eating alone? What are areas where we might choose to spend our time alone? When does this become a foolish thing? What is good about our associations with others?

17. "The Hiltons' Holiday"
Pages: 227-240 BofV
Grade Levels: 4-12

Description: Story - Story of two parents and two young daughters portraying life in rural American about 100 years ago. The story describes the genuine happiness of the father and his girls as they take a day off to go to the city to shop and visit with relatives. Politeness and civility are exemplified.

Key Points: The mother lost out in the day's enjoyment because she chose not to participate. Those who shut out others lose many opportunities.

Questions: What are some of the things you learned about the Hiltons' life. Why do you think the mother chose to stay home? Do you think she made the wisest choice? Who can think of an instance when someone chose not to get involved only to find out that they really missed out? Why does it pay to get involved even when the circumstances might seem a little threatening or unfamiliar?

18. "If You Were"

Pages: 207 BofV

Grade Levels: K-12

Description: Poem - Lists four things to keep busy at to enjoy good mental health and a happier life.

Key Points: Busy being kind, glad, good and right would leave you with no time for self-pity and criticism of others. Often we isolate ourselves from others because we substitute judgment for involvement. It is always easy to find problems when we choose to judge from a distance.

Questions: What four virtues are recommended in the poem? What promises are made to those who practice these virtues? Why do you think the author makes these promises? What happens to those who choose to stay uninvolved? Do you think this a good thing? How might you become a happier and more involved person?

19. "The Choir Invisible"

Pages: 182 BofV

Grade Levels: 7-12

Description: Poem - Argues our need to live for others. Yearns to be a strength to others and continue this service through the eternities.

20. "Count That Day Lost"

Pages: 171 BofV

Grade Levels: 4-9

Description: Poem - Argues that a day is lost if one fails to cheer another's heart or bring sunshine to another's face.

21. "The Human Touch"

Pages: 317 BofV

Grade Levels: 4-9

Description: Poem - Argues that personal concern and service are more helpful to the fainting heart than provisions of shelter and food.

22. "Cicero on Friendship"

Pages: 333-334 BofV

Grade Levels: 7-12

Description: Discourse - Argues that the highest level of friendship can only be achieved by virtuous people capable of maintaining a oneness with those of whom they associate. He further argues that great societies will cease to exist when their members lose the virtues associated with true friendship.

23. "The Arrow and the Song"

Pages: 341 BofV

Grade Levels: K-6

Description: Poem - Describes how little acts of kindness or service can have profound effects down the road.

CLIQUES

1. **"The Volunteer at Auschwitz"**
    Pages: 803-808 BofV
    Grade Levels: 4-12
    Description: Story - Describes the last years of a priest during the Nazi occupation of Poland.   He eventually was assigned to Auschwitz where he voluntarily died to spare the life of another.
    Key Points: The Nazis had little tolerance for those unlike themselves. They took elitism to new extremes and demonstrated a harshness that had not been experienced in a civilized time. We still see some of these same practices today. Usually they are more subtle than the Nazis.
    Questions: What people were targeted for Nazi discipline? Why do you think this was so? How were these people treated? What are some of the differences found in young people today? What are some of the ways we treat these individuals? Does it make it okay if our practices are less severe than those practiced in Nazi Germany?

2. **"The Loom of Time"**
    Pages: 801-802 BofV
    Grade Levels: 4-12
    Description: Poem - Describes how each person comes with unique characteristics--some comely, some awkward. Author argues that there are reasons why we are what we are and in time will come to appreciate the value and placement of each characteristic.
    Key Points: Each comes to earth with unique talents. Those who focus on certain outwardly appearances often miss the full person and what he or she has to offer.
    Questions: What do you think the colored threads represented? What might be a real life example of a gold thread? What about the darker hues? Why did the author caution against judging the piece until the entire pattern becomes clear? Can you think of individuals who had traits much like the dark hues who turned out to be very special? How does this relate to associating with friends?

3. **"The Lamb and the Tiger"**
    Pages: 800-801 BofV
    Grade Levels: 4-12

Description: Poem - Describes how both the lamb and the tiger are God's creations. Author cites the vast differences between the two. No conclusions are drawn except the fact that both exist and were made by the same hand of God.

Key Points: The poem points out that there are obvious differences in the animal world, and this can easily be extended to humankind. When we come to grips with the diversity in people, we are in a better position to accept those who look or act differently from ourselves.

Questions: What are some of the differences between the lamb and the tiger? Which is the better animal? What are some of the physical differences we find in people? Is it possible to determine what physical traits are superior over others? Why do we often include or banish individuals from our association simply because of how they look or dress or perform? Is this right?

4. "A Brother in Need"

Pages: 294-297 YP

Grade Levels: K-12

Description: Tale - Two Vietnamese brothers, one rich and one poor. When the rich brother is faced with a life and death crisis, only his brother agrees to help. All the other supposed friends turn out to be traitors.

Key Points: Seasonal friends are rarely present when needed. They have even been known to turn against former associates when a crisis develops. Family and tried and true friends are worth one's time and attention.

Questions: What were the living circumstances of each brother? Why did the wealthy brother never choose the company of his poor brother? How did he learn his lesson? How do we choose our friends? On what basis do we decide? Why must we be careful in choosing our friends? Why are groups a risky proposition at best?

5. "The Thousandth Man"

Pages: 736-737 BofV

Grade Levels: 7-12

Description: Poem - Reminds us that 100 percent loyalty and reliability are seldom found.

Key Points: Loyalty and reliability can sometimes be rare commodities. Often casual relationships are mistaken for true friendship, particularly with respect to our group associations.

Questions: What are some of the characteristics in a true friend? What distinguishes the "Thousandth Man?" Why is it important to enjoy friends for what they offer but to keep friendships, particularly group associations, in their proper perspective? What is your part in developing a true friendship?

6. "America the Beautiful"
Pages: 722-723 BofV, 298-299 YP
Grade Levels: K-12
Description: Song - Describes America, its landscape and its heritage of valor. Concludes with a plea that God crown America with brotherhood everywhere.
Key Points: A plea to God for America to "crown thy good with brotherhood from sea to shining sea." This is the final and perhaps the most important plea asked of God.
Questions: What are the four things asked of God? Why do you think the author reserved brotherhood for last? What did she mean by brotherhood from sea to shining sea? How is brotherhood practiced? Is brotherhood any less important now than it was over 100 years ago?

7. "The Kingdom of the Bees"
Pages: 387-388 BofV
Grade Levels: 7-12
Description: Poem - Shakespeare describes how the bees serve as the perfect example of a well-ordered kingdom--each with his responsibilities, each contributing to the common good.
Key Points: There should be room for everyone willing to contribute to the common good. We often determine our friendships by appearances and fail to enjoy the advantages others, not so attractive, can offer.
Questions: Why is the bee kingdom so successful in what it does? Is everyone alike in appearance and skills? What would happen to the bees if everyone was the queen or a drone? On what types of criteria are many of our friendship groups based? Why might this be a foolish way to do things? What is smart about including everyone willing to be a friend and contribute?

8. "The Sheep and the Pig Who Build a House"
Pages: 356-357 BofV
Grade Levels: K-3

Description: Poem - Describes how five animal companions agreed to contribute to the building of a house. Each did his part, and all lived happily together in the end.

Key Points: Groups can be positive if founded on a premise of working toward a constructive end. Note that everyone was included, even the rooster who could only crow in the morning.

Questions: What was the aim of the group of animals? What did each agree to contribute? What was the final result? Did they allow everyone to join? Why? Who can think of real-life reasons to establish specific groups? What should be the criteria for admission.

9. "The Little Steam Engine"

Pages: 530-532 BofV

Grade Levels: K-9

Description: Story - Describes a little steam engine's commitment and efforts to finish her work. Despite repeated refusals of help from larger and more capable engines, the little steam engine eventually prevails with the help of a second little steam engine.

Key Points: The biggest, smartest or most capable companions may not be there to assist you in your hour of need. It is wise to chose companions whose hearts are largest.

Questions: What were the little steam engine's problems? Who did the little engine go to for help? Which of the companions proved the best friend? What types of companions do we often chose to associate with? What is foolish with limiting oneself to the most popular, strongest, most skilled, etc.?

10. "Aristotle on Friendship"

Pages: 331-333 BofV

Grade Levels: 7-12

Description: Discourse - Aristotle argues that a friendship based on concern and affection for each other has the greatest likelihood of enduring. While pointing out advantages of friendships based on utility and pleasure, he recommends the cultivation of perfect friendships that have moved beyond extenuating circumstances.

Key Points: Aristotle illustrates the difficulties in basing friendships on what you can personally gain from the association. These friendships will secure advantages but will not provide the joy that only comes from friendships based on genuine concern for each other.

94

What three friendships are discussed? How does utility and pleasure differ from Aristotle's perfect friendship? What type of friendships are typically formed in a school setting? What is the danger in limiting oneself to friendships of utility or pleasure?

11. "Keep Friendships in Constant Repair"
Pages: 329 BofV
Grade Levels: 4-12
Description: Discourse - Argues that friendships cannot be trusted to endure. One should continue to add new friendships in order to assure a constant source of comradery.
Key Points: It is wise to never limit one's supply of friends. Those who place all emphasis on a single group will eventually find themselves in short supply. The wise soul continually renews his collection of friends.
Questions: What is the author's argument against limiting one's number of friends? What is the author's message when he compares friends to a well-stocked wine cellar? What are some of the reasons we restrict ourselves to a few friends? What are some of the things we can do to assure a constant source of friends? Why does this make sense?

12. "The Enchanted Bluff"
Pages: 320-328 BofV
Grade Levels: 4-12
Description: Story - Describes an evening in the lives of six boys who share a common love for a river. The boys' conversation eventually turns to the mystery and allure of a red bluff, supposedly situated in the desert of New Mexico. Story concludes with an epilogue that shares how each boy fared as an adult.
Key Points: The boys shared a friendship based on common interest. No one was excluded due to age or talents or intelligence. Some groups are appropriate because they follow logical and natural boundaries rather than artificially manipulated limits.
Questions: What common interest did the six boys share? How did the boys differ? Why do you think the group existed in the first place? Do you think they would have allowed others with a similar interest to join their group? How did this group differ from groups or cliques that are determined by such things as appearances or possessions? What do you think should be the basis for a group of friends?

95

13. "The Bear and the Travelers"

Pages: 271-272 BofV, 147 YP

Grade Levels: K-6

Description: Fable - Describes how one traveler deserts his companion when they encounter a bear along the way.

Key Points: One must be careful in the selection of companions. Those who unwisely choose their friends might find themselves all alone when times become difficult.

Questions: What caused the two travelers to temporarily halt their journey? How did each react to the bear? What did the second traveler learn about his companion?

14. "The Velveteen Rabbit"

Pages: 275-283 BofV

Grade Levels: K-6

Description: Story - Describes a rabbit's journey from her initial existence as a stuffed toy to becoming a real live rabbit.

Key Points: The rabbit was exposed to a variety of prejudices, some positive and some negative. This provides a good example of how perspectives can differ from one group to another without the person changing. Illustrates how arbitrary most judgments are.

Questions: How was the velveteen rabbit treated by the more mechanical toys? How was the rabbit treated by the little boy? How was the velveteen rabbit treated by the real rabbits when they first came in contact? Whose perspective was the most accurate? Why do people differ in their judgment of others? Why is this unfair? How can you avoid falling into this bad habit?

15. "Friendship"

Pages: 284 BofV, 145-146 YP

Grade Levels: 4-12

Description: Poem - Describes some of the characteristics of friendship by citing examples of what it is and isn't.

Key Points: This poem will provide an excellent forum to discuss the characteristics that should or should not accompany a solid friendship. This should assist those students who are too hung up on outward appearances or single issue commonalities.

Questions: What characteristics of friendship are mentioned in the poem? Which ones do you agree with? Why? How are your friendships formed? Which of these have the bonding potential of an enduring and meaningful friendship? What is unwise about forming friendships according to such things as how one dresses or how one looks?

16. "Why Frog and Snake Never Play Together"

Pages: 284 BofV

Grade Levels: K-9

Description: Tale - Describes the circumstances that led to the enmity that still exists between the frog and the snake. The reasons boil down to the influences and prejudices instilled by parents.

Key Points: The two youngsters were getting along well until they were told that they couldn't possibly get along. While not an example of cliques in the usual sense, it does illustrate how one group (snakes) can exclude another (frogs) just because this is how it has always been done.

Questions: How well did the snake-child and frog-child initially get along despite their obvious differences? What changed their perspective and relationship? What might have resulted if they had chosen to continue their positive relationship? What differences do we find between groups of young people? How do these differences often cause us to avoid positive relationships? Why is it unwise to associate only with those who have similar characteristics?

17. "Kindness to Animals"

Pages: 109 BofV

Grade Levels: K-6

Description: Poem - Asks that children be kind to helpless animals. Points out that these creatures will repay the kindness with things that will cheer us.

Key Points: If we look beyond appearance or strength, we will find that both animals and people have something to offer in return for our kindness.

Questions: What three animals are mentioned as objects worthy of our kindness? What in turn do each of these creatures have to offer in return? What are some other examples of contributions that come from the creatures around us? Might this same principle hold true for people? Why is it wise to be kind to everyone, especially those who seem different than ourselves?

18. "Beauty and the Beast"

Pages: 127-134 BofV

Grade Levels: 4-9

Description: Tale - Describes how a young lady learns to love a beast despite his horrible appearance. The beast turns out to be a prince who must appear as a beast until a beautiful maiden consents to kiss him.

Key Points: We can never judge by appearances alone. Often, much good is hidden only to be discovered by those willing to spend the time to search. We should never exclude others because of first impressions.

Questions: What circumstances brought Beauty to the Beast's castle? What was her first impression of the beast? What personal virtues eventually positioned her to free the Beast from the magician's spell? Who can think of substitutes for the "beast" we see on a day-to-day basis? Why is it wise to use patience before deciding what is good or bad about someone or something?

19. "The Indian Cinderella"

Pages: 612-614 BofV, 269-272 YP
Grade Levels: K-12
Description: Tale - Describes Strong Wind, an invisible Indian warrior, who devises a scheme to find an honest Indian maid to marry. He finally succeeds with the least likely candidate because she possessed the attribute of honesty.

Key Points: Even when, at first, it appears a lie would reward you, in the long run it never does. Two of the sisters, in effect, were part of a clique and plotted against the third sister. Cliques often benefit no one, including its members.

Questions: What test did Strong Wind require of each potential bride? Who finally succeeded in winning his heart? Why? How did the little maiden's two older sisters treat her? Why do you think they ganged up on their little sister? Was this a fair thing to do? What ultimately happened to them as a result of their behavior? What is wrong about groups excluding others and sometimes treating outsiders shamefully? How can this practice ultimately hurt the members of the group?

20. "The Athenian Oath"

Pages: 217 BofV
Grade Levels: 7-12
Description: Oath - Taken by young 17 year old men of Athens to prove loyalty to their city of Athens.

Key Points: This city became great because allegiance was given first to the entire city before consideration to groups within the city. Allegiance should first be given to school or the class if that school or class hopes to reach its greatest potential. Everyone profits under these circumstances.

Questions: What were some of the things expected of the Athenian youth? What could substitute for "city" in the Athenian oath? Why does it make sense to focus loyalties to schools, classes or homes? What is the problem with cliques or similar groups? Who usually is hurt when we focus our allegiances in the wrong places?

21. "Beautiful"
Pages: 134 BofV, 50 YP
Grade Levels: 4-9
Description: Poem - Describes how beauty is ultimately expressed in our faces, hands and feet. How we feel and act defines beauty better than the outward appearance.

22. "The New Colossus"
Pages: 179 BofV
Grade Levels: 7-12
Description: Poem - Contrasts our Statue of Liberty with a similar statue from antiquity. The author focuses on the messages conveyed by each of the statues and proudly declares our country's invitation to the tired, poor and huddled masses yearning to be free.

23. "New Friends and Old Friends"
Pages: 330 BofV
Grade Levels: 4-12
Description: Poem - Argues that there is a place for both old and new friends. States that old friends are best, but the day will come when new friends will be all that's available.

24. "A Wayfaring Song"
Pages: 312 BofV
Grade Levels: 4-9
Description: Poem - Describes the friend who is willing to share both the happy and sad times.

25. "The House by the Side of the Road"
Pages: 305-306 BofV
Grade Levels: 7-12
Description: Poem - Argues that our responsibility as people is to interrelate with others (rather than insulate ourselves within our comfort zones) with the challenge to accept others as they are and treat them as friends.

DEFEATIST ATTITUDE

1. "The Boy and the Nuts"

Pages: 46-47 BofV

Grade Levels: K-9

Description: Short Story - Little boy reaches in jar to take some nuts but finds that his fist full of nuts prevents him from pulling his hand out. Rather than think through the problem, he cries, and Mom comes to the rescue. A defeatist attitude limits our potential.

Key Points: This boy gave up trying to find a solution to getting both his hand and the nuts from the jar.

Questions: Have any of you decided to give up on something only to later find the task was simple? Who can share an example? Why is it foolish to give up on too many tasks or problems? What will this cost you in the long run?

2. "Go Forth to Life"

Pages: 103 BofV

Grade Levels: 7-12

Description: Poem - Author points to each person's heavenly birth as the reason to resist life's challenges and pitfalls and ascend to manly pureness through resolve to serve others.

Key Points: All have potential to control how they live, feel and act-- urges against giving up.

Questions: What temptations does the author acknowledge? Do you believe you are capable of controlling these desires? Why would one wish to control such things as passion's fire, a life of ease or other enticing allurements?

3. "Man's Nature Is Good"

Pages: 812-814 BofV

Grade Levels: 7-12

Description: Sermon - Argues that all men have the tendency to do good naturally. He concludes that only those who choose wisely from life's menu will retain this natural tendency.

Key Points: All have the power to control their character, but it must be continually worked, much like a muscle. Those who easily give up will lose their natural disposition for greatness and fall prey to life's temptations and misery.

Questions: What does Mencius believe about the natural state of man? What does he think determines the final state of a person's character and therefore his ability to control much of his life? How would Mencius view those who are quick to become discouraged when confronted with adversity? How can a belief in one's ability to shape one's character assist in maintaining optimism during conflict?

4. **"The Healing of the Paralytic"**
   Pages: 759-760 BofV, 373-374 YP
   Grade Levels: 4-12
   Description: Story - Describes an incident where Jesus of Nazareth healed a man who was paralyzed. The incident stood out because of the lengths taken to bring the man before Jesus. He was lowered from the roof because of the large crowd blocking the way in.
   Key Points: The friends of the paralyzed man did not allow the crowds to stand in their way. They went to great lengths to see that their friend had an opportunity to be healed of his infirmity. Their perseverance paid off.
   Questions: How did the paralyzed man get to see Jesus? What do you think prompted the men to go to these great lengths? What things are worth going the extra mile? What about little challenges that confront us each day? Why bother with them when obstacles make things difficult?

5. **"Up From Slavery"**
   Pages: 404-408 BofV
   Grade Levels: 4-12
   Description: Story - Describes select events in the life of Booker T. Washington. This particular account describes his efforts to gain the means and opportunity for a formal education.
   Key Points: Washington refused to give up on his goal for an education. He overcame numerous obstacles by sheer determination.
   Questions: What were a few of the obstacles Booker Washington had to overcome in order to enroll in Hampton School? Do you think it would have been understandable for him to give up? Why do you think he kept plugging away? What are some obstacles that must be faced today for one to get a good job or be accepted to a good college or school?

6. **"It's Plain Hard Work That Does It"**
   Pages: 409-415 BofV
   Grade Levels: K-12
   Description: Story - Describes various aspects of Edison's life. Describes many of his work habits and attitudes through anecdotes and quotes.

Key Points:	Edison had the capacity to see good arising from most failures. He viewed obstacles as opportunities to experiment.
Questions:	Did Edison ever have a failure? Can you give some examples of how Edison treated failure? Why did this turn out to be a great asset in his life? What failures can be expected as we try to live our lives? What will these failures cost us? How can these failures turn out to be blessings?

7. "Keep Your Eyes on the Prize"

Pages: 230-231 YP
Grade Levels: 7-12

Description:	Song - Celebrates the steps taken for freedom's sake and encourages continued effort by keeping one's eyes on the final prize.
Key Points:	Keeping a proper focus serves to channel one's energy toward the desired end. Freedom is worth the effort it takes to secure it. Most difficult endeavors require a sustained focus.
Questions:	What does it mean to keep your eyes on the prize? What prize does the writer focus on? Why is focus such an urgent need when one is struggling with a problem? What is the opposite of focus and how is it typically manifested?

8. "I Decline to Accept the End of Man"

Pages: 593-595 BofV
Grade Levels: 7-12

Description:	Speech - Argues that man has a responsibility to aid in his own existence by continuing to develop others' capacity to serve and understand each other.
Key Points:	Author laments a trend where many have given up their responsibility to perpetuate what is good about mankind. He challenges the rising generation to not give in to doomsday philosophy that predetermines destruction and causes people to get while they still can rather than give and serve.
Questions:	What are the author's concerns over the rising generation of writers? What does he mean when he refers to writing of matters not of the heart but of the glands? What is the problem when a writer gives up all hope of a better world? What is the problem when any individual gives up hope for a better life? Who can think of instances when people achieved great things because they refused to give up hope?

9. "Will"

Pages: 593 BofV, 242 YP

Grade Levels: 4-12

Description: Poem - argues that force of will is the only thing that determines accomplishment and happiness.

Key Points: Poem places will power over such things as chance, destiny, fate and luck. Provides an opportunity to weigh the influence of will power and resolve against such factors as chance and destiny.

Questions: What factors are compared with will power? What does the author mean by earnest purpose? Do you agree with the author's view? Who can offer an example where luck or chance might bless one and curse another? What is the stronger of the two, will power or luck? Why do you think your choice is correct? What benefits accrue to those who take responsibility for their lives and accomplishments?

10. "I Have a Dream"

Pages: 572-576 BofV

Grade Levels: 4-12

Description: Speech - Argues that the time is now to provide full liberty to all Americans. Presents a scenario of an America where no distinctions are made based on race or similar factors where all people live in harmony on equal footing under the law.

Key Points: Martin Luther King presents an attitude of optimism amid trials. While acknowledging the difficult road that lies ahead, he speaks with confidence that change for the better will occur.

Questions: What does the speaker mean when he states that the multitudes have gathered in Washington to cash a check? Describe some of the dreams mentioned in the speech? How would you describe the speaker's attitude? How does attitude factor in when one is facing significant challenge?

11. "Can't"

Pages: 567-568 BofV, 226-227 YP

Grade Levels: 4-9

Description: Poem - Argues the point that the word "can't" causes great injury to both individuals and society. Concludes that it should be despised and discarded.

Key Points: Much of what we can yet enjoy is only possible if we eliminate "can't" from our thinking, speech and actions. Those who adhere to its message will deprive themselves of much.

What things might "can't" deprive us of? Why do you think the author states that the word "can't" does more harm than slander and lies? What would our world be like if we banished "can't" as a part of our thoughts and vocabulary? Who can share an instance where someone convinced themselves that they couldn't possibly accomplish what they wanted? Why is this an unwise action?

12. "Carry On!"

Pages: 541-542 BofV, 227-229 YP

Grade Levels: 4-12

Description: Poem - argues that no obstacle is too large to cause one to quit. Concludes that there is sweetness and joy that comes in the trying and that our purpose in life is to make this a better world through our efforts.

Key Points: Focus is on effort, not results. Those who define success by how hard they tried can be assured of triumph because effort is not subject to chance or circumstances. A focus on effort removes all reason for a defeatist attitude because the individual can control effort.

Questions: What were some of life's obstacles described in the poem? Why would one choose to continue a fight when the odds are ten to one against you? How did this author measure success? Who can think of instances when the biggest winner might not be the person who scores highest or performs the best? Why does measurement in terms of effort remove one's reason to give up trying?

13. "You Mustn't Quit"

Pages: 536 BofV, 243-244 YP

Grade Levels: K-9

Description: Poem - Stresses the point to never quit no matter how dismal things may appear to be.

Key Points: Poem acknowledges that life provides its dips and curves but points out that this is no reason to give up.

Questions: What examples does the poem offer to describe life's difficulties and challenges? What advice does the author offer to people faced with obstacles? What are things that people often give up on because the obstacles seem so large? Why do people give up on certain things? Why is quitting a poor habit to develop?

14. "The Crow and the Pitcher"
Pages: 532-533 BofV
Grade Levels: K-6
Description: Fable - A thirsty crow refuses to abandon an opportunity to obtain water despite repeated failures. Eventually his persistence pays off with a plan that works.
Key Points: The crow was only successful because he was determined to find a way around his problem. Great ideas often surface after repeated efforts.
Questions: What was the crow's goal? What were some of his original plans to obtain the water? What character trait did the crow possess that allowed him to reach his goal? Why is this a valuable trait? Who can think of an instance where you told yourself, "There must be a way!" What eventually happened?

15. "Moses in the Bulrushes"
Pages: 139-140 BofV
Grade Levels: 4-9
Description: Story - Describes a mother's effort to save her son from Pharaoh's order of death. Pharaoh's daughter finds the child hidden in the rushes on the edge of the river. She takes the baby to raise as her own.
Key Points: Mother refused to accept the inevitability of losing her son to Pharaoh's death decree. She finds a way to save her son.
Questions: Why did the child's mother hide her son in a river? How did the story end? What type of attitude would be needed to go to this extent to save her child? What are some typical obstacles that often require a positive attitude to succeed?

16. "F. Scott Fitzgerald To His Daughter"
Pages: 225-226 BofV, 86 YP
Grade Levels: 4-12
Description: Letter - Father writes to his daughter at camp giving advice of what to worry about and what not to worry about. The words of counsel are intended to help shape the daughter's character.
Key Points: Much of the counsel is to help the daughter fend off discouragement. Often our defeatist attitudes arise because we focus on the wrong things.
Questions: What was the purpose in the father's letter? What were some of the things he suggested she not worry over? Why do you think he chose these particular things? Do we grow discouraged over some of these same things? Why? How can we improve our attitudes?

17. "Second Message to Congress"
Pages: 256-258 BofV
Grade Levels: 7-12
Description: Speech - Lincoln argues the need for America to remain one united nation. He confirms the rightness of the North's cause.
Key Points: Lincoln argues that the nation (North) has but one choice--that of uniting the nation and providing freedom for all its citizenry. He allows no wiggle room for those who would give up the fight.
Questions: What reasons did Lincoln cite for keeping the nation united? What were some of his points on why they must hold to their present course of action? Are there situations where we can't afford not to press forward on a situation? Who can come up with some "for instances?"

18. "The Stars in the Sky"
Pages: 542-546 BofV
Grade Levels: K-6
Description: Tale - Describes a little girl's travels to have the opportunity to touch a heavenly star. Her persistence and trust in other's advice prove an interesting combination. Eventually she accomplishes her goal.

19. "Thinking on Friendship"
Pages: 335 BofV
Grade Levels: 10-12
Description: Poem - Shakespeare laments misfortunes, missed opportunities, etc. He concludes each sonnet with an acknowledgment that all his troubles disappear each time he thinks of a highly valued friendship.

20. "L'Envoc"
Pages: 789 BofV
Grade Levels: 10-12
Description: Poem - Describes how insignificant mortal efforts are when compared with what we can expect during the eternities. Concludes by describing a future existence where we work for joy without worry of unfair judgment.

21. "Mary Wollstonecraft on Faith"
Pages: 787-788 BofV
Grade Levels: 10-12

Description: Thesis - Wollstonecraft argues that God provides opposition or allows evil to flourish in order for man to develop reason, virtue and knowledge.

22. "Amazing Grace"
Pages: 772 BofV, 347-348 YP
Grade Levels: 4-12
Description: Song - Describes how despite a wretched past, all have a great hope for the future. He attributes this opportunity to God's goodly grace.

23. "Hanukkah Hymn"
Pages: 765-766 BofV, 352-353 YP
Grade Levels: 7-12
Description: Hymn - Describes why the Jews appreciate their temple and the optimism they hold for its powerful influence in future years.

24. "Solitude"
Pages: 552-553 BofV, 244-245 YP
Grade Levels: 4-12
Description: Poem - Argues that those who focus their relationships on what is wrong about life will often walk alone. Suggests that we work out our problems discretely and maintain relationships with others.

DEFIANCE

1. **"The Story of Augustus Who Would Not Have Any Soup"**
    Pages: 45-46 YP
    Grade Levels: K-6
    Description: Poem - Describes a boy who first lost his health and eventually his life because he refused to eat his soup.
    Key Points: There is usually a good reason for customs, rules, etc. and when we refuse to follow them, there can be dire consequences. This could be likened to buckling up a seat belt, walking bikes across a busy intersections, playing with matches, etc.
    Questions: How did Augustus die? Do you think this a foolish thing to do? Are there rules in life that you can think of that could bring on tragedy if refused to be followed?

2. **"The Fiery Furnace"**
    Pages: 753-755 BofV, 370-373 YP
    Grade Levels: 4-12
    Description: Story - Describes how three young rulers in King Nebuchadnezzar's court refused to bow down to a God that was not their own. The penalty was death by fire. After refusing a second chance to bow to the idol, they were cast in the furnace but remained untouched. The king then released them and gave them greater honors.
    Key Points: The three men chose to defy the king's law because it violated their own moral and religious code. Acts of defiance can be appropriate but only under rare and specific circumstances.
    Questions: What law did the three young men violate? Was this a wrong thing to do? What was the king's penalty? When is it okay to purposely disregard a rule or a law? Who can think of examples? Why must we be careful before making such a critical choice? Do you think that the great majority of rules and laws are valid? Who can give examples of just rules and laws?

3. **"Daniel in the Lion's Den"**
    Pages: 756-758 BofV
    Grade Levels: 4-12
    Description: Story - Describes how Daniel refused to stop praying to his God despite a law prohibiting it. The king reluctantly has Daniel thrown to the lions, but Daniel remains unharmed throughout the night. The king is glad and rewards Daniel but punishes those who used the law in an attempt to destroy Daniel.

Key Points: Daniel chose to violate the law by willfully continuing his practice of prayer. He chose to remain true to a law he considered greater than the king's law.

Questions: Why was Daniel thrown to the lions? Most agree that Daniel did the right thing. Why do you think they feel this way? Why are most rules and laws enacted? How can you tell when an exception should be made? What about simple rules like not talking loudly in a library or not parking in a handicapped zone? Why is it important that they be followed?

4. "Ethical Loyalty"

Pages: 725-727 BofV
Grade Levels: 7-12
Description: Treatise - Distinguishes between blind loyalties and informed loyalties (loyalty to moral right).

Key Points: In a deep moral crisis, a soldier may have to override his oath to his profession in order to be loyal to humanity itself...that is to a higher morality. Our first loyalty is to that which we know in our heart (conscience). There are eternal truths, eternal principles, absolutes that never change despite the prevailing law.

Questions: What were the author's views on the need to follow orders no matter what the circumstances? How was the German hochverrat different from landesverrat? What situations in our day to day lives can you think of in which you might break a lesser law in order to keep a higher law? Why must you be careful in choosing?

5. "Paul Revere's Ride"

Pages: 708-712 BofV
Grade Levels: K-12
Description: Poem - Account of Paul Revere's Ride to warn John Hancock and Samuel Adams that the British were coming to destroy the colonists' arms.

Key Points: Some are willing to take quick and decisive action for the cause of liberty even when they risk violating the law of the land or those in authority. There are select times when defiance is a character virtue. It often becomes an expression of courage.

Questions: Describe the circumstances describing Paul Revere's famous ride? Who was Revere defying? Why is he considered a hero? Do you think he was justified in his actions? What circumstances need to be present before it's okay to defy the

109

rules or laws that prevail? Do we find these circumstances often in our homes and schools?

6. "Yudisthira at Heaven's Gate"
Pages: 684-685 BofV
Grade Levels: K-12
Description: Story - Describes a king's journey to heaven. He is refused entrance unless he agrees to abandon a dog who had served as a loyal companion along the way. Describes how he is willing to defy the Gods to stand on principle. Eventually he is rewarded for his convictions.
Key Points: There are times when principles should take precedence over rules. These are instances of courage rather than acts of rebellion.
Questions: Who did Yudisthira defy to remain loyal to his lowly companion? Why do you think he acted this way? What finally came as a result of Yudisthira's willingness to defy the counsel of the Gods? Can you think of instances when defiance is a good thing? Can you think of instances when it is not? What makes the difference in the two situations unfair?

7. "The Emperor and the Peasant Boy"
Pages: 264-266 YP
Grade Levels: 3-12
Description: Tale - Describes a peasant boy who obeyed an unfair law (because he believed in obeying the law) which resulted in the law being changed.
Key Points: An unfair law is not sufficient reason to break that law. The best way to change a bad law is to obey that law, but call attention to it in a way that will cause those in authority to rethink it.
Questions: Why did the emperor disguise himself? Why do you think the emperor urged the boy to break the law? What was the boy's reply? What happened as a result of the boy's honesty? Can you think of some rules or laws that seem unjust? Who can think of some factors that might determine whether a law is just or unjust? What are some ways you can change an unjust law without being defiant or disrespectful?

8. "Letter From Birmingham City Jail"
Pages: 258-262 BofV
Grade Levels: 7-12

Description: Letter - From Birmingham Jail, April 1963. Martin Luther King, Jr. sets forth reasons for breaking the law when protesting racial discrimination. He argues that there is a difference between breaking a just law and breaking an unjust law. He also outlines the steps that should be followed when breaking an unjust law.

Key Points: There are times when defiance of law is justified. The defiance should be handled in a way that avoids anarchy.

Questions: How did Dr. King define just and unjust laws? What comments did he share with respect to how one should break an unjust law? Why is his counsel on this particular subject valuable? What might happen if acts of defiance weren't conducted properly?

9. "The Declaration of Independence"

Pages: 251 BofV

Grade Levels: 4-12

Description: Document - Describes the reasoning behind the colonists' decision to dissolve themselves from the rule of Britain.

Key Points: Jefferson's reason for declaring independence from Great Britain is simply because a government loses its right to rule when it deprives its people of liberties which are a gift of God.

Questions: What was the chief message of the Declaration of Independence? What reasoning did Jefferson employ to justify the separation? Is defiance (or treason) ever justified? What conditions must be present to warrant such action? What would happen to our society if people weren't cautious in their use of defiance?

10. "The Ten Commandments"

Pages: 206-207 BofV, 117 YP

Grade Levels: 4-12

Description: List - Old Testament (Bible) list of seven "don'ts" and three "dos" so far as living our lives is concerned.

Key Points: Rules have been with us since antiquity. This particular set of rules served as a basis for the Jewish (Israelite) faith. They still have application in today's world.

Questions: Name some of the rules that are incorporated in the laws of our country. Why do you think they were formulated? What benefits might one expect when following these rules? What consequences might arise when violating one or more of these rules?

11. "The Cattle of the Sun"

Pages: 79-81 BofV

Grade Levels: 4-12

Description: Myth - Describes an incident in Homer's Odyssey where Ulysses and his men meet with disaster because they fail to heed wise counsel. The men's resolve to avoid enticements quickly evaporates when they react to the foolish words of a crew member. Their impulsive reaction ends up costing them their lives.

Key Points: The crew members chose to defy Ulysses' warnings because they were first weary and then hungry. They lost their lives as a result of their defiance.

Questions: Why do you think the crew members chose to ignore Ulysses' warnings? What happened as a result? Can you think of instances when defiance can cause serious trouble for the individual involved?

DISHONESTY

1. "Fading Favor"
Pages: 305 YP
Grade Levels: 7-12
Description: Chinese Tale - Describes a king whose fidelity to his maidens lasted only so long as they remained young and physically attractive to him.
Key Points: Our fidelities should not change because another's physical appearance changes. Recalling past infractions (some imagined) to justify morally wrong decisions is a form of dishonesty.
Questions: What changed the king's perspective on Hua? Was his change of attitude a fair one? Could you consider this dishonest even when it's done by a king? Who can think of some forms of dishonesty in our day to day lives? What makes something honest or dishonest?

2. "Knute Rockne"
Pages: 732-735 BofV
Grade Levels: 4-12
Description: Story - Highlights of the life of Knute Rockne who is considered one of the greatest coaches of all time. It was not what he did, but how he did it, that made him great.
Key Points: His example of how he treated the Army scout demonstrated his honesty. Those who work hard never need to be dishonest.
Questions: Describe some of the reasons why Knute Rockne is considered the greatest college football coach of all time? What example from the story described his honesty? Why is honesty such an esteemed virtue? What are examples of honesty in the classroom (or home)? Does honesty pay?

3. "A Devoted Friend"
Pages: 674-683 BofV
Grade Levels: 7-12
Description: Story - Describes the relationship between a wealthy miller and a poor gardener. The friendship turns out to be one-sided and illustrates that friendship should work both ways.
Key Points: Loyalty-friendship is a two-way street. The only way we can understand this virtue is through practice. Often we distort our views to accommodate our wants. The story is also an illustration of dishonesty toward one's self.

113

Questions: Who can describe how the miller practiced his friendship? Why didn't the miller understand what true loyalty and friendship was? Why didn't the water rat want to hear about a story with a moral? Can you think of an instance when someone you know managed to convince himself that his actions were okay when they clearly were not?

4. "Hercules Cleans the Augean Stables"

Pages: 389-390 BofV, 153-154 YP

Grade Levels: 4-9

Description: Myth - Describes how Hercules promises to clean out the stables if the king rewards him with a tenth of his cattle. Hercules fulfills his part of the bargain, but the king denies making the agreement and is eventually forced to reward Hercules when his son testifies against the king.

Key Points: Those who choose not to keep their word eventually end up losing more than they would have otherwise.

Questions: What agreement did the king make with Hercules? Was it a fair deal? How was it that the king was forced to pay his debt? What did the king give up in addition to the cattle? Do you think it was worth it? What sorts of things do we lie about today? What often happens? What might we lose besides certain privileges?

5. "Emerson on Friendship"

Pages: 336-337 BofV

Grade Levels: 7-12

Description: Discourse - Argues that a true friend is a masterpiece of nature-- open, caring without ulterior motive. The author provides insights on why genuine friendships are difficult to develop.

Key Points: Emerson's key characteristic of a true friendship is complete honesty. He contrasts this with the hypocrisy that directs a typical relationship. "We cover up our thoughts from him under a hundred folds."

Questions: What is Emerson's point when he states, "A friend is a person with whom I may be sincere?" What examples does he offer to define what friendship is not? How does everyday honesty relate to the honesty required of a true friendship? Why is the constant practice of honesty a worthy enterprise?

6. "Rocking Horse Land"

Pages: 286-291 BofV

Grade Levels: K-6

Description: Tale - Describes the relationship between a young prince and a magical rocking horse. Story illustrates positive examples of keeping one's commitments.

Key Points: Story provides clear illustrations of keeping one's word. Good example for younger students to examine one important expression of honesty.

Questions: What agreement did the prince and rocking horse enter in to? What changed in the relationship that caused the prince to forget his commitment? How did he make up for his mistake? What good eventually resulted from the prince's resolve to keep his promise? Who can think of an agreement they made with a friend? Was it always an easy thing to keep up your part of the agreement? Why? Why is it important to be honest in your dealings with others?

7. "The Wisdom of Solomon"

Pages: 147-148 BofV

Grade Levels: 6-12

Description: Story - Describes how King Solomon uses great wisdom in determining which of two women is the real mother of a child.

Key Points: Dishonesty will eventually come to light.

Questions: What was the problem King Solomon was asked to solve? How did he determine the real mother of the child? Why is it that dishonesty usually is found out? Why do people do dishonest things? Why is it foolish to practice dishonesty?

8. "The Honest Woodman"

Pages: 602-603 BofV

Grade Levels: K-12

Description: Fable - Describes a woodcutter who, because of his honesty, recovered not only his own lost axe but gained a gold and silver axe in the process.

Key Points: The woodman was happy and satisfied with his work and didn't need to gain more by deceit. He had developed the habit of telling the truth and therefore was not tempted. Often, honesty in the face of temptation provides unexpected rewards.

Questions: What misfortune did the man suffer? How was the man's honesty tested? How did he respond when tempted? Can you think of real-life situations similar to what happened in this fable? How can you prepare yourself to choose honesty when temptations come your way? Why do you think they say, "Honesty always pays?"

9. "Pinocchio"
Pages: 609-612 BofV
Grade Levels: K-9
Description: Tale - Story about Geppetto's wooden puppet who was provided numerous opportunities to prove himself truthful. Each time he lied his nose grew longer until he was helplessly trapped.
Key Points: Only a portion of the story of Pinocchio is told in this version. Telling one lie usually leads to telling more lies, a habit that must be stopped completely in order to again have peace of mind and a clear conscience.
Questions: What opportunities did the fairy provide for Pinocchio to tell the truth? What ultimately happened in the case of the four gold pieces? Do we have our noses grow each time we tell a lie? What does happen to us each time we lie? How is it similar to a nose growing larger?

10. "Truth Never Dies"
Pages: 661-662 BofV
Grade Levels: 4-12
Description: Poem - The author argues that truth never dies. It may be obscured, scoffed at or ignored, but eventually it will manifest itself again.
Key Points: While sometimes it appears that dishonesty prevails or pays dividends, the truth will eventually surface and reward those who take the path of honesty.
Questions: What are some of the ways the author uses to drive home her point that truth never dies? Who can think of an instance where the truth was hidden for a time but eventually manifested itself? What is foolish about the thinking that one can evade the truth forever? What short-term consequences always follow dishonesty? What long-term consequences usually occur once the truth comes out?

11. "The Boy Who Never Told a Lie"
Pages: 601 BofV
Grade Levels: K-6
Description: Poem - Describes a boy everybody loved because he always told the truth and never told a lie.

116

Key Points: Our reputation is determined to a great degree by our honesty. People like to associate with honest people, and this often opens avenues of opportunity. Shakespeare said, "No legacy is so rich as honesty."

Questions: What did the little boy's classmates have to say about him? Do you think his reputation helped him in his later years? Why? Why do people admire those who can always be counted on to say the truth?

12. "Nobility"
Pages: 654-655 BofV
Grade Levels: 9-12
Description: Poem - Outlines the ingredients of nobility. . ."For he who is honest is noble, whatever his fortunes or birth."

13. "Lady Clare"
Pages: 639-641 BofV
Grade Levels: 9-12
Description: Poem - Describes Lord Ronald's love of Lady Clare for her own true worth and not for her wealth. Lady Clare's total honesty likewise proves her love for Lord Ronald.

14. "Truth"
Pages: 642 BofV
Grade Levels: 7-12
Description: Poem - Reminds us that faith and love depend on truth.

15. "Francis Bacon on Truth"
Pages: 660-661 BofV
Grade Levels: 10-12
Description: Essay - Bacon argues that truth stands independent of all things and serves as the guidepost of man's existence. He envisions man's greatest pleasure as grasping the truth of all things and conforming one's actions to its precepts.

16. "Plato on Justice"
Pages: 657-660 BofV
Grade Levels: 10-12
Description: Dialogue - Socrates argues that the exercise of justice (integrity) is always superior to the exercise of injustice. His rationale is that virtue is the health, beauty and well-being of the soul while vice is disease, weakness and deformity.

17. "The Way to Tao"
   Pages: 815-816 BofV
   Grade Levels: 9-12

   Description: Sermon - Describes the need to rid oneself of obstructions in order to free oneself to that degree where all things can be accomplished. The twenty-four obstructions that are listed are considered impediments to the full discovery of Tao.

DISORGANIZED

1. **"For Everything There Is a Season"**
   Pages: 103-104 BofV
   Grade Levels: 4-12
   Description: Descriptive Counsel - Biblical extract that extols patience by stating that there is a proper time for every action.
   Key Points: When one takes care of business at the proper time, there are rewards that follow. Conversely, when one chooses not to act at the proper time, there are often penalties. Often this is simply a matter of organization and resolve.
   Questions: How many can think of instances when things didn't work out because of timing? How can you assure yourselves that you are getting things done in their proper order and time? What can go wrong when a person fails to act at the proper time?

2. **"Flag Day"**
   Pages: 724-725 BofV
   Grade Levels: 4-12
   Description: Editorial - Describes the flag and the love of country that it stands for.
   Key Points: The flag symbolizes all that our country was and is, tangible and intangible. It represents tens of thousands of factors that each play their part in keeping America great. The flag represents the order that characterizes our country.
   Questions: What are a few of the things represented by our flag? Why is it necessary for each part of America to play its part if America hopes to retain its identity and greatness? Why does this require order? What organizational aids in your life help you to be a success at school or home or wherever? What happens when something breaks down?

3. **"Opportunity"**
   Pages: 408-409 BofV
   Grade Levels: 4-12
   Description: Poem - Describes how opportunity for fame, love and fortune come to all people, but only those who grasp them when available will profit. Those who doubt or hesitate are condemned to failure.
   Key Points: Those prepared to take advantage of life's opportunities will gain the best life has to offer. Often this boils down to those who are organized to go at a moment's notice.

Questions: What goals or opportunities does the poem mention? Where or when do these opportunities present themselves? Besides doubt or hesitation, what other things might serve as obstacles when opportunities do arise?

4. "Robinson Crusoe Builds a Boat"

Pages: 394-396 BofV

Grade Levels: 4-12

Description: Story - Describes how a man marooned on an island decides to build a boat without first planning the matter through. After much labor and time, he must give up because he is unable to transport his heavy boat to the sea.

Key Points: Sometimes, all the work in the world will not compensate for a poorly organized plan.

Questions: What was Robinson Crusoe's reason for building the boat? Why did he ignore the problem of getting his boat to the water until the very end? What was his thinking? What eventually happened? Who can think of some activities that require that they first be thought out and organized for success? Who can think of times that they did poorly just because they failed to organize themselves to succeed?

5. "The Three Little Kittens"

Pages: 188-189 BofV

Grade Levels: K-9

Description: Poem - Describes how three little kittens learn responsibility by rewards and punishments.

Key Points: By taking responsibility to correct a problem, you will be rewarded one way or another, sooner or later. However, many problems can be avoided with proper planning. Proving you can handle small responsibilities will lead to being given larger responsibilities. Often this requires good organization. Many little mistakes are preventable with good organization.

Questions: What was the kittens' original problem? What did they lose as a result? What was their second mistake? Could these mistakes have been avoided? What are some of the reasons why we make mistakes? Which of these can be prevented? How?

DISRESPECT

1. "George Washington's Rules of Civility"
Pages: 20-25 YP, 74-78 BofV
Grade Levels: 4-12
Description: List - Rules that George Washington wrote when he was fourteen years old. Most have to do with respecting others.
Key Points: Washington was greatly respected for his tact and manners. The majority of his rules have to do with showing proper respect.
Questions: Washington lived almost 200 years ago. Which of these rules makes sense in today's world? Who can pick out a rule that they either followed or ignored and came to profit or suffer as a result?

2. "Little Fred"
Pages: 44 BofV
Grade Levels: K-3
Description: Poem - Describes how little Fred goes to bed each night using the best of manners.
Key Points: Illustrates example of young child showing good manners in going to bed.
Questions: Why do you think Fred is used as an example for good manners? Who can tell us about a time when you didn't use good manners in going to bed? Why do you think some parents insist on early bed times? What other things should be respected?

3. "The Little Gentleman"
Pages: 43 BofV
Grade Levels: K-3
Description: Poem - Lists the table manners required of little gentlemen.
Key Points: This poem provides a lengthy list of appropriate table manners for young gentlemen. This entry is helpful as a teaching primer for proper behavior at the dinner table.
Questions: Why do you think these particular manners are considered good? Can you think of reasons why they were chosen? What is the reasoning behind these various rules of behavior?

4. "Table Rules For Little Folks"

Pages: 42-43 BofV

Grade Levels: K-3

Description: Poem - Describes in some detail what is expected of young people with respect to table manners.

Key Points: There is a sizeable collection of actions that constitute proper table manners. Many students are not aware that they exist.

Questions: Can you think of table manners that are enforced at your home? What is the point of table manners? What does it accomplish? Who can think of animals with manners that are different from what is expected of children? How do the two standards differ?

5. "Jim"

Pages: 33-35 BofV

Grade Levels: K-9

Description: Poem - Humorous poem of a little boy who ran away while visiting the zoo and as a consequence was eaten by a lion.

Key Points: There are consequences to disobedience. Often the initial consequences are subtle but eventually can add up to significant things.

Questions: Can you think of a reasons why the writer would choose being eaten by a lion as the consequence to disobedience? In real life situations, what might happen to a disobedient young person that is a lot like being eaten bit by bit until it's too late to save oneself?

6. "My Own Self"

Pages: 30-32 BofV

Grade Levels: K-6

Description: Fairy Tale - Describes how a young boy defiantly refuses to heed his mother's warning to take refuge in his bed when the fairies might be out for mischief. Eventually he learns for himself that his mother's counsel is wise.

Key Points: The young boy in this tale almost paid a severe price for his disobedience and disrespect. He was lucky in this instance, but are we willing to trust on luck alone? This boy seemed wise in that he used this near-disaster to learn his lesson.

Questions: Is this little boy that different from children of today? What sort of counsel do young people ignore today? What consequence might replace the penalty described in this fairy tale?

7. **"Rebecca"**

Pages: 26-27 BofV

Grade Levels: K-12

Description: Poem - Rebecca has a nasty habit of purposely slamming doors to annoy others. Eventually she slams a door that disrupts a marble bust which falls on her head and kills her. Other children take note and resolve not to follow her example.

Key Points: Good people can lose sight of the fact that what amuses them may cause others problems. When we treat others badly, there is often a consequence down the road.

Questions: Do you think you can expect to be killed if you perform rude acts? What is more likely to happen? Is it possible to be acting rude toward others without even realizing it? Can anyone think of an example where this could happen?

8. **"Please"**

Pages: 24-25 BofV

Grade Levels: K-6

Description: Tale - Supposedly each person has a 'please' that lives in one's mouth. To live, the little 'please' needs air which is provided each time the person says please. This is told from the please's perspective. The please is saved when an impolite little boy follows the example of his older brother.

Key Points: Sometimes we learn from the example of others, especially older brothers and sisters. It is a good thing to set a good example so others may follow. The 'please' represents those who benefit from the polite acts of others.

Questions: Who can think of what the 'please' represents? Can anyone give us a real-life example of a 'please?' Has anyone here been a 'John' because of acting as a good example?

9. **"Good and Bad Children"**

Pages: 23 BofV

Grade Levels: K-3

Description: Poem - Contrasts the fate of virtuous children (grew to be kings and sages) versus unvirtuous children (became as geese). Bright, quiet, content, innocent, honest and happy children are contrasted with unkind, unruly, cruel and crying children.

Key Points: Poem points out causes and effects--The good become kings and sages (wise), and the bad are hated and become as geese. How we treat others can effect what we become and how well we are liked.

Why do you think the good children later became kings and the bad were thought of as geese? Instead of becoming kings or geese, what might you become today as a result of your behavior? Why would people like the geese become hated?

10. "The Boy Who Tried to Be the Sun"

Pages: 28-30 YP
Grade Levels: K-6
Description: Legend - A boy who is fathered by the sun returns to earth only to be teased about not having a father. The boy goes to great lengths to prove he has a father only to lose his life in the process.
Key Points: The young boy chose to ignore the counsel of his father despite his father's pleadings and logic.
Questions: How many have been given advice by parents? Can you remember a recent occurrence? Why is it wise to listen to the advice of parents?

11. "Deucalion and Pyrrha"

Pages: 775-777 BofV, 349-352 YP
Grade Levels: 4-12
Description: Myth - Describes Jupiter destroying the earth by flood because the people had grown contentious, lazy and irreverent. When only one couple remained (kind and respectful), Jupiter removes the water and shows them how to repopulate the earth.
Key Points: The issue of respect is of ancient origin. Here is an instance where an entire planet was targeted for destruction because this virtue had been grossly violated. This myth brings home the importance of this particular virtue.
Questions: Why was Jupiter so angry that he decided to destroy all the inhabitants of the earth? Why did he stop his work of destruction when he found that only Deucalion and Pyrrha remained alive? Why would the ancient Greeks put such great emphasis on the virtue of respect? What occasions do we have today to show respect? Do you think there should be consequences for those who show disrespect? Why?

12. "The Steadfast Tin Soldier"

Pages: 536-540 BofV
Grade Levels: K-6
Description: Tale - Describes a toy soldier whose sense of duty causes him to accept circumstances that he otherwise might have avoided. After a series of calamities, he is reunited with his life's love.

Key Points: Respect for one's duties and beliefs can cause occasional inconvenience or discomfort but often result in good outcomes. Sometimes we need to do something because it's our duty.

Questions: What were some of the reasons the soldier had for not trying to avoid some of his problems? What trait caused him to act this way? What were some of his difficulties? How did the story end? Do you think this was a happy ending? Why or why not? What instances do we have that show our respect for something? Are any of these instances awkward or embarrassing? What should you do in these particular instances?

13. "The Gettysburg Address"

Pages: 568-569 BofV

Grade Levels: 4-12

Description: Speech - President Lincoln dedicates a burial site for many of the soldiers who died in defense of the nation. He eloquently states that his own words are inadequate when compared to the deeds of those who gave their lives in the battle. Concludes with a challenge to not let these men and their cause die in vain.

Key Points: One way of expressing respect for the martyrs of freedom is to adhere to the principles of freedom that they died for.

Questions: Who was President Lincoln honoring in his speech? For what cause did these soldiers sacrifice their lives? In what ways did the president show his respect to these soldiers? How might we show our respect to those who died for freedom's sake? Why is this an important virtue to develop?

14. "A Time to Talk"

Pages: 331 BofV, 122 YP

Grade Levels: 4-9

Description: Poem - Argues that maintaining friendships is sometimes more important than completing a task.

Key Points: We should always give time to our friends however strong our desires to complete a task. This goes beyond maintaining friendships. It also has to do with respect for others.

Questions: What does the author recommend when a worker is interrupted by a friend? Do you agree with this counsel? What virtue is required to put aside an important task in order do give another some attention? Who can share some possible outcomes that would stem from each course of action? Why should respect be a key factor in one's decision despite the outcomes?

15. "Ruth and Naomi"

Pages: 296-298 BofV, 141-144 YP

Grade Levels: 4-12

Description: Story - Describes how a daughter-in-law demonstrates her love and respect for a widowed and destitute woman.

Key Points: Provides a vivid example of proper respect for the aged. It also illustrates how respect goes beyond attitude. It often boils down to acts of sacrifice and compassion.

Questions: What was Ruth's relationship to Naomi? What predicament did they find themselves in? How did Ruth's response to the crisis differ from the other daughter-in-law? Who can think of reasons why it's important to show respect for the aged? How can we show the respect through actions?

16. "Grandmother's Table"

Pages: 143-144 BofV

Grade Levels: K-9

Description: Story - Describes how two parents learn a lesson about respect for the aged from their little daughter.

Key Points: What goes around, comes around. This is a classic example of how we might reap what we sow. Sometimes respect requires that we allow ourselves to be inconvenienced.

Questions: Why did the parents place Grandmother in a corner off by herself? How did Grandmother feel about this? How did the parents come to find the error of their ways? Why is it important to respect the elderly even if it causes some inconvenience?

17. "The Boy We Want"

Pages: 196 BofV

Grade Levels: K-12

Description: Poem - Lists the qualities in a boy that are needed to help solve the grave problems in the world. Points out that these boys are the hope for the future.

Key Points: Good example of a young person who respects many of the important institutions in life.

Questions: What are some of the qualities of this boy that are described in the poem? What does it mean to respect something? Why do you think the poem is entitled "The Boy We Want?" What are some other things worthy of respect that are not mentioned in the poem?

126

18. "Etiquette in a Nutshell"
Pages: 201-202 BofV
Grade Levels: K-12

Description: List - Describes rules of good etiquette that help us get along with others.
Key Points: Good manners never go out of style. They help us get along with others and be accepted. This is an excellent list for discussion purposes. The basis for each rule of respect is an excellent medium for analysis and introspection.
Questions: What are some examples of good manners mentioned in the poem? Pick out an example and explain why the advise is good to follow. Who does it help? What are some classroom or home courtesies that might also be included in the list?

19. "Men Without Chests"
Pages: 263-265 BofV
Grade Levels: 7-12
Description: Speech - Author argues that there are rights and wrongs in life. He suggests that young people should be provided opportunity to develop likes and dislikes and that these virtues are received through proper training.
Key Points: There are attitudes and doctrines that should be determined as rights or wrongs. It is the responsibility of the wise to inculcate the correctness or truth of those things essential to a meaningful life. Young people need to acquire the respect of certain truths and institutions.
Questions: What was the author referring to when he described "men without chests" (see last paragraph) who have virtue and enterprise expected of them? What might be an example of something that the author might treat as an absolute good thing? Why is respect for these things essential to our well being as a people?

20. "Respecting the Flag"
Pages: 219-220 BofV
Grade Levels: K-12
Description: List - Covers a few rules for respecting the U.S. flag and why we should do so.
Key Points: These rules are supportive of the United States code which states: "The flag represents a living country and is itself considered a living thing." Only through our respect for our

country and its laws will we maintain our freedoms and opportunities.

Questions: What rules listed in this code were unfamiliar to you? Why do you think the flag has so many rules governing its proper use? What might happen if we fail to show respect for our flag? What are some other things we are asked to respect? Why is it important to show respect in these instances? What happens when people stop showing respect to something?

21. "The Duties of a Scout"

Pages: 217-218 BofV

Grade Levels: 4-12

Description: Rules - Boy Scout and Girl Scout Oath, Promise and Law

Key Points: These rules have worked well for the scouting program. Most have to do with displays of respect.

Questions: What are some of the duties of a scout? Why do you think these particular duties were selected? Can the virtues that embody the duties of a scout become habit forming? How? How do you think these virtues will help a person confront many of the challenges facing today's youth?

22. "Baucis and Philemon"

Pages: 303-304 BofV

Grade Levels: K-9

Description: Tale - Describes how the Roman Gods, Jupiter and Mercury, were treated by the inhabitants Phrygia. Only Baucis and Philemon treated them with the respect due weary travelers, and only this kindly couple were spared the destruction imposed on the city's inhabitants.

23. "A Legacy"

Pages: 343 BofV

Grade Levels: 7-12

Description: Poem - Describes a friendship that should not diminish nor incur sadness when death arrives. Some specific characteristics of this type of friendship are listed.

24. "The Path of Virtue"

Pages: 810-812 BofV

Grade Levels: 7-12

Description: Proverbs - These statements of wisdom are attributed to Buddha. They describe many of the virtues that make for greatness.

25. "Going to Church"
Pages: 798-799 BofV
Grade Levels: 4-12

Description: Speech - Teddy Roosevelt cites ten reasons for regularly attending a church. His reasons range from the sublime to the more practical outcomes to church attendance.

26. "The Farewell Address"
Pages: 794-795 BofV
Grade Levels: 7-12
Description: Speech - Washington cautions that our government will fail if we fail to exercise morality and reason. He predicts that we will always find political prosperity with an adherence to virtue even though we may forfeit some short-term advantages.

27. "Only a Dad"
Pages: 706-707 BofV
Grade Levels: K-12
Description: Poem - Reminds us to be thankful for devoted fathers who may not be famous or highly successful but are always there when needed.

DISTRUST

1. **"Phaeton"**
   Pages: 69-74 BofV
   Grade Levels: 4-12
   Description: Myth - Describes how Apollo grants his mortal son one wish in order to prove his fatherhood. The son chooses unwisely and, despite his father's pleadings, refuses to abandon his wish. The son almost destroys the earth and loses his own life in the process.
   Key Points: Here is an instance where a boy was so set in his mind that he refused to heed the wise advice of a parent. The result was ruinous for both himself and others.
   Questions: Why didn't Apollo (his father) refuse this foolish request? Who suffered as a result of the boy's stubbornness? Why do you think the boy chose to disregard his father's advice? What types of advice do young people often reject when it comes from parents, teachers or other adults? Why is this so?

2. **"The Captain's Daughter"**
   Pages: 760-761 BofV
   Grade Levels: K-12
   Description: Poem - Describes how a ship is struggling in a violent storm and how the captain orders the mast to be cut down. The passengers grow the more despondent when the captain concedes that all is lost. Perspectives change when the captain's daughter points out that God must be on the ocean if he is on the land.
   Key Points: Sometimes one individual's courage or trust is all that is needed to strengthen the entire group. Fear and helplessness are a frame of mind that can be changed with a change in perspective.
   Questions: Why were the crew and passengers worried? What was said that changed everyone's attitude? Who can think of events that happen in our lives that cause us to give up hope? How do you develop the trust needed to work your way through the adversity? What about little things that seem to go wrong? Why is it wise to not give up trying?

3. **"A Mighty Fortress Is Our God"**
   Pages: 770-771 BofV, 346-347 YP
   Grade Levels: 4-12

Description:	Song - Describes Satan's influence and destructive presence in each of our lives. States how all will work out for the good due to God's power and love.
Key Points:	Song admits to life's challenges but passes them off as insignificant if one places trust in God's power to overcome all obstacles.
Questions:	How does the song writer judge Satan's influence? Why is he not concerned over Satan's destructive power? Viewing today's world, what are some of the manifestations of troubles that the author referred to? What sorts of things might we put our trust in so that we might not grow too discouraged when we see things go wrong?

4. "Nearer Home"

Pages: 769-770 BofV
Grade Levels: 4-12

Description:	Poem - Describes how we are constantly growing closer to the time when we pass by mortality and enter a life where we lay our burdens down and enter the mansions prepared for us. Author concludes that we must endure through trust and faith, especially during the troubling times.
Key Points:	Those who keep their final end firmly in mind will have little difficulty when life provides its challenges.
Questions:	What did the author mean by stating that I'm nearer my home today than I have ever been before? How does she use this thought to help her through the tough times? What things happen to us that could be considered winding down through the night in the unknown stream? What thoughts or beliefs might help us to keep up our trust in the future despite the times when things go wrong?

5. "A Child's Dream of a Star"

Pages: 766-769 BofV
Grade Levels: K-12

Description:	Story - Describes how a young boy continually loses his loved ones to death. He is sustained by a recurring dream that has each of these loved ones waiting for him to join them in a glorious star that is now their home.
Key Points:	The young boy had occasion to grow to be distrustful of life and its tragedies. Instead he developed the trust that life was fair and if patient, he would be reunited with his loved ones.
Questions:	What dream caused the little boy to change his outlook about death? What hope did he harbor that kept him optimistic?

Must we wait for a dream to obtain a perspective that develops and sustains our trust? What are ways we can develop trust that things will eventually work out if we are patient and do our best?

6. "The 23rd Psalm"

Pages: 758 BofV, 369-370 YP
Grade Levels: 4-12
Description: Psalm - The words of this "song" speak of the author's trust in his God. He describes some good things about his life and mentions his lack of fear when bad things might occur. He concludes, expressing his trust in his God.
Key Points: The writer of the 23rd Psalm acknowledged the good and bad in life but confirmed his belief that good would always prevail in the end. This is a strong testament of trust and faith.
Questions: What examples does the author cite to illustrate some of the good things in his life? How does the author describe the bad times? What attitude do you think the author is trying to describe? What are some of the good things in your life? What are some of the bad things? Would the attitudes we discussed work today?

7. "I Never Saw a Moor"

Pages: 753 BofV, 354 YP
Grade Levels: 4-12
Description: Poem - Emily Dickinson describes how she believes that certain things exist despite her lack of proof. She cites her belief that moors, seas and heaven exist even though she has never seen them.
Key Points: One need not have tangible evidence to believe in something. There is much around us that we will never see evidence of but is none the less real. We will miss much if we distrust everything and everyone until proven otherwise. We end up spending undue time and energy searching for evidence.
Questions: What things did the author believe in despite her lack of evidence? What are things around us that we believe in even though we can't see or understand how they work? What about people? Do you know of anyone who automatically distrusts until they have evidence to the contrary? Why is this a bad practice?

8. "Penelope's Web"

Pages: 701-705 BofV

Grade Levels: 4-12

Description: Myth - Describes Queen Penelope's wait of over 20 years for the return of her husband Ulysses. Most everyone but Penelope assumed Ulysses was dead. She puts off unwanted suitors long enough for Ulysses to return.

Key Points: Patience, resourcefulness, constancy and love are qualities that bring happiness and remembrance. Penelope never lost hope or complained of being a victim. She continued to run the kingdom left in her charge.

Questions: What were the circumstances of Penelope's and Ulysses' separation? What were some of the temptations and hardships Penelope was forced to endure in order to remain faithful? What trait kept her going? Do you feel you are sometimes unjustly dealt with? Why is trust a handy virtue to possess in times of strife or hardship?

9. "The Rebellion Against the Stomach"

Pages: 386-387 BofV, 166-168 YP

Grade Levels: K-12

Description: Story - Describes how a man dreams that different parts of his body grow resentful of the stomach who seems to do little but accept the food. The other parts refuse to work but soon learn that the stomach contributes to the overall good just like everyone else.

Key Points: It is easy to distrust certain types of people or things when all one sees is what's on the surface. The stomach is a good example of something that appears to do little but is vital to the health of a body.

Questions: Why do you think the stomach was singled out for distrust? What plan did the rest of the body devise to teach the stomach a lesson? What did they find out about the stomach? Who are people that we have a tendency to distrust without knowing much about them? Is this a wise habit to fall into? Why?

10. "The Long, Hard Way Through the Wilderness"

Pages: 555-560 BofV, 245-253 YP

Grade Levels: 4-9

Description: Story - Biblical account of Israelites' trials and activities during the forty years between the time they left Egypt and the time they entered their promised land.

Key Points:	Moses continually battled those who judged every obstacle as a sign that they should return to Egypt and captivity. This persistent attitude eventually stalled their opportunity to enter the promised land. Too great a focus on distrust will divert the energy and commitment required to achieve success.
Questions:	What were some of the reasons for the widespread distrust and discontent? What problems did this cause for Moses and those with faith in his judgment? What was the eventual result of this distrust? What instances of distrust in our day to day lives can hurt our opportunities for success? How does the distrust affect our actions?

11. "Helen Keller and Anne Sullivan"
Pages: 312-317 BofV, 128-134 YP
Grade Levels: 4-12

Description:	Story - Describes the events surrounding a deaf and blind child's first discovery of communication.
Key Points:	Young Helen Keller demonstrated one of the primary reasons for distrust--lack of understanding. Once Helen learned more about her teacher and what she was teaching, she was able to place the trust that is often essential to learning.
Questions:	What handicaps hindered Helen's learning? How did she view her teacher during their first weeks together? What changed Helen's attitude about her teacher and what benefits did this change provide? What are some of the reasons for distrusting others? Which of these reasons can we do something about to increase our ability to trust? What benefits often follow a demonstration of trust?

12. "Damon and Pythias"
Pages: 306-308 BofV, 125-127 YP
Grade Levels: 4-12

Description:	Story - Describes how a man offers himself as collateral for his convicted friend to first return home and say good-bye to his wife and children. The king, whose unjust sentence caused the problem, learns a lesson about friendship and trust.
Key Points:	Story shows the depth possible in a true friendship. This is also a fine illustration on the value in trust.
Questions:	Why was Pythias sentenced to death? What did his friend do to allow Pythias the opportunity to bid farewell to his family? What lesson did the king learn? Do you think Damon worried that his friend would abandon him? Why? What reward goes

to those who develop the capacity to trust others? Where are instances when it pays to be trusting?

13. "The Boy Who Cried 'Wolf'"

Pages: 602 BofV

Grade Levels: 4-12

Description: Fable - Describes a boy who is not believed when a real crisis develops because of previous lies.

Key Points: Those who develop a reputation for lying will lose the trust of others. Little white lies may seem harmless but can develop into habits that eventually will cause great harm.

Questions: What trick did the boy play? Why didn't the people trust him the third time he cried wolf? What do you think the boy learned from this experience? How should we determine whether or not to trust another?

14. "The Injustice of Mere Suspicion"

Pages: 647-648 BofV

Grade Levels: 4-12

Description: Folktale - Describes a man who suspected his neighbor's son of stealing his axe. The more he observed the boy, the more convinced he was that he had stolen the axe. After learning the boy had not stolen the axe, he could observe nothing that might make him suspect the boy. Only the man's attitude changed, not the boy or his actions.

Key Points: Distrust is often based on groundless perceptions or first impressions. A wise person gives others the benefit of the doubt until sufficient is known to base a judgment on fact.

Questions: Who did the man suspect of stealing his missing axe? Why do you think his sight of the suspected boy only strengthened his conviction? What changed his perspective? Was the man fair in his initial distrust? Can anyone remember being critical of someone or something based on a first impression? Did the perspective change after greater exposure? What are the dangers of mistrust without basis?

15. "Federalist No. 55"

Pages: 252-253 BofV

Grade Levels: 7-12

Description: Document - James Madison discusses the question of whether Legislators (who represent the people in a republican form of government) can be trusted to safeguard the public liberty. The importance of virtue among men for self-government is discussed.

Key Points: Elections for Representatives (state and federal) every two years is designed to prevent any scheme of tyranny or treachery. We must employ some trust if our government is going to survive.

Questions: What were some of Madison's arguments against those who claimed that the new Constitution would soon rob the citizens of their liberties? What importance did Madison place in trust? According to Madison, what place does the exercise of virtue have in the success of a republican form of government? To what degree should we trust our institutions of today? What should be the criteria for our trust?

16. "Over in the Meadow"
Pages: 187-188 BofV
Grade Levels: K-3
Description: Poem - Illustrates parent's responsibility to nurture their children. It is the children's responsibility to respond.
Key Points: Poem illustrates the trust that is possible between parent and child. Children need to be motivated and challenged. Parents need to have faith the children can do it. This same level of trust is needed for schools to be effective particularly in the primary grades.
Questions: What four directives or requests were mentioned in the poem? How did the toads, fishes, birdies and ratties respond? Was this a good thing? Why do you think parents or teachers ask certain things of young persons? Who can think of some of these things? Why is trust usually a good thing?

17. "The Stars in the Sky"
Pages: 542-546 BofV
Grade Levels: K-6
Description: Tale - Describes a little girl's travels to have the opportunity to touch a heavenly star. Her persistence and trust in other's advice prove an interesting combination. Eventually she accomplishes her goal.

18. "Little Thumbelina"
Pages: 120-122 BofV
Grade Levels: K-6
Description: Tale - Describes how a very tiny girl is helped by many friends. Her trusting nature and gentle disposition attract the love and support of those she associates with.

136

FIGHTING

1. "The Duel"
Pages: 35-36 YP
Grade Levels: K-3
Description: Tale - Describes a terrible fight between a gingham dog and a calico cat that ends with each of their deaths.
Key Points: The witnesses to the fight knew beforehand that it was going to happen. This indicates that the gingham dog and calico cat had tendencies to quarrel and fight. The tendency to fight developed much the same as other habits and can lead to disastrous results. Here was an instance where the fight proved fatal to each.
Questions: Who was involved in the fight? How do you think the clock and the place knew the fight was going to occur? Why is it that some people seem prone to fight when confronted with a problem? Did either combatant win? Do you think most fights will end in deaths? What is more likely to happen to young students who have a problem with fighting?

2. "Battle Hymn of the Republic"
Pages: 797-798 BofV
Grade Levels: 7-12
Description: Song - Describes how God is watching over the northern troops during the Civil War. Concludes that there will be no retreat from the cause to make all men free.
Key Points: The song provided a rationale for the North's involvement in the conflict. It was implied that there are certain things worth fighting for. An extension of this thought is that there are certain things not worth fighting for.
Questions: Who did the author favor in the war and why? Could one conclude that this was an instance where fighting was warranted? Did it make a difference which side you were on? Who can cite an instance where fighting is appropriate? What makes it so? What are instances where fighting or serious conflict are not appropriate?

3. "Castor and Pollux"
Pages: 699-700 BofV, 303-304 YP
Grade Levels: 7-12

137

Description: Myth - Describes the stars Castor and Pollux and how they came to be. Pollux, an immortal, finding Castor dead chooses to spend half of his time throughout eternity with his mortal half brother. This arrangement allowed Castor to live on in the heavens.

Key Points: The greatest relationship is when we seek out ways to assist others rather than fight over differences. Compassion and not pride make for the best relationships. Pride usually leads to conflict in one form or another.

Questions: What was the relationship between Castor and Pollux and how did they fundamentally differ? What great sacrifice was Pollux willing to make? What could he have done? How does this relationship differ from the intrigues we find in our classrooms, playgrounds and neighborhoods? What is the good in the half brother's approach to life?

4. "In Flanders Field"

Pages: 723 BofV

Grade Levels: 7-12

Description: Poem - Famous description about the allied dead buried in Belgium (World War I) and the expressed hope that they did not die in vain.

Key Points: This poem honored the dead who died in World War I, fighting for the sake of their cherished freedoms. It described a situation where fighting was considered honorable.

Questions: Who is saying the words, "We are the Dead?" What do they mean when they ask that we take up our quarrel with the foe? When is fighting a just thing to do? How can one tell when one has crossed the line between justifiable conflict and self-serving conflict? Who can cite examples of each?

5. "I Have a Dream"

Pages: 572-576 BofV

Grade Levels: 4-12

Description: Speech - Dr. Martin Luther King argues that the time is now to provide full liberty to all Americans. He presents a scenario of an America where no distinctions are made based on race or similar factors, where all people live in harmony on equal footing under the law.

Key Points: Dr. King urged immediate action including a commitment to struggle together, to go to jail together and to stand up for freedom together. But he cautioned that the struggle must be conducted on the high plain of dignity and discipline, not physical violence and force.

Questions: What were some of the freedoms Dr. King was fighting for? What type of fighting was he recommending? Why do you think he cautioned against violence and widespread distrust? What are some legitimate ways to fight for what you believe? What is the risk that you run when you adopt measures that are as wrong as the things you are opposed to?

6. **"We Shall Fight in the Fields and in the Streets"**
Pages: 569-572 BofV
Grade Levels: 4-12
Description: Churchill illustrated some of the reasons that justify fighting. He also credited valor under the conditions of defeat and retreat.
Key Points: This might help young people sort out when a fight is appropriate and when it is not. It should also show that there can be dignity and honor in how we respond to provocation.
Questions: What were some of the battle results that Churchill was reviewing? Why did he place so much attention on Britain's Air Force pilots? How was he able to praise soldiers in a conflict that they had lost? What do you think was Churchill's purpose in giving this speech? Who can think of instances where fighting is justified? Are there times that the true victor in a fight is not the one that won the fight?

7. **"Little Girls Wiser Than Men"**
Pages: 318-319 BofV
Grade Levels: K-9
Description: Story - Describes how a minor spat between two little girls prompts a near brawl from their parents and relatives. All learn a lesson when it's noticed that the two little girls have made up despite the growing hostilities of the adults.
Key Points: This story illustrates the foolishness of many fights. What was a minor altercation between two little girls escalated to what was approaching a major fight amongst the adults. Some people foolishly view minor disagreements as invitations to do serious battle.

What caused the two little girls conflict? How did the adults react to the situation? What lesson did the adults learn from observing the two little girls resumption of play? What could have happened had the adults continued to carry on? Who can think of an instance where a fight transpired that just wasn't necessary? What were the circumstances? What would have been the wiser thing to do?

8. "How Robin Hood Met Little John"
Pages: 308-311 BofV
Grade Levels: 4-9
Description: Story - Describes the circumstances of Robin Hood's and Little John's first introduction to each other. The encounter boils down to a test of wills and pride where neither man is willing to yield without a fight.
Key Points: Each man was ready to fight at the first provocation. While it eventually turned out fine, it was possible that one of these two (who later became devoted friends) might have received serious harm or even death as a result of their tempers.
Questions: What caused the two to fight? How do we know that one of the two might have been seriously hurt? How did they eventually feel about each other? Why was the fight unnecessary? Has anyone ever been involved in a conflict because one or the other was simply too stubborn to give in without a fight? What disastrous results can occur when one is compelled to fight to "save face."

9 "O Captain! My Captain!"
Pages: 178 BofV, 55-56 YP
Grade Levels: 7-12
Description: Poem - Describes much of the tragedy in Abraham Lincoln's senseless death. Lincoln is likened to a captain whose life is cut short before he is able to enjoy the fruits of his successful voyage.
Key Points: Cites the senselessness that accompanies violence. Points out how tragedy can overshadow any gains that might be achieved especially when the violence serves no constructive purpose.
Questions: Who was the captain described in the poem? What prize was won? Why did the author seem forlorn despite the war's end and the reunification of the country? What are some of the consequences that befall both the winners and losers in a conflict? How about conflicts at school or home? Are there

ever clear winners and losers? What are alternatives to physical conflict?

10. "Vigil Strange I Kept on the Field One Night"
Pages: 175-176 BofV
Grade Levels: 7-12
Description: Poem - Describes how a soldier loses a friend in battle and returns to the battlefield to spend the night with his fallen comrade. With the onset of daylight, he buries his friend where he fell.
Key Points: This illustrates some of the tragic consequences of conflict. It reveals the human cost that is easily forgotten in our preoccupation with winners and losers and gains and losses.
Questions: What brought the soldier back to this particular battle field? How did he spend his night? What last act of love did he perform for his fallen friend? What are some of the costs to war? Who can cite other forms of conflict other than armies fighting it out on a battlefield? What human costs accompany these conflicts?

11. "The Quality of Mercy"
Pages: 151-152 BofV
Grade Levels: 7-12
Description: Poem - Shakespeare describes the noble attributes of mercy. Explains how it is greatest when exercised by the mightiest. Finally, it describes how mercy transcends a monarch's power and might, and it places a man in the company of God.
Key Points: The exercise of mercy is stronger than the exercise of might.
Questions: What did Shakespeare mean when he stated that the exercise of mercy is mightiest in the mightiest? Do you agree or disagree? Where are opportunities for mercy found in our day-to-day lives? Who can describe why mercy is often considered a stronger expression of strength than fighting?

12. "The Piece of String"
Pages: 648-654 BofV, 274-282 YP
Grade Levels: 4-12
Description: Story - Describes how a falsely accused man allows his obsession with the situation to ruin his life. The man's obsession continues to control him even after his innocence is established.

Key Points: A long-standing grudge was the basis for the man's strange behavior over the string, and this led to him being accused of the crime. Fighting, grudges and animosities can cause us to do foolish things that can lead to further problems. Those held hostage to bitterness and anger will often lose perspective and distort reality.

Questions: Why did the man act strangely over picking up the string? Why did the authorities fail to believe the man when he told them the truth? What didn't the man tell the authorities about the episode? Why? Who can think of situations where anger and hurt feelings can cause someone to act differently than they would otherwise? What bad things can follow as a result?

13. "Let Dogs Delight to Bark and Bite"

Pages: 37 YP

Grade Levels: K-3

Description: Poem - Short (eight verses) illustration of how children should differ from dogs, bears and lions with respect to anger and fighting.

Key Points: Poem points out that while it appears natural for certain animals to be aggressive, it should not be the case for children. The inference is that children who fight are patterning their actions after animals of lesser intelligence than humans.

Questions: What animals did the author mention in his poem? Why do you think these animals were chosen? Do you agree that children should act differently than animals with respect to fighting? What do you think the rising of angry passions means? Can you think of examples? Are these good things to do?

GUILT DENIAL

1. "The Fiery Furnace"
Pages: 753-755 BofV, 370-373 YP
Grade Levels: 4-12
Description: Story - Describes how three young rulers in King Nebuchadnezzar's court refused to bow down to a God that was not their own. The penalty was death by fire. After refusing a second chance to bow to the idol, they were cast in the furnace but remained untouched. The king then released them and gave them greater honors.
Key Points: The three young men had ample opportunity to make excuses for not bowing down to the golden idol. Instead, they clearly admitted to their actions. They eventually were rewarded for their honesty.
Questions: Were the three men guilty of breaking the law? How could the three men have avoided the fiery furnace? Why did they choose to face up to their actions? Did it turn out to be the right thing to do? What do you think would have happened if they lied to avoid the punishment? Have things in our day changed? What types of punishments do we usually face when we violate a rule or law? Does it make sense to follow the example of the three young men of Babylon?

2. "Nathan Hale"
Pages: 714-717 BofV, 316-320 YP
Grade Levels: 4-12
Description: Story - Describes the circumstances that led to the execution (hanging) of Nathan Hale by the British during the Revolutionary War.
Key Points: Nathan Hale expressed his commitment to his role by saying, "Every kind of service necessary to the public good, becomes honorable by being necessary (even being a spy... assuming the garb of friendship)." Nathan Hale boldly admitted to being a spy and gave his name and rank. He was willing to accept the consequences of his actions.
Questions: Why did Nathan Hale choose to be a spy? Was this a good thing to be? What were the usual consequences if caught spying? How did he react when caught? Is it ever okay to lie about guilt? Why or why not?

3. **"Judas and Peter"**
   Pages: 695-699 BofV
   Grade Levels: 4-12
   Description: Story - Describes the accounts of Judas' betrayal of Jesus and Peter's denial of Jesus.
   Key Points: The test of our loyalty and character is tested in times of crisis. Pride and money (Judas) and fear (Peter) can cause us to betray (Judas) or deny (Peter) a friend. Denial of guilt can bring on every thing from sorrow to eventual destruction.
   Questions: When did Judas deny his guilt of duplicity? What were the circumstances when Peter denied the guilt of association of Jesus? How did each react when they realized the folly of their actions? What types of things are we apt to deny? Why do we do it? How often does it come back to haunt us?

4. **"Abraham Lincoln Denies a Loan"**
   Pages: 402-404 BofV
   Grade Levels: 4-12
   Description: Letter - Lincoln replies to his step-brother's request for another loan. Lincoln seems to indicate that his brother has never come to grips with the real problem of his not being willing to work hard enough to care for his family.
   Key Points: Until we come to grips with what the true nature of our problem is, we will never get it solved. Acknowledging our own failings or misdeeds to ourselves is as important as confessing to others.
   Questions: What did Lincoln's step-brother ask of him? What reasoning did Lincoln use in turning Johnston down? Why do you think he was so candid and harsh in his comments? What do you think Lincoln was trying to accomplish? Who can think of instances where we continually hide from the truth? Why do you think we do these sorts of things? What is the problem with it?

5. **"Rebecca's Afterthought"**
   Pages: 608-609 BofV
   Grade Levels: K-7
   Description: Poem - Rebecca broke a china basin while alone in the house. She could have denied it, yet she told her mother, who commended her.
   Key Points: The time to admit a mistake is immediately. This leaves little time to reconsider and brings immediate peace of mind.

Questions: What mistake did Rebecca make? What temptation first entered her mind? What did she finally decide to do? Who can share a time when they were tempted to hide the truth? What are the problems with this sort of dishonesty?

6. "Honest Abe"

Pages: 620-623 BofV, 258-262 YP

Grade Levels: K-12

Description: Story - Tells of Lincoln returning a few pennies to correct an overcharge and also working three days to pay for a soiled book that had been entrusted to his care. In each case he acknowledged his error and set about to correct it.

Key Points: Habits of honesty should begin early in life. Honesty takes many forms including acknowledgment of one's mistakes. Lincoln was a good example of being true to one's convictions, even at personal cost or inconvenience.

Questions: Who can describe the circumstances of each of the three instances? How might Lincoln have avoided any consequences to his mistakes? What would have been required of Lincoln to evade his responsibilities? How difficult would it have been to follow one's conscience in these instances? Who can think of instances today that might require this same soul-searching? Why bother to follow your conscience?

7. "Cain and Abel"

Pages: 205-206 BofV

Grade Levels: K-12

Description: Story - Recounts world's first recorded murder--that of Cain killing Abel. Cain denies his crime, does not accept responsibility and is not repentant.

Key Points: Accepting responsibility for our actions is an age-old struggle. Concealing a misdeed or mistake often brings more self-remorse and pain than a consequence imposed by another. There is no freedom from the consequences of our acts. Eventually, all must pay for their actions.

Questions: What wrong did Cain do? How did Cain respond when confronted by the Lord? Did it do any good to deny his actions? What are some excuses we give to justify wrong doing? Does this practice do us any good? Can we avoid consequences by lying about our actions?

8. "The Conscience of a Nation Must Be Roused"

Pages: 253-256 BofV

Grade Levels: 4-12

Description: Speech - Speech given by Frederick Douglass (raised a slave) on July 4, 1852, Rochester, N.Y. denouncing slavery. Douglass holds the "scorching iron" of moral reproach to the nation's conscience.

Key Points: As long as slavery persisted in America, Independence Day was a sham to people like Frederick Douglass. Here was an instance where much of the nation denied the wrongness of slavery and refused to accept any guilt in the matter.

Questions: What was the principal message of the speech? How was it that much of a nation managed to deny any quilt over slavery? What are some of the reasons we use to deny some of the wrongful acts we do today (vandalism, cheating, theft, murder)?

9. "The Bell of Atri"

Pages: 208-210 BofV, 101 YP

Grade Levels: K-12

Description: Story - The King of Atri installs a "bell of justice" to be rung by anyone who feels they have been wronged. Finally an old, mistreated horse inadvertently pulls on the bell's rope. The horse's treatment is judged, and the owner is punished for his neglect.

Key Points: Justice demands that we live up to our obligations to one another including our obligations to be kind to animals. Eventually we must face the consequences of our acts. Often the price is more costly than it would have been had we owned up to our mistakes.

Questions: What wrong did the miserly man commit? How was it that it came to the attention of the people? How did the miser respond to his punishment? Do you think he ever accepted his guilt in the matter? How is it that we can come to believe that our misdeeds are okay? Where does "habit" come into play? What can become the cost of habitual denial of guilt?

10. "King Alfred and the Cakes"

Pages: 196-198 BofV, 94-96 YP

Grade Levels: K-12

Description: Story - King Alfred, preoccupied with all his troubles, failed to pay attention to the small responsibility of watching over some cakes baking over the fire. He was severely criticized, admitted his mistake and commended the women who criticized him, promising never to be neglectful of large or small duties again.

Key Points: Great leaders do not ignore small responsibilities. When the king's mistake was pointed out to him, even calling him a lazy-good-for-nothing fellow, he candidly admitted his mistake, promised to learn from it and commended the women for telling him.

Questions: What did King Alfred fail to accomplish? What was his response when chastised by the woodcutter's wife? What could he have done? Why is owning up to one's mistakes a worthwhile thing? What does it often lead up to? Why is it hard to admit a mistake? Should we call attention to someone else's mistake even when that person is very important? What may be some small duties that, if neglected, may turn out to be important?

11. "The Chest of Broken Glass"

Pages: 202-204 BofV, 109-111 YP

Grade Levels: K-12

Description: Tale - describes how a dying old man plays a trick on his three sons as a test for them to determine if they had kept the commandment to honor thy father and mother. They fail the test and realize their mistakes.

Key Points: The boys realized their mistake and faced the mental and emotional consequences. It is reasonable to project that they grew more responsible as a result.

Questions: What were the three sons guilty of? What was their response when they figured out what their father had done? How could they have reacted? Do you think they did the right thing? Do you think it helped them in the future?

147

IMPULSIVE

1. **"For Everything There Is a Season"**
   Pages: 103-104 BofV
   Grade Levels: 4-12
   Description: Sermon - Biblical extract that extols patience by stating that there is a proper time for every action.
   Key Points: Patience is a necessary virtue to act in unison with life's dictates. Those who are wise will be careful to await the best circumstances for their actions.
   Questions: Science has allowed us to control certain seasons and thereby act on immediate need. Can you think of other things that require patience until times and conditions are right? What are some possible consequences to acting on impulse without regard for proper timing and/or conditions?

2. **"The Magic Thread"**
   Pages: 57 BofV
   Grade Levels: K-8
   Description: Story - A very impatient and impulsive boy is given a magic thread that enables him to soar ahead in time each time he pulls the magic thread. He ends up rushing through life and missing many moments that would have been worth experiencing.
   Key Points: Those who always want things immediately fall into a thought pattern that can never be satisfied. Nothing can be enjoyed because the next thing is always foremost in one's thoughts.
   Questions: Who can share something they are looking forward to? Is it a pleasant feeling or one that drives you crazy with anticipation? Who has lost valuable moments or experiences because they were too focused on something up the road?

3. **"The Frogs and the Well"**
   Pages: 39 YP, 52 BofV
   Grade Levels: K-9
   Description: Fable - Two frogs are forced to find a new home due to a drought. The more impulsive of the two is stopped from jumping into a deep well by his more prudent companion.
   Key Points: There can be dire circumstances when someone acts before first thinking things through, especially when major decisions are involved.
   Questions: Which of the two frogs seemed to be the more impulsive? Was this a major decision the two frogs were making? What major decisions can you think of that should be carefully thought out?

Can anyone think of examples where someone rushed into a major decision only to meet problems or disaster?

4. "Mr. Vinegar and His Fortune"

Pages: 48-52 BofV

Grade Levels: K-9

Description: Story - A man and wife, in seeking their fortune, come upon robber's gold. On impulse, the man trades the gold for a cow and then continues trading until he is left with nothing but a walking stick.

Key Points: When you always act on first impulse and never think things through, you eventually may find yourself with nothing.

Questions: Do you think the old man was a wise trader? What did he base his trades on? What are real-life examples of things we immediately decide on that later turn out to be disasters? How can we avoid this?

5. "To the Little Girl Who Wriggles"

Pages: 32-33 YP

Grade Levels: K-6

Description: Poem - Humorous account of why a little girl shouldn't wriggle in her chair. She is threatened that if she keeps it up she might turn into an eel where sea animals might harass her and possibly consume her as dinner.

Key Points: We might be surprised at the consequences resulting from uncontrollable behavior. Why run the risk of unwanted consequences because of our failure to maintain control of our actions.

Questions: What terrible things are predicted in the poem if the little girl continues to wriggle? Can you think of a real-life consequence that might result because someone never learned to sit still or hold their tongue? How can we overcome actions or habits that are not really bad but annoying or distracting to others?

6. "There Was a Little Girl"

Pages: 29-30 BofV

Grade Levels: K-3

Description: Poem - Describes a little girl who goes from the extreme of very good behavior to the other extreme of very poor behavior. Eventually she is spanked for misbehavior.

Key Points: Sometimes, like this little girl, we show two types of behavior, good and bad. If we never learn to control our behavior, then we run the risk of having someone else make the decisions.

Sometimes we have to give extra effort to maintain good behavior, but the effort is worth it.

Questions: What "terrible" thing did the little girl do? Who can think of behaviors that we all have a tendency to do from time to time? Why do you think many of us suffer with this flip-flop behavior? How can we avoid these sudden changes? Where do habits fit into this problem?

7. "The King and His Hawk"

Pages: 37-39 BofV

Grade Levels: 4-12

Description: Story - Genghis Khan, upon returning from a hunting trip, stopped by a stream for a cup of water. His trained pet hawk repeatedly knocked away his filled cup before he drank. Eventually in temper, Khan slew the hawk only to find that the hawk knew the water would have killed Khan.

Key Points: Khan chose to make his decision before further investigating the situation. His impulsiveness cost him his prized pet.

Questions: Why did Genghis Khan kill his favorite pet? Did he later regret his decision? Why? What are examples in our day-to-day life of hastily made decisions? Can anyone think of ways to avoid making hasty decisions?

8. "The Cattle of the Sun"

Pages: 79-81 BofV

Grade Levels: 4-12

Description: Myth - Describes an incident in Homer's Odyssey where Ulysses and his men meet with disaster because they fail to heed wise counsel. The men's resolve to avoid enticements quickly evaporates when they react to the foolish words of a crew member. Their impulsive reaction ends up costing them their lives.

Key Points: The crew members chose to ignore Ulysses' warnings, because they were first weary and then hungry. They were killed as a result of their hasty and foolish decision.

Questions: Why do you think the crew members chose to ignore Ulysses' warnings? What happened as a result? Can you think of situations today where we act foolishly because we want something right away?

9. "The Honest Disciple"

Pages: 762 BofV

Grade Levels: 4-12

Description: Story - Describes how a rabbi poses a question to three disciples. Each answers differently, and the rabbi ponders their answers. He finds most worth in the third reply that shows some deliberation before settling on a final course.

Key Points: The rabbi values the deliberate response over the correct but hasty response and the honest but wrong response.

Questions: What question did the rabbi pose? Whose response pleased the rabbi the most? Why did you think this occurred? What is wrong about the hasty response? Why do people value those who think things through before making a decision?

10. "How Queen Esther Saved Her People"

Pages: 689-695 BofV, 306-314 YP

Grade Levels: 4-12

Description: Story - Describes how Esther and Mordecai, because of their loyalty and courage, save the Jewish people in Persia from being destroyed.

Key Points: Major decisions should be preceded by careful though and counsel with wise people. They should not be made hastily in the way Haman and the king reacted when circumstances and the counsel of others pleased them. Impulsive decisions often demand costly and painful change in order to avoid the problems they will cause.

Questions: What were some of the impulsive decisions made by the king and Haman, his advisor? What was the difference between Mordecai's approach to decisions and that of the king and Haman? Who won out in the end? What are some crucial decisions you expect to face soon? In the years ahead? Who should you go to for advice when faced with a major decision?

11. "Success"

Pages: 422-423 BofV

Grade Levels: 4-12

Description: Poem - Describes how success is achieved through hard and dedicated effort on a step-by-step basis.

Key Points: A strong point is made that few accomplishments come through sudden flashes of insight and effort. Most require deliberate, sustained effort where many small achievements eventually lead to great ends.

What did the author mean to convey when he contrasted sudden flight with toiling upward in the night? What steps might we expect before achieving something worthwhile in school, work or leisure? Why should we fight the temptation to get everything accomplished in a hurry? What are some of the things we are tempted to rush?

12. "Tom Sawyer Gives Up the Brush"

Pages: 398-402 BofV

Grade Levels: 4-9

Description: Story - Describes how Tom Sawyer is able to convince the boys in his town that painting a fence is a privilege. He manages to free himself up from his chore while actually having the boys pay him to do his work.

Key Points: Sometimes something can be presented in a way that distorts its true nature. Those who act before they think will often be fooled under these circumstances.

Questions: How did Tom really feel about painting the fence? What did he say that convinced the other boys that it is a privilege to paint the fence? What did each of the boys end up doing? Do you think it is possible for people to believe so foolish a thing? What might they have done to get a better perspective on the matter? What advertisements can you think of that are intended to convince us to act (or buy) without first giving careful thought to the matter?

13. "The Choice of Hercules"

Pages: 390-392 BofV

Grade Levels: 4-9

Description: Myth - Describes how Hercules is feeling overworked and angry. He happens on a fork in the road where two beautiful ladies greet him and suggest that he follow their path. Hercules eventually chooses the path of virtue over the path of pleasure despite realizing that the pay of virtue will require sacrifice and work.

Key Points: All the conditions were present for Hercules to choose the easier path, that of immediate pleasure. Rather than follow his first impulse, he backed away and thought the matter through.

Questions: What was Hercules feeling when he first encountered the two paths? Which path sounded the most desirable? Why do you think Hercules chose as he did? What was wrong with the path of pleasure? What are some of the paths offered to you each day? What would happen if you developed the habit of immediately choosing the path that appears the most pleasurable?

14. "Persevere"
Pages: 529 BofV
Grade Levels: K-9
Description: Poem - Describes need to be patient and to follow through on tasks. This formula insures success.
Key Points: Those in a hurry to finish reduce their likelihood for success. Patience and deliberation are two keys to accomplishment.
Questions: What examples does the author use to make his point? What usually will happen if a fisherman draws in his net too soon? Who can give examples of things we often rush only to find that our hurry caused us to fall short of what we could have accomplished?

15. "The Piece of String"
Pages: 648-654 BofV, 274-282 YP
Grade Levels: 4-12
Description: Story - Describes how a falsely accused man allows his obsession with the situation to ruin his life. The man allows the obsession to continue to control him even after his innocence is established.
Key Points: The man lost control of his emotions and self-control and worsened his reputation and health. His impulsive denials became a compulsion that eventually came to control his every waking hour.
Questions: What was the man accused of doing? What had he actually been doing? Why did people begin to disbelieve his words even when his innocence should have been plain to see? What habit did he develop from this situation? Have you ever allowed something to become so important that it controlled what you said?

16. "Truth, Falsehood, Fire, and Water"
Pages: 636-637 BofV, 288-289 YP
Grade Levels: 4-9
Description: Tale - Describes how Falsehood schemed to get rid of Fire and Water but failed to destroy Truth. Concludes by stating that Truth and Falsehood are fighting to this day.
Key Points: Both Water and Truth were easily tricked because they acted without thinking the matter through. The results for each were disastrous.

Questions: What trick did Falsehood play on Water? What trick did he play on Truth? What happened to Water and Truth as a result of their hasty decision to follow the advice of Falsehood? Can anyone think of instances when a hasty decision or action came back to hurt you? How can you avoid these unfortunate occurrences.

17. "The Boy Who Went to the Sky"

Pages: 634-635 BofV

Grade Levels: K-12

Description: Tale - Describes a star ball player who became overly anxious to win the game and flagrantly broke one of the rules. The ball that he illegally threw went into the sky along with the boy and became the moon. On the surface of the moon could be seen the face of the boy who had not played fair in the ball game.

Key Points: Our desire to win in sports, business, grades, etc. must never allow us to forget the rules (standards, ethics) of the game. Too strong a desire to want something can distort our perspectives and cause us to act impulsively and foolishly.

Questions: What do we know about the Indian boy? How did he feel about winning? What do you think caused him to break the rules? What were the consequences of this impulsive act? How could he have avoided this temptation to win at all costs? What are some examples of things we do without thinking things through because of our passion for winning or getting what we want? What can be the consequences of these impulsive acts to win?

INATTENTIVENESS

1. "The Ants and the Grasshopper"
Pages: 354-355 BofV
Grade Levels: K-6
Description: Fable - Describes how some ants are interrupted in their work by a starving grasshopper begging for food. The ants give him nothing after he admits to wasting away his summer singing.
Key Points: Those who give little thought to important responsibilities will find themselves wanting when it's too late.
Questions: What was the grasshopper's excuse when asked why he had no food of his own? Did the ants share their food? Was this a fair thing to do? What little responsibilities do we often pay little attention to because we are occupied with other thoughts or activities? Are there prices to pay for this inattentiveness?

2. "The Little Red Hen"
Pages: 352-353 BofV
Grade Levels: K-6
Description: Poem - Describes how five companions are given the opportunity to assist in the farming of a grain of wheat. Four refuse to do the work, and the fifth, the little red hen, ends up doing it all. Finally, the hen is the only one who enjoys the finished bread.
Key Points: Those who are inattentive to the routine chores and responsibilities often fail to gain the rewards that eventually come.
Questions: What chores were asked of the four other animals? What was their reply? How did they respond to the hen's last question? Did they receive what they asked for? Why? What little things are asked of us on a daily basis? Which of these things do we have a choice in? What happens to those who pay no mind to seeing that these things are worked on or finished?

3. "Eureka"
Pages: 562-564 BofV
Grade Levels: 4-12
Description: Poem - Describes how Archimedes invents a means to determine whether or not his king has been cheated by a goldsmith. Observing how bulk displaces water, he realizes that he can use this same principle in determining if the king's crown is made of pure gold. His experiment proves that the goldsmith cheated the king.

Key Points: Paying attention to life around you can trigger the imagination and cause great things to be accomplished.

Questions: What question did the king place before Archimedes? Did Archimedes have an immediate answer? How did Archimedes eventually come up with the means to determine if the crown was made of pure gold? What things should a person pay attention to? What are things that usually aren't worth our attention? What advantage is there in staying in focus?

4.   "Bruce and the Spider"

Pages: 553-554 BofV, 224-225 YP

Grade Levels: 7-12

Description: Poem - Robert Bruce, King of Scotland (1274-1329) in flight from the enemy after five successive defeats, finds himself hiding in a hut. Here he observes a spider succeed in spinning a web after six failed tries. The perseverance and patience of the spider inspire the King, and he goes on and wins for Scotland.

Key Points: Bruce's attention to the spider rewarded him with the resolve to continue on despite his repeated battlefield losses. Often those who pay attention to life's happiness will find answers, inspiration or opportunities that otherwise would allude them.

Questions: What recent problems had Bruce encountered? What caused him to focus his attention on a spider? What lesson did he learn from the spider? Why did this prove a wise thing to understand? Who can think of an instance where paying attention to a little thing really paid off?

5.   "The Little Hero of Holland"

Pages: 533-535 BofV

Grade Levels: K-9

Description: Story - Describes how a little boy shows foresight and courage when he plugs up a small hole in a water dike with his finger and then holds on until help finally arrives.

Key Points: Good example of how attention to a small detail can lead to great things.

Questions: What little thing did the boy notice? What did he do to fix the problem? What great thing did he accomplish? Can anyone relate a situation where paying attention and acting on what was learned proved a wise thing to do? What types of people are most prepared when opportunity knocks?

6. **"Little Sunshine"**
   Pages: 110-111 BofV
   Grade Levels: K-9
   Description: Story - Describes how a little girl notices how her aged grandmother has no opportunity to enjoy the sunshine. Eventually, she determines that she will bring the sunshine to her grandmother through daily visits.
   Key Points: The grandmother's plight would have gone completely unnoticed except for her granddaughter's attention. We can accomplish much when we develop our capacities to pay attention to the important things.
   Questions: What concerned Elsa about the location of her grandmother's bedroom? How do you think she noticed this problem in the first place? What finally came about as a direct result of Elsa's attention to this matter? Who can think of something important that you noticed that no one else seemed to pick up on? Did this notice allow you to do something about it? How do you develop the ability to notice the things that are important? How might this ability help in school? Home?

7. **"Icarus and Daedalus"**
   Pages: 211-213 BofV, 90-93 YP
   Grade Levels: K-12
   Description: Myth - To escape from prison on the island of Crete, ingenious Daedalus builds a pair of wings for himself and his son, Icarus. They work perfectly but only at the proper altitude. However, Icarus fails to notice that he is flying too high, and it costs him his life.
   Key Points: We should pay attention to the advice of older people who have had much more experience. Doing so may save us a lot of trouble. Our inattentiveness to detail or important advise can prove costly.
   Questions: Do you have difficulty remembering that parents, teachers, etc. were once young like you? What caused Icarus to forget his father's advice? How often are decisions a matter of life and death? What is more apt to happen when we are inattentive to wise counsel? What are some of the things we pay little attention to but later find important?

8. "Little Orphan Annie"

Pages: 190-191 BofV

Grade Levels: K-6

Description: Poem - Describes how important it is to be constantly on the watch concerning our manners and obedience. Otherwise we must suffer the consequences

Key Points: Paying attention to little things, like respectful behavior, can help us avoid much of life's troubles.

Questions: How many things can you find in the poem about good manners? What was the consequence when the little boy and the little girl failed in their responsibilities? Even though goblins won't get you, what do you think happens to those who don't pay attention to what they should be doing? What are some of the little things (or big) that we should be paying attention to?

9. "Work While You Work"

Pages: 355 BofV

Grade Levels: K-3

Description: Poem - Describes how one must do things to their fullest to do the job right. The poem states that this holds true for both work and play.

158

INDULGENT

1. "The Goose That Laid the Golden Eggs"
Pages: 47 BofV
Grade Levels: K-6
Description: Fable - A couple in possession of a goose which laid golden eggs lost everything when their greed caused them to butcher the bird. They figured that the bird must have a golden inside, and they would no longer have to wait for their daily egg.
Key Points: Example of the pitfalls that may result when you are never satisfied with what you have. This story has implications for those not satisfied with modest gains or pleasures (i.e.; gambling, alcohol, television watching, etc.)
Questions: Why was the goose so valuable? Why did the man and his wife kill the goose? What did they hope to gain? Who can remember an instance where someone lost what they had because they continually whined for more?

2. "The Flies and the Honey Pot"
Pages: 37 YP, 48 BofV
Grade Levels: K-9
Description: Fable - Flies greedily eat only to find themselves stuck to the honey and unable to get away.
Key Points: People who insist on excess of anything usually find that they would have been better off with moderation.
Questions: Can anyone remember when they actually tired of a good thing? Too much sun? Too much summer vacation? Too many treats? How is it that excess can cause something to lose its initial appeal?

3. "The Fisherman and His Wife"
Pages: 30-37 YP, 53-57 BofV
Grade Levels: K-9
Description: Tale - Fisherman catches a fish that has the ability to grant wishes. The fisherman's wife keeps prodding her husband to ask for bigger and bigger gifts until they are left with nothing.
Key Points: Once we decide that more possessions are the only thing that will make us happy, then we will never be satisfied. Those who complain too much soon find themselves complaining when there is nothing to complain about.
Questions: How did the fisherman differ from his wife? When do you think she should have been satisfied? Have any of you found yourselves or a friend not being satisfied even after a great gift?

159

Who can remember a Christmas when they were disappointed with their presents?

4. "Plato on Self-Discipline"

Pages: 97-101 BofV

Grade Levels: 9-12

Description: Dialogue - Socrates and Callicles argue over the means to happiness. Callicles champions unrestrained appetites and the ability to satisfy them. Socrates appears to win the argument with his position that self-control accomplishes good and eventual happiness.

Key Points: The argument is over how one pursues happiness. Socrates argues that it can only be achieved through temperance and self-control. Callicles argues for unrestrained appetites and the ability to satisfy those appetites.

Questions: Who can agree with Callicles that unrestrained appetites with the money and means to satisfy the appetites is the key to happiness? What can go wrong with this philosophy? What are some appetites that can never be completely satisfied no matter how much money or power you possess?

5. "How Much Land Does a Man Need?"

Pages: 88-94 BofV

Grade Levels: 6-12

Description: Story - Describes a man whose desire to own land becomes a compulsion. Eventually he enters into a contract to acquire land that causes him to lose everything.

Key Points: Contentment is a matter of mind, not of possessions or achievements. Those who look for contentment in possessions will always be wanting.

Questions: What did Pahom want from life? Had he achieved his goal? Why not? Could Pahom ever become contented? What are some of today's goals that drive people? How can you tell when they become compulsions? How can you guard against unhealthy compulsions?

6. "David and Bathsheba"

Pages: 81-84 BofV

Grade Levels: 7-12

Description: Story - King David lusts after another man's wife and secretly has him killed in battle. David then feels sorry for his actions but loses a son as a consequence for his murder.

Key Points: Overindulgence has its risks. David had nearly everything, but it still wasn't enough. He decided he needed someone who belonged to another and lost sight of some of the standards and virtues that he had followed.

Questions: What great sin did David commit? Why did he do it? Why was it that David failed to see that the prophet Nathan's story was really about himself? What are some of the things that blind us so that we are not able to see our own desires for over indulgences?

7. "Aristotle on Self-Discipline"
Pages: 101-102 BofV
Grade Levels: 7-12

Description: Treatise - Aristotle defines moral virtue as the mean between excess and deficiency. He states that virtue is not inherent, only the capacity to develop is inherent. We are to practice virtue to acquire it as a habit.

Key Points: This treatise describes a means to determine a proper balance of virtue so far as our feelings and actions are concerned. Practice, constant reassessment and modifications are emphasized.

Questions: Can anyone think of instances where you judged in error that you had too much or too little of something? What about kindness, sympathy or work? Is it possible to overindulge in these areas? How can you determine the proper balance in the exercise of virtue?

8. "The Golden Touch"
Pages: 63-66 YP
Grade Levels: K-6

Description: Story - King Midas is granted the ability to turn everything he touches into gold. His joy is quickly lost when he finds he has lost everything important, and all his gold cannot bring them back.

Key Points: Classic example of how excess will turn a good thing into a disaster. Difficulties often follow those who are never satisfied and continually cry out for more. Greed can distort reality.

Questions: Why was King Midas delighted when he saw that he had the golden touch? Why did the golden touch turn out to be a bad thing? Can anyone think of something where it is okay to never be satisfied with what you have? What about happiness, money, muscles, friends? Can any of these things be overdone?

161

9. "Land of the Pilgrim Fathers"

Pages: 790-791 BofV, 359-361 YP

Grade Levels: 4-12

Description: Poem - Describes the difficult circumstances faced by our pilgrim ancestors. Concludes by citing their purpose in coming: To be free to worship God as they wished.

Key Points: The pilgrims' priorities are much different from those we value today. The early pilgrims were an example of those who valued life's basics. They endured deprivation, destitution and death for the right to be free.

Questions: How did the author describe the conditions that accompanied the arrival of the pilgrims? Why did she spend so much time focusing on what they didn't have? What was their reason for enduring the hardships that beset them? What is the prevailing notion of how one gains happiness in today's world? How was it that the pilgrims paid these priorities little heed?

10. "Faith of our Fathers, Living Still"

Pages: 773 BofV

Grade Levels: 4-12

Description: Song - The poem thanks those martyrs who sacrificed their lives and fortunes for freedom's sake.

Key Points: Many have sacrificed much to defend their countries and freedoms. This poem honors those whose faith sustained them despite having great hardships, including death.

Questions: What are some of the hardships endured by those who refused to give up their freedoms? Why does the author feel so strongly devoted to these individuals? How do we treat people today who endure hardship for the sake of their principles? How do these people differ from those who always are searching for what they feel life owes them? Which of the two attitudes do you think will bring the most happiness?

11. "The Sermon to the Birds"

Pages: 761-762 BofV

Grade Levels: K-9

Description: Story - Describes an incident in the life of St. Frances where he spoke to the birds who he considered his brothers and sisters of the air. He pointed out how much God had given them and how this demonstrated God's love for them. He concluded by urging them to always be grateful.

162

Key Points: This story points out many of the blessings that all enjoy. It brings focus to what is good about life despite the challenges that affect all.

Questions: What do you think is the message of this story? What reasons did St. Frances give for stating that God must love the birds? Why did he conclude his sermon with a plea that they be grateful? What are some of the things we enjoy as living organisms on this earth? How many of you actually think about some of these things rather than simply take them for granted? Why is gratitude such a powerful tool?

12. "Job"

Pages: 749-752 BofV, 354-359 YP
Grade Levels: 4-12
Description: Story - Describes the story of Job, a prosperous and wealthy man. Satan is given power to torment Job to see if he will remain faithful to God. Job loses his wealth, his family and his health but never wavers in his trust. He eventually is rewarded for his unwavering trust and gratitude.
Key Points: Each of us choose how we will accept what life provides. To some, there is never enough. To others, they are grateful for the little they have.
Questions: What was Job's life like before Satan was given power to torment him? What were some of the misfortunes that beset him? How did Job react to these misfortunes? Who has had a run of bad luck where nothing works out? How did you feel inside? What were your options in dealing with the misfortunes? Why is it that some are grateful despite having little and others are never satisfied?

13. "In Flanders Field"

Pages: 723 BofV
Grade Levels: 7-12
Description: Poem - Famous dramatization about the allied dead buried in Belgium (World War I) and the hope that they did not die in vain.
Key Points: Others' sacrifice is one reason for loyalty. It is a reminder to those of us remaining to pick up the torch of those who sacrificed their lives for the freedoms we enjoy. We sometimes forget the sacrifices of those who preceded us in our quest to satisfy our ever-present needs and wants.

Questions:	How many of you would like to trade places with those on the battlefields who fought for the freedoms we enjoy? What are some of the little things that we complain over not having enough? Why are some of these complaints foolish when compared to the important things in life like freedom, good health and sufficient sustenance?

14. "Elias"

Pages: 431-435 BofV

Grade Levels: 4-12

Description:	Story - Describes how a man and his wife accumulated great wealth and power only to lose it all in their aged years. The story concludes with their confession that they had finally found the happiness they had long sought because their climb to the top and great responsibilities had blinded them of the opportunity to serve each other, their neighbors and their God.
Key Points:	There is a downside to having too much success and wealth. One can easily lose perspective while trying to maintain what one has and miss out on the simple joys of life.
Questions:	How did Elias and his wife come to lose all their worldly possessions? How did they come to view this great loss? Why do you think the guests were surprised at what they heard? Do you agree with this argument? What can happen to those who focus too much on acquiring possessions at the expense of all else?

15. "The Week of Sundays"

Pages: 380-384 BofV

Grade Levels: 4-12

Description:	Tale - Describes how a lazy man is granted his wish for a week of Sundays only to find out that this is not so desirable a thing. He learns that too much free time soon becomes a liability.
Key Points:	Only those who earn their free time are in a position to enjoy it. Too much of anything is usually a liability in the end.
Questions:	Why did the man desire every day to be a Sunday? What did he expect it would provide him? What lessons did he learn about life when he received his wish? Who can think of good things that become bad when there is too much? Why do you think some people always want more of the things they enjoy? Is this smart?

16. "The Donner Party"

Pages: 576-582 BofV

Grade Levels: 4-12

Description: Story - Describes some of the trials, tragedies and heroism that accompanied a party of settlers immigrating to the west coast of America.

Key Points: This story illustrates why we should be thankful for what we have rather than fret and complain over what we are denied.

Questions: What were a few of the conditions that made life difficult for the Donner party? What became most important to those stranded in the mountains? What does it often take to point out our daily blessings? Why would it be wise to be thankful for what we have rather than complain over what we lack? Who is usually the happier, those who are grateful or those who can rarely be satisfied? Why?

17. "Echo and Narcissus"

Pages: 152-154 BofV

Grade Levels: 7-12

Description: Myth - Describes how Narcissus is cursed for his vanity and self-absorption. He eventually wastes his life away gazing at his own image in the water.

Key Points: One can consume himself in his own lusts until it rules and ruins his life.

Questions: Who can describe Narcissus? What was Narcissus' problem and how did it manifest itself? What finally happened to him? What are some of the things we are vain about? What is wrong with desiring more and more of something?

18. "A Legend of the Northland"

Pages: 148-151 BofV

Grade Levels: 4-9

Description: Poem - Describes how a woman's greed causes her to treat another poorly. As a consequence of her actions, she is turned into a woodpecker.

Key Points: When we focus on ourselves, we can easily lose our compassion toward others. Those who practice greed can lose everything in the end.

Questions: What did Saint Peter ask of the woman? What changes in her generosity happened as she thought the matter through? What was the final result? Who can recall a situation where it was difficult to share with another? How do you feel when you choose not to share? Is greed worth it? Why or why not?

19. "The Little Match Girl"

Pages: 124-126 BofV

Grade Levels: K-12

Description: Story - Describes how a little girl with little to enjoy in life finds joy in striking matches on a cold December night. The light from each match conjures a vision of warmth and love. Eventually she dies but in so doing returns to her loving Grandmother.

Key Points: This story helps each of us appreciate our blessings in life. It also provides hope for a better life to those who struggle with life's great challenges.

Questions: Why was the little girl outside and ill-clothed on a cold winter night? Why did she decide to strike the first match? What were some of the things she saw each time she struck a match? Have any of you lost perspective over something you wanted badly? How can the little match girl help you to keep a proper perspective?

20. "The Legend of the Dipper"

Pages: 122-124 BofV

Grade Levels: K-9

Description: Myth - Describes how a little girl labors to obtain water for her sick mother. Despite her needs, the little girl cannot refuse others in need. Eventually her acts of kindness are rewarded, and the Big Dipper is created as a memorial to the little girl's generosity.

Key Points: While each of us always seems to have needs, we still have an obligation to the needs of those around us. Those who forget themselves for others will eventually be rewarded for their kindness.

Questions: Why was the little girl in search of the water? Why would she have been justified in refusing others? Who can think of times when we have unfulfilled needs but choose to help others first? Why would we do something like this?

21. "The Bridge Builder"

Pages: 223 BofV, 105 YP

Grade Levels: K-12

Description: Poem - Describes old man who, after crossing a dangerous stream in a deep and wide chasm, turns around and builds a bridge so that others can cross easier and more safely. He did this though not obligated to do so.

Key Points: We have a responsibility to build a foundation that is safe and secure for the next generation. Willingness to work for the good of those to follow is a critical need today. All gain when the emphasis is placed on others' needs rather than our own.

Questions: What did the old man accomplish? Why did he do it? What legacy did your parents, grandparents, etc. leave for you? What legacy do you wish to leave? What bridges can you build for your family and friends today? How can too much a focus on yourself curtail your ability to serve the next generation?

INTIMIDATION

1. **"John, Tom and James"**
   Pages: 29 YP
   Grade Levels: K-9
   Description: Poem - Links rude and intimidating actions with eventual ugliness and loneliness.
   Key Points: Poem suggests that bullies eventually get their due. The "ugly" and "nobody caring" actually can happen. The ugly can be manifested in many ways that go beyond physical attractiveness.
   Questions: Do you believe that rude bullies actually grow ugly? Are there different ways that ugliness can manifest itself? Who can think of examples of ugliness? Why do you think nobody cares when something bad happens to a bully?

2. **"The Volunteer at Auschwitz"**
   Pages: 803-808 BofV
   Grade Levels: 4-12
   Description: Story - Describes the last years of a priest during the Nazi occupation of Poland. He eventually is assigned to Auschwitz where he voluntarily dies to spare the life of another.
   Key Points: Intimidation arises for different reasons and takes various forms. The degree of severity doesn't determine whether it is right or wrong. Subtle acts can be as damaging as extreme acts of violence.
   Questions: What were some of the ways the Nazis bullied those who they perceived as deserving of such intimidation? Why do you think they chose to pick on certain groups of people? Did things seem to get out of hand? Why do you think that happened? What types of people are bullied today? Do you think the bullies have valid reasons for their actions? What are some of the ways we bully people in school? Could we be acting as a bully without realizing it?

3. **"The Lion and the Mouse"**
   Pages: 110 BofV
   Grade Levels: 4-6
   Description: Fable - Describes how a powerful lion could have eaten a mouse but took pity and released him. As a result, the mouse lived to save the lion in his hour of need.

Key Points: What goes around, comes around. Kindness will often be repaid. Acts of intimidation will leave the bully helpless in his hour of need.

Questions: How did the lion treat the mouse? What could the lion have done to the mouse but chose not to? What happened as a result of the lion's kindness? Who can think of how some students are much like the lion and some like the mouse? Why does it make sense for people to treat others in the same way the lion treated the mouse?

4. "Let Dogs Delight to Bark and Bite"

Pages: 37 YP

Grade Levels: K-3

Description: Poem - Short (eight verses) illustration of how children should differ from dogs, bears and lions with respect to anger and fighting.

Key Points: Poem points out that while it appears natural for certain animals to be aggressive, it should not be the case for children. The inference is that children who bully are patterning their actions after animals of lesser intelligence than humans.

Questions: What animals did the author mention in his poem? Why do you think these animals were chosen? Do you agree that children should act differently than animals with respect to fighting? What do you think the rising of angry passions means? Can you think of examples? Are these good things to do?

5. "Last Lines"

Pages: 817-818 BofV

Grade Levels: 7-12

Description: Poem - Argues that God's existence supersedes all the concerns and activities of life. Concludes that God will remain even if all earths, men and universes cease to exist.

JUDGMENTAL

1. **"The Dying Christian to His Soul"**
    Pages: 810 BofV
    Grade Levels: 7-12
    Description: Poem - This poem questions all the attention we give to death. It argues that death only opens the door to a better existence.
    Key Points: This poem argues that the ultimate misfortune, death, is something not worthy of attention or concern. It puts in perspective many of our prevalent gripes about life's unfairness.
    Questions: What were the author's views on death? What perspective allowed him this casual approach to such a serious event? How do you think the author feels about the misfortunes of life that fall short of death? What are some of the things that upset us and cause us to complain about unfairness? Are the complaints warranted in light of the poem's message?

2. **"We Understand So Little"**
    Pages: 774-775 BofV
    Grade Levels: K-12
    Description: Story - Describes how two brothers from the city observed a farmer in his work. One boy continually criticized each step in the farmer's work because he didn't understand the purpose. His brother was patient and came to see the reasoning behind each of the farmer's tasks.
    Key Points: It is easy to be critical when we react to isolated events. We need to withhold judgment until we have the full picture.
    Questions: Why did the first brother continually find fault with the farmer's actions? Why did the second brother have an advantage over the first brother? Who might wish to relate an instance when you made a hasty decision without learning all of the facts? How did you feel afterward? What damage might you do to yourself or others?

3. **"All Things Beautiful"**
    Pages: 748-749 BofV
    Grade Levels: 4-12
    Description: Poem - Describes many of nature's endowments and attributes all to the hand of God.
    Key Points: Nature offers much to enjoy, and those who focus on the good will find much that pleases. Those focused on what is wrong will often miss what is right.

Questions: What examples did the author use to describe nature's gifts? What are some of nature's other bounties provided for mankind's enjoyment? Why is it that there are times when we fail to see the beauty around us? What do we lose when we fail to see the beauty around us?

4. "Of Studies"
Pages: 423-424 BofV
Grade Levels: 7-12
Description: Lecture - Bacon argues that studies are conducted for various reasons and as such should be handled differently. He spends considerable time on the third reason, that for ability.
Key Points: Studies must be judged for their ultimate aim. Many who complain about relevance do so because their aims are inconsistent with the nature of the material. Once they understand their own aims and that of the material, they are in position to adjust the learning to suit the circumstances.
Questions: How did the author contrast studies for "delight," for "ornament" and for "ability?" What does he mean when he states, "Some books are to be tasted, others to be swallowed and some few to be chewed and digested."? How can one decide which studies need to be chewed and digested and which need to be treated in some other manner? How does this understanding help us to view the worth in most studies? What might we lose if our overly critical perspective dominates our conscious thought?

5. "The Shoemaker and the Elves"
Pages: 370-372 BofV
Grade Levels: K-6
Description: Tale - Describes how a destitute shoemaker is helped by some elves. He and his wife repay their kindness by making them little articles of clothing.
Key Points: The shoemaker and his wife could have been angry and judgmental when the elves failed to return, especially after the elves were given gifts in return. Instead, they dismissed any feelings of anger by concluding that the elves must be helping someone else.
Questions: What did the elves do for the shoemaker? How did the shoemaker and his wife repay the kindness? How did the shoemaker react when the elves failed to return? Who can think of instances when we are hurt because we don't completely

understand the actions of another? Is this a wise way to react? What does it usually lead to?

6. "The Husband Who Was to Mind the House"
Pages: 364-366 BofV
Grade Levels: 3-12
Description: Story - Humorous story that describes how a complaining husband agrees to switch roles with his wife who keeps house. Expecting a day of leisure, he has nothing but trouble trying to manage all the chores and responsibilities asked of a homemaker.
Key Points: It is easier to find fault when one looks at a situation from the outside. We first need to learn about something firsthand before deciding on an opinion.
Questions: What first upset the husband? What type of day did he expect when he first agreed to switch places with his wife? How did things actually turn out? How many of you have had someone question your actions without first understanding all the circumstances? Can you think of times you have been guilty of the same offense?

7. "Alice's Supper"
Pages: 359-360 BofV
Grade Levels: K-6
Description: Poem - Describes the process involved that eventually produces a loaf of bread. This is built around the theme of providing little Alice with her supper.
Key Points: Each of these individuals involved in the work have a common focus--that of providing bread for a little girl's supper. They are focused on serving another rather than what's in it for themselves.
Questions: Why was everyone so cheerful in their labors? Can it work this way in real life? What are things we can do for others that help us keep our focus on service rather than our own misfortunes or complaints?

8. "Five Little Chickens"
Pages: 353-354 BofV
Grade Levels: K-3
Description: Poem - Five chicks spend their day wishing for things for breakfast. Their wise mother reminds them that the only way they can have what they want is to come and scratch.

Key Points: The little chicks put off the chores needed to obtain their breakfast while they whined over what they wanted. Life is no different. Often we are late getting to things that will bring us success and happiness because we spend too much time whining and complaining.

Questions: What are some of the things the little chicks wished for? Why would they be late in getting their wishes? Is this a foolish approach? What are some of the things we are always asking for but unwilling to get started to make them happen?

9. "In Memory of L. H. W."
Pages: 582-592 BofV
Grade Levels: 4-12
Description: Story - Bittersweet tale of a man who faced life with courage and compassion despite undue amounts of criticism, ridicule and misfortune.

Key Points: Those who base judgment on outward appearances often underestimate or overestimate the worth of an individual. Greatness stems from the heart and is manifested through valiant deeds performed under duress. It is foolish to base an opinion of another on initial appearances.

Questions: What were some of the characteristics that Lem was commonly judged by? What acts did he perform that could be considered great? Why didn't his neighbors recognize these wonderful acts of courage and compassion? How do we commonly judge our friends and companions? Why should we be cautious in making judgments about others? Does the same reasoning hold true for judging things?

10. "The Good Samaritan"
Pages: 141 BofV
Grade Levels: 4-12
Description: Parable - Describes how a man beaten and robbed is eventually assisted by one who is often frowned upon by the victim's people. This act of kindness came after two of the victim's own people ignored his need for help. The parable illustrates the true nature of a neighbor.

Key Points: People should be judged by their deeds rather than their race, culture or some similar characteristic.

Questions: What happened to the man? Who ignored his need for help? Who eventually assisted him? What message did the parable teach? Who can think of examples of people who are judged for reasons other than what they are like inside? Why is this judgment unfair and unwise?

11. "The Question"

Pages: 643-644 BofV, 282 YP

Grade Levels: 7-12

Description: Poem - Poses the question: If the whole world were as good as you, would this be a better world?

Key Points: First examine your own virtue before examining the actions of others. This is a good yardstick in determining your right to challenge another's actions.

Questions: What is the basic message of the poem? Do you agree with this message? What are some occasions where we have a tendency to pass judgment on others? In these instances, how could you use the message of this poem to avoid hypocrisy?

12. "The Woman Caught in Adultery"

Pages: 642-643 BofV

Grade Levels: 9-12

Description: Story - Describes a woman brought to Jesus of Nazareth who had been taken in adultery. When asked if she should be stoned according to the Law of Moses, Jesus said, "He that is without sin among you, let him first cast a stone at her." Apparently the words struck the conscience of those present because each left without further comment.

Key Points: Hypocrisy is one of the most common varieties of dishonesty. Often those who are the most critical of others (judgmental) have the most to hide in their own lives.

Questions: What was the woman's offense? What did the accusers ask of Jesus? What was his reply? How did the accusers respond? Why is it important that we use caution when we judge others? What conditions, preparations and self-analysis should be seen to first before we judge others?

13. "Death, Be Not Proud"

Pages: 809 BofV

Grade Levels: 7-12

Description: Poem - Describes how we shouldn't fear death. It is pointed out that death only ushers in an existence of rest and pleasure and how death then ceases to exist.

14. "The House by the Side of the Road"

   Pages: 305 BofV

   Grade Levels: 7-12

Description: Poem - Argues that our responsibility as people is to interrelate with others (rather than insulate ourselves within our comfort zones) with the challenge to accept others as they are and treat them like a friend.

15. "Beauty and the Beast"

   Pages: 127-134 BofV

   Grade Levels: 4-9

Description: Tale - Describes how a young lady learns to love a beast despite his horrible appearance. The beast turns out to be a prince who must appear as a beast until a beautiful maiden consents to kiss him.

LAZINESS

1. "Godfrey Gordon Gustavus Gore"
Pages: 27-28 YP
Grade Levels: K-6
Description: Poem - Short poem about a boy who refused to shut doors despite his parent's pleadings. Eventually he is threatened with banishment to Singapore if he continues. He promises to mend his ways for a reprieve.
Key Points: Sometimes we pay no attention to counsel for no other reasons than we don't wish to be bothered or we are just too lazy. Often our laziness becomes a habit, and this in turn causes others to eventually step in and say or do something that we might not like. Little acts of laziness can grow to be major problems to both ourselves and others.
Questions: Do you think parents would really threaten to send their child off to another country just because he never shuts a door? What might parents more likely do? What are other examples that we often do that are similar to not shutting doors? Why would others care if we don't shut doors?

2. "The Magic Thread"
Pages: 57-63 BofV
Grade Levels: K-12
Description: Story - A very impatient and impulsive boy is given a magic thread that enables him to soar ahead in time each time he pulls the magic thread. He avoids much of life's challenge and ends up losing many opportunities to experience the joys and sorrows of life that would have been worth experiencing.
Key Points: The boy had a lazy mental approach to life where he avoided anything he perceived as taxing or boring. In essence, he avoided responsibility and the joys that accompany accomplishment and effort.
Questions: How did the magic thread work? What eventually happened to the boy? How many would like a magic thread so they could avoid all of life's undesirable parts? What would you choose to avoid? What would you lose out on as a result?

3. "The Bramblebush"
Pages: 377-378 YP
Grade Levels: K-12
Description: Parable - Describes how a man puts off the removal of his bramblebush which is obstructing passage on a road. As he

waits, the bush grows younger and healthier while he grows older and weaker.

Key Points: The bush is a metaphor for bad habits. He who puts off the correction of a bad habit will soon find it has become his master. It requires effort to master our environment. Lazy habits will curtail growth.

Questions: Why do you think the man first ignored the requests to remove his bramblebush? Do you think the reasons for his refusal changed with time? Why did he resist at the end? What are some of the bramblebushes that we face today? How do you think laziness plays a factor in whether or not we are willing to remove the problem?

4.   "The Coming of Maize"
Pages: 375-377 YP
Grade Levels: K-9
Description: Tale - Describes how a young boy encounters a messenger from the Great Spirit while fasting and praying for a means to help his impoverished family. He is told he must wrestle the messenger on successive nights. Eventually, he prevails, buries his opponent and finds that the gravesite produces maize which is the answer to his prayers.

Key Points: The boy did not allow hunger or weariness to stop him from following the bidding of the messenger. He eventually finds the reason for his efforts and gains a great reward.

Questions: Why was the lad in a weakened position when he first encountered the messenger from the Great Spirit? What kind of effort would it take to wrestle under these conditions? Why did the young boy do it? What came of his efforts? Who can think of times when even a small chore seemed an overwhelming burden? What benefits are gained by ignoring the difficulties and getting the job done?

5.   "Loyalty to a Brother"
Pages: 706 BofV
Grade Levels: K-12
Description: Story - Describes a soldier in World War II risking his life to bring his injured brother off the battle field even though his brother is presumed dead and he has been advised against the venture. His brother's dying words were: "Tom, I knew you would come."

Key Points: It took courage and effort to find his dying brother. The effort seemed a fruitless and foolish thing to do. This often is the case when we go the extra mile, particularly when things seem hopeless or no one is watching. The rewards eventually will come.

Questions: Why was the one brother cautioned against saving his brother? Do you think it would have been easy to accept orders, particularly in light of the danger and the likelihood that his brother was already dead? Why is it that we often give up or grow lazy when we see little hope for success? Why is this a foolish habit to get in to?

6. "The Song of the Bee"
Pages: 349-350 BofV
Grade Levels: K-6
Description: Poem - Describes the industry of a bee in its daily activities and tasks. Point is made that it is better to be busy than have nothing to do.
Key Points: The bee is an example of an organism that always seems busy. The point is made that being busy is far superior to having nothing to do at all.
Questions: What are some of the bee's activities? It is described that the bee is singing. What do you think the author is trying to tell us? Why do you think it is said that being busy is better than having nothing to do? What opportunities do you have to keep busy? What can you do to see that you are busy?

7. "The Three Little Pigs"
Pages: 357-358 BofV
Grade Levels: K-3
Description: Story - Describes how three little pigs build their own homes. Only one of the pigs survives the wolf's assault because he has built his house out of bricks.
KeyPoints: Those who extend little energy usually get what they deserve. In the pigs' case, the consequence was rather harsh. Life is much like the example of the pigs.
Questions: What materials were chosen to build each of the three houses? Why did each pig choose as he did? What happened to each of the pigs when the wolf came? Was this a fair thing to happen to the first two pigs? What are some of the things we must work hard at if we wish to be prepared for the future? What often happens if we are prepared? What often happens if we are not?

8. "Hercules and the Wagoner"

Pages: 359 BofV, 152 YP

Grade Levels: K-6

Description: Fable - A wagoner, stuck in the mud, calls for Hercules' help. The Greek God arrives and chides the wagoner for asking assistance before first trying to resolve the problem on his own.

KeyPoints: There will always be obstacles. Those who first make effort are in the best position to secure the help of others.

Questions: What was the wagoner's problem? Why did Hercules refuse to help him? What are some of the day-to-day obstacles that confront us? Why is it wise for us to first rely on our own efforts before seeking help?

9. "Mother Holly"

Pages: 366-369 BofV

Grade Levels: K-9

Description: Tale - Describes how two sisters are provided opportunity to receive rewards through their service. One is industrious and is rewarded well, while the other is lazy and gains nothing.

KeyPoints: Often the rewards of work come unexpectedly.

Questions: What caused the beautiful and industrious sister to arrive in the beautiful meadow? What was her response to the repeated requests for her help? What was her eventual reward? Did she expect it? How did the second sister's experience differ from the first sister's? Who can think of instances where we were expected to work without hope for any payment or reward? Is this fair? Do some rewards come unexpectedly or in a concealed form?

10. "The Farmer and His Sons"

Pages: 370 BofV, 164 YP

Grade Levels: K-6

Description: Fable - Describes how a farmer tricks his sons into believing that a treasure is hidden in their vineyard. After much searching, through hard work, they find that the treasure is in the bounteous crop produced by the hard work.

KeyPoints: There are few easy paths to fortune or success. We must work for what we hope to achieve.

Questions: How did the farmer trick his sons? What treasure did their efforts produce? Why was their father wise? What are some of the treasures we seek after? What happens to those who try very hard but fail to achieve their goal? Was all their effort wasted?

11. "How the Camel Got His Hump"

Pages: 373-376 BofV

Grade Levels: K-6

Description: Tale - Describes how the idle camel is punished with a hump because of his laziness. It turns out that the hump is a fitting punishment because it allows the camel to make up for lost time by storing the food he would otherwise have to stop work for.

KeyPoints: Work or laziness brings its just reward. Often the reward or punishment is as a direct result of our industry.

Questions: How did the camel differ from the other animals? How did the Djinn punish the camel for his laziness? What is the significance of the hump so far as work is concerned? What are some of the punishments we receive when we fail to do our share of the work? What are some of the rewards?

12. "Results and Roses"

Pages: 389 BofV, 161 YP

Grade Levels: 4-9

Description: Poem - Describes how we must work if we wish for results or roses. It adds that there are few things that come as a result of wishing.

KeyPoints: Nothing good comes without effort. The goal is not as important as how hard one works to achieve the goal.

Questions: Why do you think the author used the example of a garden to share his message? What do you think he was trying to tell us? Do you believe it? Does work always pay off immediately? How about a garden? Does it always produce well the first year? What benefits always follow hard work given a chance?

13. "The Ballad of John Henry"

Pages: 393-394 BofV, 161-164 YP

Grade Levels: 4-9

Description: Poem - Describes the heart and courage of a man who put his principles above all else. Poem concludes with John Henry giving up his life due to his commitment to his work.

KeyPoints: Pride in one's work is a sure way to encourage industry and effort.

Questions: What was John Henry's trade? What contest did he enter? How did he lose his life? Who can tell us something that you do very well? How do you feel when you are doing this? What did it take you to become skilled in this area? Was it worth it? Does this process work for other things?

14. "It's Plain Hard Work That Does It"

Pages: 409-415 BofV

Grade Levels: 2-12

Description: Story - Covers aspects of Edison's life. Describes many of his work habits and attitudes through anecdotes and quotes.

KeyPoints: Edison typically worked 18-hour days. While this schedule won't work for most, it does provide a clear example of what long and hard effort can produce.

Questions: What did Edison mean when he stated, "Genius is one percent inspiration and 99 percent perspiration." What did he mean when he said, "Sleep is like a drug. Take too much at a time, and it makes you dopey. You lose time, vitality and opportunities." Do you agree with Edison? Where are areas where much work is required for success? Are these efforts worth it?

15. "A Psalm of Life"

Pages: 436-437 BofV

Grade Levels: 7-12

Description: Poem - Describes the author's discovery that involvement and personal growth are the keys to happiness.

KeyPoints: Those who embrace life's opportunities are far better off than those who give up trying. Action in various forms is a cure to much of what ails us.

Questions: What do you think was the author's cure for depression? Do you agree with him? Why is this wisdom often ignored? What is required of those who are struggling but lack the resolve to get involved with life? How might one develop this capacity to work at life?

16. "Dust Under the Rug"

Pages: 376-380 BofV

Grade Levels: K-9

Description: Tale - Describes how a young girl goes off to earn money for her mother and lame sister. Some dwarfs employ her and promise her a reward if she is diligent. On her last day she goes the extra mile and sweeps under the rug only to find some gold coins that are to serve as her reward.

KeyPoints: The young girl would not have received the reward if she failed to do her job well. Often the real reward in a job comes when we stretch ourselves as far as we can.

Where had the little girl failed to clean on her last day? How was she rewarded for her extra effort? What would she have received if she failed to finish her job? Who can think of instances where we can go the extra mile in a chore or assignment? What might be the hidden rewards?

17. "What A Baby Costs"

Pages: 224-225 BofV

Grade Levels: K-12

Description: Poem - Describes the cost of a baby in time, attention, tears, worry, money, pain, loneliness, etc.

KeyPoints: Raising a baby is a good example of why hard work is worth the effort. It also points out the critical importance of hard work. We would cease to exist as a people if we failed to take care of our young.

Questions: What are some of the "costs" of babies? Does it sound like hard work? Why do people do it? What other things require hard work but seem to be worth the effort? What types of benefits arise from these situations? How would we all suffer if everyone became lazy?

18. "Which Loved Best?"

Pages: 204 BofV

Grade Levels: K-12

Description: Poem - Illustrates that it takes more than just words to prove your devotion to your mother. It takes deeds.

KeyPoints: Actions speak louder than words. "When all is said and done, more is said than done."

Questions: Describe how the expression of love differed between the three children? Which expression do you think is the most correct? Why? What does it often require to practice love in the correct way? What are some ways that we can practice love on a day-to-day basis? Does it work the same way when showing our love to friends or others?

19. "The American's Creed"

Pages: 219 BofV

Grade Levels: 4-12

Description: Essay - Nationwide contest winner (1917) for the best summary of American political faith. The primary point is that we as citizens should be loyal to our constitution.

KeyPoints: Citizens have a duty to support the principles upon which their government stands. "Responsibility" rather than "rights" is emphasized. It requires effort to be a good citizen, but it pays off for everyone.

Questions: What are some of the principles listed in the essay as critical for the proper functioning of our government? Why do you think these principles are considered important? How do we practice these principles in our day-to-day lives? Who can describe an America without the constitution?

20. "Wynken, Blynken and Nod"

Pages: 351-352 BofV

Grade Levels: K-3

Description: Poem - Describes the imaginings of a child dreaming of fun adventures while falling asleep listening to his mother's song.

21. "I Meant to Do My Work Today"

Pages: 385 BofV

Grade Levels: K-6

Description: Poem - Describes how intentions and actions are two completely different things.

22. "Heaven Is Not Reached in a Single Bound"

Pages: 415 BofV

Grade Levels: 7-12

Description: Poem - Describes the process one must follow to reach heaven. Author argues that noble deeds are steps that when added together provide the means to return to God.

23. "Perseverance"

Pages: 565 BofV

Grade Levels: 4-9

Description: Poem - Argues that we reap what we sow. Only those who act on life will harvest life's blessings.

PEER PRESSURES

1. **"The Lovable Child"**
   Pages: 28 BofV
   Grade Levels: K-6
   Description: Poem - Describes the attributes of a well-behaved child and reinforces the notion that these types of children are admired and loved.
   KeyPoints: This poem points out some characteristics that attract friends. These are also the characteristics of the friends we would want to seek out for advice.
   Questions: How did the author describe a lovable child? Why would you choose a friend who is lively bright, gentle and happy? What can you expect from a friend such as this? Why would it be wise to heed advice from a friend such as this?

2. **"Boy Wanted"**
   Pages: 39-41 YP, 78-79 BofV
   Grade Levels: K-9
   Description: Want Ad - Appeared almost 100 years ago and described the qualities of the boy they were looking for.
   KeyPoints: Many of the qualities required in this want ad are different from what other boys of the same age would be showing. Note: This type of boy is wanted everywhere--family, school, office, girls and all creation.
   Questions: What were some of the virtues asked for in the advertisement? Why would a young person like this be wanted in a family, school or office? Why would it be wise to make a friend of a person with these qualities? How might you judge the example and advise from such an individual? What types of individuals should you be wary of their influence?

3. **"The Cattle of the Sun"**
   Pages: 79-81 BofV
   Grade Levels: 4-12
   Description: Myth - Describes an incident in Homer's Odyssey where Ulysses and his men meet with disaster because they fail to heed wise counsel. The men's resolve to avoid enticements quickly evaporates when they react to the foolish words of a crew member. Their impulsive reaction ends up costing them their lives.

184

KeyPoints: In two instances the crew members chose to follow the wishes of the group despite stern warnings from the authority figure. Eventually, it cost them their lives.

Questions: Why do you think the crew members chose to disobey Ulysses' warnings? Surely some believed Ulysses' counsel. Why did they ignore it? Do similar situations exist in your lives? What perils might you face rather than go against the wishes of your friends?

4. "The Boy Who Tried to Be the Sun"
Pages: 28-30 YP
Grade Levels: K-6
Description: Legend - A boy who is fathered by the sun returns to earth only to be teased about not having a father. The boy goes to great lengths to prove he has a father only to lose his life in the process.
KeyPoints: A young boy was willing to risk everything to gain acceptance from other children of the village.
Questions: Has anyone ever felt different from everyone else? How did it make you feel? Did this young boy use good judgment in trying to prove he was like everyone else? Can anyone think of instances where it is okay to be different?

5. "Vaulting Ambition Which O'erleaps Itself"
Pages: 85-87 BofV
Grade Levels: 10-12
Description: Story - Macbeth is convinced by his wife, against his better judgment, to murder Duncan the King in order to gain the throne.
KeyPoints: Macbeth caves in to the pressure of his wife despite his recognition of the evil involved.
Questions: What act of violence did Macbeth and his wife plot? What arguments against the plot did Macbeth put forth? What caused Macbeth to act against his common sense and conscience? Why is it that our friends often lead us to behaviors we know are wrong and the consequences weighty? How can we guard against the destructive influence of others?

6. "Noah and the Ark"
Pages: 745-748 BofV
Grade Levels: K-12
Description: Story - Describes story of Noah. Accounts how the people of the earth grew wicked. Noah is instructed to build a large ship

to house his family and representatives of the animal kingdom. Floods destroy the earth and all on it. Noah and his group are spared because they heed the counsel of God rather than the voices of their neighbors.

KeyPoints: Close associations with people can unify thoughts and actions that can be good or bad. In Noah's time, the people unified in evil. Sometimes it requires a complete removal of association to change behavior and thoughts.

Questions: What caused all the people to grow evil in their thoughts and actions? What was God's solution to this problem? To whose influence did Noah pay heed? What happens today when we spend great amounts of time with a friend or group of friends? Does the association usually mean a change? How might you judge the nature of the change?

7. "Home Sweet Home"

Pages: 707-708 BofV

Grade Levels: K-12

Description: Poem - Reasons why "There's no place like home."

KeyPoints: Home can be a place of strength, peace and above all reality. Often in our quest to follow the enticements and expectations of the world and friends, we need a place where we can regain a healthy perspective.

Questions: What are some of the descriptions of home listed in the poem? Has anyone noticed how home can help put some of our yearnings and ambitions in proper perspective? Why do you think this is so? Why is it good to limit your time associating with the same friends? How can this distort your perspectives?

8. "The Cap That Mother Made"

Pages: 668-671 BofV

Grade Levels: K-9

Description: Tale - Describes a boy who wouldn't trade his new cap for anything, even a king's crown.

KeyPoints: Convictions, even to such simple things as a cap mother made, tell something about our character. This boy resisted some strong pressure to trade his cap for things that appeared enticing. He held to his conviction that what he had was worthy of saying no to all the offers.

Questions: Who can remember some characteristics about the cap? Who can describe some of the offers he received to trade the cap? Do you think it would have been difficult to turn some of these offers down? Why? What might you be asked to give up that

186

is of real worth? Must it always be a tangible possession like a cap or a toy?

9. "George Washington Rejects A Crown"
Pages: 717-718 BofV
Grade Levels: 4-12
Description: Letter - George Washington, emphatically rejects the idea that he become King and America become like Britain.
KeyPoints: Washington resisted the pressure to become King. This took courage to say no. It took even more courage to reprimand those who wanted to bestow this great honor on him.
Questions: Who was it that offered Washington the opportunity to be king? How did Washington react? Would this have been an easy thing to say no to? Can anyone think of instances when our friends desire something of us that appeals to our pride but is inherently wrong? Why is it wise to listen to our conscience rather than the flattery of others?

10. "The Lover Pleads with his Friend for Old Friends"
Pages: 330 BofV, 145 YP
Grade Levels: 7-12
Description: Poem - Argues that new friends should not be made at the expense of old friends.
KeyPoints: Sometimes in our quest for attention or acceptance, we follow a path charted by others who haven't our best interests at heart. Ultimately this can cost us our tried and true friends when things begin to unravel.
Questions: What "shining days" might the author be alluding to? What counsel does the author give about maintaining true and time-tested friendships? Who can think of instances where there may be a temptation to ignore old friends? What can happen as a result?

11. "Jonathan and David"
Pages: 299-303 BofV, 135-140 YP
Grade Levels: 4-9
Description: Story - Describes some of the incidents in David's life after his slaying of Goliath. Particular emphasis is placed on David's relationship with King Saul and Jonathan, the king's son.

KeyPoints: Story describes a situation where Jonathan is receiving pressure from his father to assist in David's destruction. While not technically "peer pressure," it does illustrate the courage required to act against the wishes of those who have close associations.

Questions: Why was King Saul trying to kill David? How did Jonathan react to his father's pressures? What could Jonathan have achieved if he gave in to his father's wishes? Why do you think he followed his conscience? What do you think was his reward for his loyalty to David? Why is it sometimes difficult to put conscience over peer pressures?

12. "The Angel of the Battlefield"
Pages: 144-146 BofV, 58-61 YP
Grade Levels: 4-12
Description: Story - Describes incidents in the life of Clara Barton, the founder of the American Red Cross. Her determination and courage on the battlefields of the Civil War are described.

KeyPoints: Clara Barton had the courage to follow her convictions rather than accept the common practices of the day. Her resolve eventually led to great accomplishments despite fighting against the prevailing notions of the times.

Questions: What troubled Clara Barton? How did the General react to her idea? What did the General use as the basis for his denial? How did the matter eventually work out? What kind of prevailing pressures do young people face today? What do you do when these prevailing practices or attitudes run counter to what you know is right?

13. "Truth and Falsehood"
Pages: 636-637 BofV, 286-287 YP
Grade Levels: 4-12
Description: Tale - Portrays truth and falsehood as people. Falsehood tricks Truth into making a promise he later regrets. Concludes with the two going their separate ways and resolving to never travel together again.

KeyPoints: Be cautious about who you allow to do you a favor. You may compromise your integrity. While being honest may not be easy, deceit is far more difficult and painful.

Questions: Why did Truth agree to tag along with Falsehood? What compromising situation arose as a result of the partnership? Do you think Truth was wise to allow Falsehood to talk him into something he had little understanding of? What are some of the things that have resulted because an individual foolishly allowed himself to be talked into something he knew was wrong or knew little about? How can you guard against this sort of thing?

14. "The Story of Regulus"

Pages: 617-618 BofV, 283-286 YP

Grade Levels: 4-12

Description: Story - The account of a heroic Roman general who willingly gave up his freedom rather than break a solemn oath.

KeyPoints: Keeping your word inspires others. Sometimes an entire nation will rally around the efforts of one truthful person. Make promises you can keep. Regulus agreed to only one of the two conditions set forth, the one he knew he could keep. He agreed to return to prison and fulfilled his oath. He didn't let others influence his decision despite their persistence.

Questions: What did Regulus' captors require of him? How did the Roman general respond? What did his family and friends urge him to do? Do you think it took courage to keep his word? Who would he let down if he returned to Carthage? Who would he let down if he remained in Rome? How would you have decided?

15. "The Emperor's New Clothes"

Pages: 630-634 BofV

Grade Levels: 4-12

Description: Tale - An emperor, obsessed about wearing new clothes, is duped by two rascals who claim they are making clothes that will be invisible to every person unfit for office. Though no clothes were made, the emperor and his people pretended they existed to prove they were fit for office. It took a child to show the folly in everyone's actions.

KeyPoints: We often do or say things because everyone else is doing it. Occasionally the things we do make little sense.

Questions: What trick did the tailors play on the Emperor and his subjects? Why do you think everyone acted like they saw the clothes? How difficult would it have been to admit that you didn't see anything? Do you think this courage would have paid off in the end? Who can think or examples of things we do or wear or say because we fear to be different from everyone else? What might we lose in the long run?

16. "Plato On Responsibility"

Pages: 246-250 BofV

Grade Levels: 10-12

Description: Dialogue - Between Crito and Socrates (by Plato). Socrates has been unjustly imprisoned and condemned to death. He refuses to escape on the grounds of breaking the law and hence abusing all that he has stood for.

Key Points: Socrates believes that his first responsibility is to follow the dictates of his conscience, to be honest to his convictions and to remain responsible to community, family and self. He could have succumbed to his friends' urgings and disregarded the law.

Questions: What issue was Socrates and his friend discussing? What was the advice of Crito? What were some of the reasons Socrates had for not following the advice of his friend? What course had Socrates chosen? Why didn't Socrates give in to peer pressure (Crito)? Can you think of some helpful things you can do to choose conscience over peer pressure?

17. "Jefferson Urges an Examination of Faith"

Pages: 791-794 BofV

Grade Levels: 7-12

Description: Letter - Jefferson counsels nephew to pay no heed to the opinions of others but employ his own faculties in determining morality. Jefferson does caution that one must first practice morality to strengthen one's faculties of discernment.

SHOW-OFF

1. "Ozymandias"
Pages: 68-69 BofV
Grade Levels: 7-12
Description: Poem: Describes how a monument now lays in ruin in stark contrast to its inscription of boastful grandeur.
Key Points: One's accomplishments of the moment, however wonderfully perceived, are rarely significant after the lapse of time. Those who pay too much mind to their own accomplishment and boast to others may find personal disappointment and even embarrassment when others are not as impressed.
Questions: How do you think Ozymandias felt about his accomplishments? How did this particular monument appear today? How do you think the sculptor saw this king? Who remembers an accomplishment that turned out less than originally supposed? Were you disappointed, embarrassed? How could each of these emotions been avoided?

2. "King Canute on the Seashore"
Pages: 25-27 YP, 67-68 BofV
Grade Levels: K-12
Description: Story - A king of England who recognized the pitfalls of receiving too much praise, taught his subjects a lesson on humility.
KeyPoints: An example of a wise king who went to great lengths to avoid boasting and pride. He took pains to remain level-headed and humble because he understood the problems induced through false pride.
Questions: What lesson did the king teach his subjects? Why do you think the king was so concerned over the praise he was receiving? What could it hurt? Can you think of instances when too much attention can be a bad thing?

3. "The Fox and the Crow"
Pages: 38 YP, 66 BofV
Grade Levels: K-9
Description: Fable - A crow is tricked by a hungry fox into releasing a juicy piece of meat. The fox accomplishes the trick by flattering the crow into singing.
KeyPoints: Often we pay a price for showing off.

Why would the crow be so foolish as to drop his meat? Can you think of an instance where showing off could cost you dearly? Who has seen a situation where showing off caused an accident or an embarrassment?

4. "Our Lips and Ears"
Pages: 25 YP, 44 BofV
Grade Levels: K-3
Description: Poem - Cautions against gossip and boasting.
KeyPoints: Provides excellent advice about bragging, boasting, etc. It warns that jeers may follow the boaster.
Questions: Who can give examples of any of the five things that should be observed with care? What is gossip? What is a jeer? Why would talking about yourself cause others to jeer?

5. "A Name in the Sand"
Pages: 777-778 BofV
Grade Levels: 4-12
Description: Poem - Describes how easily the tide destroys any impressions we might make in the sand. It relates this thought to our earthly contributions. Poem concludes that with God all impressions are recorded and honored for the eternities.
KeyPoints: Those who hope to impress others will find that their efforts are soon forgotten. Often, boasting or other forms of showing off are the only things remembered, and these usually leave negative impressions.
Questions: What happened when the person wrote her name, year and day in the sand? How did she relate this to life? How many of us feel a need to be noticed when we do something well? What are ways we use to draw attention to ourselves? Does the metaphor of the sand and tide apply to our attempts at recognition?

6. "St. Nicholas and the Golden Bars"
Pages: 763-765 BofV
Grade Levels: K-9
Description: Story - Describes incidents in the life of St. Nicholas. He comes to the aid of a nobleman who has fallen on hard times and anonymously shares some of his wealth.
KeyPoints: Many realize that their gift is only meaningful when it doesn't embarrass the receiver. Giving should be for the receiver's benefit and not for the giver's glory.

Questions: How did Nicholas come to be so wealthy? What was the problem the nobleman and his daughters were facing? How did Nicholas choose to help them? Why did he do it anonymously? Who can remember doing something nice for another without letting your generosity be known? Why did you do this? Why is it wrong to show off when you are doing something worthwhile? Who can it hurt?

7. "George Washington Rejects A Crown"
Pages: 717-718 BofV
Grade Levels: 4-12
Description: Letter - George Washington emphatically rejects the idea that he become King and America become like Britain.
KeyPoints: The Revolutionary War was fought to free the people from the tyranny of England. Washington did not want America to take that risk. Washington had opportunity to place himself at the highest level of power and recognition. He chose to reject this opportunity and allow his actions to speak for themselves.
Questions: What was the purpose of the letter? What opportunities would a kingship provide? Do you think Washington was unwise to give up this opportunity to show off his power? Why is Washington considered one of the greatest of leaders? What opportunities to show off present themselves in a school or home setting? What might happen if one chooses to flaunt his success? What might happen if one chooses to let the actions speak for themselves?

8. "The Story of Cincinnatus"
Pages: 671-674 BofV
Grade Levels: K-12
Description: Story - Describes how a humble Roman farmer leads Rome to victory. Concludes with the man willfully giving up his power and returning to his farm.
KeyPoints: True character does not expect recognition or material reward when something is accomplished. The quiet, steady approach to life will eventually be recognized and rewarded.
Questions: What did the people of Rome face? Why did the Roman Elders come to Cincinnatus in the first place? What was Cincinnatus able to accomplish? What did he choose to do after the threat of war ended? What successes might we achieve today? What often happens to those who seek out recognition? What often happens to those who do not?

9. "The Noble Nature"

Pages: 431 BofV

Grade Levels: 7-12

Description: Poem - Describes how we must view life as small snatches of growth that eventually come together to mold the virtuous man.

KeyPoints: Those who limit their focus to ostentatious expression or showmanship miss the point of life. Greatness is earned through small, but constant accomplishment.

Questions: How did the author feel about focusing on the 300-year-old oak as opposed to the lily-of-a-day? What does this mean in our everyday lives? Who are the popular role models of today? Why should we be careful in choosing a role model? What types of individuals achieve lasting fame because of the good lives that they lead? What characteristic do most of these individuals possess?

10. "The Village Blacksmith"

Pages: 397-398 BofV, 168-170 YP

Grade Levels: 4-12

Description: Poem - Describes an ideal individual who seems to always do the right thing but in a quiet way without notoriety or fanfare. He eventually is recognized for his dedication and industry.

KeyPoints: Those who allow their actions to speak for themselves eventually win the admiration and respect they deserve.

Questions: What characteristics of virtue were demonstrated by the village blacksmith? Did you see any indications that he boasted of these virtues? Do you think this was one of the reasons he was so admired by the author? How did the blacksmith find his joy? What are some of the valiant acts we can perform that often go unnoticed at first? What can result from making this sort of behavior a habit?

11. "The Darning Needle"

Pages: 360-362 BofV

Grade Levels: K-9

Description: Tale - Told from the perspective of a darning needle who had a tendency to view herself as an ornament rather than a tool. Her misguided pride caused her trouble after trouble. She rationalized each new degradation as yet another extension of her comeliness until she was left with nothing.

KeyPoints: Some place their energies with vain imaginations and boasting rather than in constructive efforts. These usually are left with nothing in the end.

Questions: What was the initial role of the pin? What were some of the things she saw in herself? Why did the practice prove disastrous? What are some of the things we dream and brag about at the expense of working hard? Why is this a foolish way to expend our energies?

12. "The Tortoise and the Hare"
Pages: 529-530 BofV
Grade Levels: K-9
Description: Fable - Describes how a boastful hare (rabbit) is beaten in a foot race by a tortoise. The tortoise's slow and deliberate pace proves a greater advantage than the hare's spurts and lulls.
KeyPoints: The hare brings on the eventual humiliation of defeat due to his boasting. The tortoise won because he focused on the race and not on who was paying attention to all the boasting and showing off.
Questions: What caused the tortoise to agree to a race? What was the hare's attitude? Who finally prevailed? What is foolish about boasting or other forms of showing off? Who do you think the fox was rooting for? Why?

13. "As Rich as Croesus"
Pages: 135-137 BofV, 46-50 YP
Grade Levels: 4-12
Description: Story - Describes a rich king who takes great pleasure in displaying his immense wealth. Eventually he is defeated in battle and scheduled for execution. He is saved, not for his wealth, but for another's compassion.
KeyPoints: Those who devote all time and attention to wealth or other possessions may find they do little good in a crisis. It's our associations that often make the difference when troubles occur.
Questions: What did Croesus choose to show Solon? How did he expect Solon to react? How did Solon react? What crisis occurred in Croesus' life? How important was his wealth at this time? Why? What are some things that people typically boast about today? How important are those things in a crisis? Why do you think it is wise to focus on developing friends or learning skills rather than vain boasting?

195

14. "Matilda, Who Told Lies, and Was Burned to Death"

Pages: 607-608 BofV

Grade Levels: K-9

Description: Poem - A little girl creates a stir by falsely claiming there is a fire in her house. Later, when a real fire occurs, she loses her life because no one responds to her alarm.

KeyPoints: The young girl enjoyed bringing attention to herself even when at the expense of others. Ultimately, there is always a price to pay. In this particular case, the consequence was rather extreme.

Questions: What trick did Matilda pull? Why do you think she did this? What finally happened to Matilda? What can happen when people tell lies or do too many things that bring attention to themselves? What are some other ways we can lose the respect of our friends and family?

15. "The Lie That Deserved Another"

Pages: 273-274 YP

Grade Levels: 4-12

Description: Tale - Describes a traveler who exaggerated about the sights he saw. His friends exposed his lies with an exaggeration of their own.

KeyPoints: Boasting or exaggerations usually are recognized for what they are. Those who show off by stretching the truth will soon lose the trust and respect of their friends.

Questions: What was the traveler's tale? Why did his friend chose another exaggeration? Who made the final point? Is it easy to recognize when someone is showing off by stretching the truth? Who can describe an instance where they gave in to this temptation. What happened as a result? Why is it foolish to show off in this way? What can one ultimately lose as a result of this foolish practice?

16. "Truth in Advertising"

Pages: 655-657 BofV

Grade Levels: 9-12

Description: Lecture - P.T. Barnum defines humbug as one who secures public attention but does it honestly and often for the public good. His example was the advertising of Warren's Blacking in large lettering on the pyramids of Egypt.

Key Points: This illustrates the difference between showing off in a business or political maneuver and showing off for the sake of vanity.

Questions: How did the author define humbug? How do you think the
author viewed the ploy of placing bold lettering on the
Pyramids of Ghiza? What would have been his argument?
What is the difference between showing off for sound reasons
and showing off for vanity? Is one more acceptable than the
other? Why? Who can cite a few examples of each?

17. "The Emperor's New Clothes"

Pages: 630-634 BofV

Grade Levels: 4-12

Description: Tale - An emperor, obsessed about wearing new clothes, is
duped by two rascals who claim they are making clothes that
will be invisible to every person not fit for office. Though no
clothes were made, the emperor and his people pretended they
existed to prove they were fit for office. It took a child to show
the folly in everyone's actions.

Key Points: Everyone was too concerned about appearances to see the
foolishness of their behavior. Those caught up in showing off
run the risk of losing perspective which can lead to foolish or
embarrassing behavior.

Questions: Why did the people lie about being able to see the clothes?
How did the people behave in order to show off their fitness for
office? What do you think of their behavior? What are other
forms of boasting or showing off that often occur? What
foolish behavior results from this showing off? Is it worth it?

18. "Insincere Honesty"

Pages: 647 BofV

Grade Levels: 4-12

Description: Tale - Describes a young man named Honest who reported his
father's theft of a sheep and then offered to bear the penalty.
All this was done, not for the sake of honesty, but to show off.

SLOPPY

1. "Washing"

Pages: 41-42 YP

Grade Levels: K-3

Description: Poem - Describes a little child who has trouble understanding why personal grooming is important but prays that someday he will understand and do it.

Key Points: This child is having difficulty accepting cleanliness as worth the effort it requires, yet he wants to see its value. Poem provides a clue as to how one changes behavior and values. "Please show me how I always can do simple things that lead to..."

Questions: Have any of you failed to see the reason for looking your very best? Can you remember occasions when your parents insisted on proper grooming and clothes? Why do you think they chose to be so insistent about how you look?

2. "Dirty Jim"

Pages: 40-41 YP

Grade Levels: K-6

Description: Poem - Describes a boy who refuses to maintain personal cleanliness despite the urging and assistance of his friends. The author points out that being poor is not an excuse.

Key Points: Despite encouragement from his friends, Jim refused to make the effort to be clean. Eventually his friends began to complain, and most chose playmates other than Jim. You may still have few riches yet still maintain cleanliness of clothes and body.

Questions: If you asked Jim why he was always dirty, how do you think he would reply? Did the poem give a clue of whether or not Jim was too poor to stay clean? Why is it important to develop the habit of maintaining good personal grooming? What might happen if you choose not to?

3. "Up From Slavery"

Pages: 404-408 YP

Grade Levels: 4-12

Description: Story - Describes select events in the life of Booker T. Washington. This particular account describes his efforts to gain the means and opportunity for a formal education.

Key Points: Booker T. Washington learned to value neatness and order.

Questions: Why did Washington learn to look on Mrs. Hampton as one of his best friends? What did he learn from her? What value is there in learning to appreciate order and cleanliness? What are ways we practice the habits of neatness and cleanliness? Where are some areas we can work on? Why are these virtues wise things to develop?

4. "Quality"
Pages: 425-430 YP
Grade Levels: 4-12
Description: Story - Describes selected events in the life of a bootmaker who stood for the highest standards of quality.
Key Points: Some have come to value quality beyond normally expected levels. These serve as examples to those who accept shoddiness and fail to see value in higher expectations.
Questions: What distinguished these bootmakers from their competitors? Was this a good trait or bad trait? Where do you draw the line? Why is concern for one's efforts and appearances an important thing? What can happen to those who acquire a tolerance for sloppiness or halfhearted effort?

5. "Rebecca"
Pages: 191-192 BofV
Grade Levels: K-6
Description: Poem - Describes a little girl's deep sense of responsibility in tending to the many needs of her doll including grooming.
Key Points: The young child found a sense of accomplishment in maintaining a high sense of grooming for her doll. This sense of accomplishment will follow any act or project that is done well.
Questions: What were some of the things the girl did for her doll? Why do you think she did these sorts of things? How do you think she felt afterwards? Why do you think we gain a feeling of accomplishment when we put the finishing touches on projects? What are some of the things we should keep up with?

6. "For Want of a Horseshoe Nail"
Pages: 198-200 BofV, 88-90 YP
Grade Levels: K-12
Description: Story - Describes how, for the want of a horseshoe nail, the battle and kingdom were lost. With his horse unable to run, King Richard failed to rally his troops and consequently lost the battle and his kingdom.
Key Points: Neglect of the little things can cause catastrophe. It usually pays to give heed to the small details. Sloppy and careless work can ruin an entire venture.

Why did Richard's horse fail to perform? Who was at fault? What happened as a result of the missing horseshoe? Why is neatness and careful work a good thing to practice? Where are areas where these traits can and should be practiced?

7. "Sir Walter Raleigh"

Pages: 200-201 BofV
Grade Levels: 4-12
Description: Story - Describes the chivalry of Sir Walter Raleigh who placed his beautiful scarlet cloak in the mud as a bridge way for the Queen of England. He was later rewarded for his chivalry.
Key Points: Courtesy and careful attention to detail rest on a deep moral foundation. Being observant for opportunities to be courteous and chivalrous can be habit forming--a habit that brings much satisfaction and occasional reward. Raleigh saw to it that the queen had a means to cross the muddy street without personal affront. This concern for detail paid off handsomely for Raleigh.
Questions: What act of courtesy did Sir Walter Raleigh perform? What does this have to do with caring greatly for the quality of your efforts? What could Raleigh have done otherwise? Would any other act have impressed the queen as much? What similar situations warrant our consideration?

8. "The Man Who Tossed Stones"

Pages: 113-114 YP
Grade Levels: 4-9
Description: Tale - Describes how a rich man eventually paid for his habit of cluttering the road with stones he had no use for. Now poor and desolate, the man stumbled on the very rocks he had carelessly discarded.
Key Points: The man channeled his disregard for others' welfare by cluttering areas that were not his own. He paid the price for his actions down the road. This often happens when neatness and appearance are limited to one's personal satisfaction. We often pay a personal price when we pay little heed to our environment.
Questions: What habit had the rich man practiced during his years of plenty? What does this say about his concern for others? What price did he ultimately pay? Who can think of instances where we show our disregard for everyone but ourselves? How might life pay us back?

STEALING

1. "Seeing Gold"
Pages: 28 YP
Grade Levels: 4-9
Description: Short Story - Man steals gold jewelry in a crowded marketplace and is apprehended by police. When asked why he would steal with so many people around he confesses to not seeing the people because of being blinded by the gold.
Key Points: Greed can blind us to possible consequences to our actions. Eventually, we will pay the consequence to stealing or similar crimes.
Questions: What crime did the man commit? How is it possible that the man did not notice the number of people witnessing his theft? Can anyone think of instances where an overwhelming desire for something caused someone to lose track of what they were doing.

2. "Thunder Falls"
Pages: 686-689 BofV, 333-338 YP
Grade Levels: 4-12
Description: Story - Describes two brave Indian women who sacrificed their lives in order to save their tribesmen from additional massacre.
Key Points: The attacking Shawnee were not content with the success of their first acts of theft and destruction. They continued on until they lost everything including their lives.
Questions: What did the Shawnee accomplish in their first raid? Why did they choose to continue in their quest for further bloodshed and spoils? What finally happened as a result of their greed? What are some of the things we steal today? What often happens to those who continue to want more and more? Is it worth it in the long run?

3. "The Cattle of the Sun"
Pages: 79-81 BofV
Grade Levels: 4-12
Description: Myth - Describes an incident in Homer's Odyssey where Ulysses and his men meet with disaster because they fail to heed wise counsel. The men's resolve to avoid enticements quickly evaporates when they react to the foolish words of a crew member. Their impulsive reaction ends up costing them their lives.

Key Points: The crew members chose to ignore Ulysses' warnings because they were weary and hungry. They chose to take matters into their own hands by stealing and butchering cattle that were not theirs to enjoy. Here is an instance where the men tried to justify their actions and came to pay a heavy price for their misdeed.

Questions: Why do you think the crew members chose to ignore Ulysses' warnings? What happened as a result? Can you think of situations today where we act foolishly because we feel like our circumstances warrant breaking the law? Why is this a foolish pattern of thought and action?

4. "Eureka"

Pages: 562-564 BofV

Grade Levels: 4-12

Description: Story - Describes how Archimedes invents a means to determine whether or not his king has been cheated by a goldsmith. Observing how bulk displaces water, he realizes that he can use this same principle in determining if the king's crown is made of pure gold. His experiment proves that the goldsmith cheated the king.

Key Points: Stealing can take many forms. Eventually someone will figure out a deceitful plan and bring the thief to justice.

Questions: What question did the king place before Archimedes? Did Archimedes have an immediate answer? How did Archimedes eventually come up with the means to determine if the crown was made of pure gold? What things should a person pay attention to? What are things that usually aren't worth our attention? What advantage is there in staying in focus?

5. "Cat and Mouse in Partnership"

Pages: 272-274 BofV

Grade Levels: K-9

Description: Tale - Describes how a mouse is betrayed by his partner and "would be" friend, the cat. The cat uses deceit to steal the mouse's portion of their winter food supplies.

Key Points: This tale illustrates a form of stealing that might not be recognized by all young people. Someone taking more than his fair share is a common practice that often leads to greater conflict down the road.

Questions: What agreement had the mouse and cat entered into? What trick did the cat use to eat all the honey? What eventually happened when the mouse confronted the cat with the truth?

Did the cat steal from the mouse? Who can think of instances where people steal from others by taking more than their fair share? Why is this wrong?

6. **"The Pied Piper of Hamelin"**
   Pages: 627-629 BofV
   Grade Levels: 4-12
   Description: Story - For a set fee the mayor and town council make a deal with the Pied Piper to rid the town of its rats. Once the rats are gone the mayor refuses to pay the agreed upon amount. As a result the Pied Piper lures all the children away from the town.
   Key Points: Agreements should be kept even when it appears that the one with whom you have made the agreement got the better of the deal. Those who refuse to honor a contract are practicing a form of stealing, and the consequences can be severe.
   Questions: What were the terms of the original contract concerning the removal of the rats? What reasons did the mayor have for refusing to pay the full $50? What were the consequences of this broken promise? Could it be considered stealing to break a contract of this nature? Why? Can anyone think of other examples of stealing that do not fit the basic pattern for theft?

7. **"Someone Sees You"**
   Pages: 604 BofV
   Grade Levels: K-12
   Description: Folktale - Describes a farmer's scheme to steal wheat from his neighbors' fields without being seen. The man asks his daughter to warn him if anyone sees his stealing. His daughter reminds him that someone always sees him from above.
   Key Points: Stealing always hurts another. In this case, the greatest loss was suffered by the thief. He lost the respect of his daughter. One can also lose respect for one's self.
   Questions: What plan did the man devise to steal from his neighbor? What part was the man's daughter to play? How did she respond? What effect do you suppose the father's stealing had upon his daughter? Who do you think suffered as a result of the stealing? Why?

8. **"The Devoted Son and the Thief"**
   Pages: 112-113 YP
   Grade Levels: K-9
   Description: Tale - Describes how a young man accepts his losses as he watches a thief rob him and his elderly mother. He only

protests when the thief takes the pot the young man needs to prepare food for his mother. The thief is moved by this devotion and returns all that he has taken.

Key Points: Often we don't realize the hurt we cause in others when we steal. Usually there is an undeserving victim when we steal or commit similar acts.

Questions: What items did the thief steal? Why did the young man react to the taking of the old pot? Why do you think the young man's words changed the thief's attitude? Do you think most thieves stop to think of who they might be harming? Why is it important to think things through when one is tempted to steal something that isn't his to begin with?

9. "The Chest of Broken Glass"

Pages: 202-204 BofV, 109-111 YP

Grade Levels: K-12

Description: Tale - describes how a dying old man plays a trick on his three sons as a test to determine if they had kept the commandment to honor thy father and mother. They fail the test and realize their mistakes.

Key Points: It is easy to rationalize away our responsibility to honor our father and mother. This is a form of stealing when we fail to assume the burdens of our loved ones. In effect we are stealing the blessings due them because of our neglect.

Questions: What trick did the father play? How did the three sons react? What finally happened? How did the sons react when they realized what their father had done? What had the sons been denying their father? How might this be considered stealing? What responsibility do we have to our loved ones and close friends?

SUBSTANCE ABUSE

1. **"Terence, This Is Stupid Stuff"**
Pages: 95-97 BofV
Grade Levels: 10-12
Description: Poem - Describes our tendency to resort to intoxication rather than endure the pain and troubles of life. Author suggests alternatives and cites the example of an ancient king who purposely ingested small doses of poison to build up immunity.
Key Points: Author concedes that life has more bad than good but advocates defenses or cures less destructive than intoxication. It is pointed out that one always comes off a "high" with the same circumstances, problems, etc.
Questions: According to the author, what is the problem with temporary escapes through intoxication? What alternative to intoxication does the author suggest in dealing with life's troubles? What are alternatives that might replace today's tendency to abuse drugs for escape from the troubles in life?

2. **"The Vulture"**
Pages: 46 YP
Grade Levels: K-9
Description: Poem - Compares a vulture's unflattering characteristics with the effects from eating between meals.
Key Points: This has to do with self-control with regards to our eating. It takes courage to say no to our appetites.
Questions: How serious a matter is overeating or steady eating? Why was a vulture a good choice for showing the results of poor eating habits? Who can remember instances where they overdid their eating? Why is it a good thing to be in control of what and when you put things in your body? What can happen to a person who has no control over appetites?

3. **"The Bramblebush"**
Pages: 377-378 YP
Grade Levels: K-12
Description: Parable - Describes how a man puts off the removal of his bramblebush even though it is obstructing passage on a road. As he waits, the bush grows younger and healthier while he grows older and weaker. Eventually he is unable to remove the bush.
Key Points: The bush is a metaphor for bad habits. The hold of the bramblebush was insignificant at first and could easily have

been removed. Eventually it gained too large a hold on the situation, and the man was nearly powerless to cast it away. So it is with drugs and the like.

Questions: Do you think it would have been an easy matter to remove the bramblebush immediately? Why didn't the man act immediately? Why was it that the bush eventually grew too difficult a thing to cast away? What bramblebushes must we deal with in today's world? How do these addictions relate to the bramblebush? Why is it that we allow them to grow so strong?

4. "The Kids Can't Take It If We Don't Give It"

Pages: 778-781 BofV

Grade Levels: 4-12

Description: Story - Babe Ruth describes his early youth and the training he received about right and wrong. He confesses how difficult it was for him to remember and live the principles he had learned but conceded that they still had their effects during his years of rough living. He pulled things together in his late years.

Key Points: Ruth's greatest regrets were when he let down the kids because he was too anxious to enjoy life to the fullest. In these instances, he let everyone down--himself, his ball team and the fans.

Questions: Who can recall from the story the Babe's worst moments in life? How can he say these were his worst moments when he described these times as those when he was anxious to enjoy life to the fullest? What sorts of things do you think he did in living life to its fullest? What new abuses are available today for those who think they are living life to the fullest? What happens to the abusers of today?

5. "Tom Sawyer Gives Up the Brush"

Pages: 398-402 BofV

Grade Levels: 4-9

Description: Story - Describes how Tom Sawyer is able to convince the boys in his town that painting a fence is a privilege. He manages to free himself up from his chore while actually having the boys pay him to do his work.

Key Points: Sometimes things are presented in such a way that they sound much better than they are.

Questions: How was Tom able to get the boys to pay him to do his work? Does it make sense to you? Why do you think it made sense to them at the time? What are some of the things in today's world that are made to sound much better than they really are? How can you be sure that you don't make a mistake and do something that might turn out to be very foolish and perhaps destructive?

6. "The Sword of Damocles"
Pages: 213-215 BofV, YP 114
Grade Levels: K-12
Description: Story - Describes a king (Dionysius) who was much envied by his friend (Damocles). Damocles was made "King for a Day" and learned of the awesome burdens that accompanied the benefits of kingship.
Key Points: The thrill of being king was offset by the constant risk of the sword's sharp point. So also is the situation with substance abuse. The risks are not worth the anticipated rewards.
Questions: What did Damocles expect when he was given the opportunity to be king for a day? How did it actually turn out? Why do you think Damocles decided that being king wasn't such a good thing? What things in our lives seem like fun but carry great risks? What are some of the risks that accompany drug abuse? What means can you think of to turn these temptations down when they are offered?

7. "The Little Hero of Holland"
Pages: 533-535 BofV
Grade Levels: K-9
Description: Story - Describes how a little boy shows foresight and courage when he plugs up a small hole in a water dike with his finger and then holds on until help finally arrives.
Key Points: Boy could see how a little problem could lead to a big problem. He had the foresight and courage to stop the tragedy before it was allowed to spread and worsen. Substance abuse is an easy problem to correct at first. Those with foresight and courage will never allow its spread.
Questions: What little problem did the little boy discover? Why did he chose to do what he did? Why was his timing a major factor in this story? What major disaster did he avoid? Who can think of things that are easy to correct at first, but left unattended will eventually prove an almost overwhelming problem? What is the best way to handle these situations?

8. "The Rich Man's Feast"

Pages: 50-51 YP

Grade Levels: 4-9

Description: Poem - Illustrates an extreme example of obsessive greed. Here, a man too poor to own a lamp is driven from an obscure place where he shared another's light because it was perceived that this somehow deprived the wealthy owner.

Key Points: Developing a strong need for something can distort our sense of reality. One must guard against desires that have the capacity to rule thoughts and compromise compassion and sound judgment.

Questions: What did the poor man desire of his wealthy neighbor? What was the wealthy man's response? Can one steal light? Why then was the poor man cast out? What was the problem here? Can anyone think of something that people will want so much that they willingly will compromise what they know is right? What distortions of reality can occur when one becomes "hooked" on something?

9. "George Washington and the Cherry Tree"

Pages: 605-606 YP

Grade Levels: K-9

Description: Story - George Washington, as a small boy, used his new hatchet to cut down a valuable cherry tree. In a thoughtless moment, the boy destroyed the tree's future just for the sake of a few moment's pleasure.

Key Points: Young George abused the tree and destroyed its future--all because he wanted a few moments of pleasure. Much like this tree, a life can be destroyed simply because a person desired a few moments of pleasure.

Questions: How did the father feel about the tree? What abuse did the tree suffer? What did the future now hold for the tree? Would the tree ever be provided a second chance? How are we like the tree? What kind of abuse might cause us to lose our future?

10. "The Character of a Happy Life"

Pages: 619 BofV, YP 263

Grade Levels: 4-12

Description: Poem - Describes a person of the highest form. Honesty truth, self-control, purity, humility, prayerfulness, etc. are all part of this person's makeup. It concludes with stating that this individual has it all.

Key Points: The path to a happy life "whose conscience is his strong retreat" is honesty and self-control. Our bodies are much like this wonderful individual. We have it all so long as we maintain the virtue (or health) that earns us the right to have it all. What a shame it is to destroy this perfect state of happiness through acts of abuse.

Questions: What are some of the attributes of this esteemed, happy individual? What do you think is meant by "having nothing, yet having it all?" What changes must take place for this person to lose what he has? Who can see how this might compare with our bodies? What changes could occur that would rob us of our physical gifts? What sorts of abuses might force these changes? Why are these actions costly and very foolish?

11. "The Frog Prince"

Pages: 623-626 BofV

Grade Levels: 4-12

Description: Tale - Describes how a prince, who had been turned into a frog, was once again made prince. This was made possible because the king's daughter kept her promise (at the king's insistence).

Key Points: Make promises only after gaining a full understanding of all the implications. The promises may turn out to be more than one bargains for. Promises made to friends can lead to involvement with drugs and other abuses.

Questions: What agreement did the princess and frog make? Why did the princess neglect her end of the agreement? Why do you think she made the promise in the first place? What should the princess have done prior to making such a strange agreement? Can anyone think of agreements that we might make without counting all the costs? What might be the consequences of these agreements? Who might serve the king's part and pressure you to keep your agreement?

12. "Mr. Vinegar and His Fortune"

Pages: 48-52 BofV

Grade Levels: K-9

Description: Story - A man and wife, in seeking their fortune, come upon robber's gold. On impulse, the man trades the gold for a cow and then continues trading until he is left with nothing but a walking stick.

Key Points: When you always act on first impulse and never think things through, you eventually may find yourself with nothing.

209

Questions: Do you think the old man was a wise trader? What did he base his trades on? What are real-life examples of things we immediately decide on that later turn out to be disasters? How can we avoid this? What things do we trade off when we choose to get involved with drugs?

13. "The Cattle of the Sun"
Pages: 79-81 BofV
Grade Levels: 4-12

Description: Myth - Describes an incident in Homer's Odyssey where Ulysses and his men meet with disaster because they fail to heed wise counsel. The men's resolve to avoid enticements quickly evaporates when they react to the foolish words of a crew member. Their impulsive reaction ends up costing them their lives.

Key Points: The crew members chose to ignore Ulysses' warnings, because they were first weary and then hungry. They were killed as a result of their hasty and foolish decision.

Questions: Why do you think the crew members chose to ignore Ulysses' warnings? What happened as a result? Can you think of situations today where we act foolishly because we want something right away? Who can think of things we feel we must have now only to learn of their destructive nature down the road?

NOTE: THE AUTHORS SUGGEST THAT THE READER REFER TO SECTIONS ON "IMPULSIVE," "INDULGENT" AND PEER PRESSURE" FOR ADDITIONAL MATERIAL THAT ADDRESSES "SUBSTANCE ABUSE."

TARDINESS

1. "The Last Lesson"
Pages: 727-731 BofV
Grade Levels: 4-12
Description: Story - Describes the last school day of a French schoolmaster who has taught his lessons in his native French for the past forty years. The country, now occupied by Nazi Germany, is losing its right to teach its own curriculum and own language. Describes how certain individuals became mindful that they had let precious learning opportunities slip by.
Key Points: We seldom appreciate our heritage and freedoms until after they are taken away from us. Here is a dramatic instance where those who postponed learning opportunities lost their opportunity to make up the lost ground.
Questions: What were the circumstances accompanying this sad day? Why were so many thinking back to what they hadn't gotten done? What are some things we have a tendency to be late on? Why is punctuality such a wise virtue to practice? What usually happens to those who allow tardiness to become a habit?

2. "Mr. Meant-To"
Pages: 364 BofV
Grade Levels: K-6
Description: Poem - Describes how those who postpone their tasks, rarely win.
Key Points: Those who put off or postpone their tasks will often fail to get the job done. Habitual tardiness can lead to many lost opportunities.
Questions: What types of individuals do you think Meant-To and Didn't-Do are? Why do you think they live in the house of Never-Win? What are some of the things we often postpone? Which of these things never get done or are completed inadequately? Why is tardiness a foolish habit to develop? What might you lose?

3. "The Sin of Omission"
Pages: 138-139 BofV, 69-70 YP
Grade Levels: 4-9
Description: Poem - Describes how the key to service is in acting on a problem without compulsion or hope for recognition. It concludes with the thought that slow compassion or things left

undone will forfeit the satisfaction that accompanies true service.

Key Points: Subtle message that those who are slow (tardy) to act when they see a problem will find little sense of accomplishment. The timing of service is often the determinant of its worth and its personal reward.

Questions: What were some of the author's thoughts on what constituted a person's standing so far as serving others is concerned? What did the author mean by "slow compassion" or "tarrying until too late?" Why does the author talk about heartache? Who can think of instances when tardiness might deny one that feeling of accomplishment?

4. "What Have We Done Today"

Pages: 384-385 BofV
Grade Levels: 4-9
Description: Poem - Describes how our intentions, however noble, are nothing if they are not acted upon.

5. "The Little Hero of Holland"

Pages: 533-535 BofV
Grade Levels: K-9
Description: Story - Describes how a little boy shows foresight and courage when he plugs up a small hole in a water dike with his finger and then holds on until help finally arrives.

TEMPER DISPLAYS

1. "The King and His Hawk"

Pages: 37-39 BofV

Grade Levels: 4-12

Description: Describes Genghis Khan, upon returning from a hunting trip, stops by a stream for a cup of water. His trained pet hawk repeatedly knocks away his filled cup before he drinks. Eventually in temper, Khan slays the hawk only to find that the hawk knew the water was poisonous.

Key Points: Genghis Khan didn't take the time to find out why his pet hawk was acting strangely. Instead, he allowed his temper to flare until it overcame his better judgment.

Questions: Why did the Khan kill his pet? Was this action a foolish thing to do? Can anyone recall a personal example when they lost their temper without understanding the full situation? How did you feel afterwards? Why is it wise to allow yourself enough time to learn all the facts before making judgment? What might this extra time do for you?

2. "Let Dogs Delight to Bark and Bite"

Pages: 37 YP

Grade Levels: K-3

Description: Poem - Illustrates how children should differ from dogs, bears and lions with respect to anger and fighting.

Key Points: Poem points out that while it appears natural for certain animals to be aggressive, it should not be the case for children. The inference is that children who fight are patterning their actions after animals of lesser judgment.

Questions: What animals did the author mention in his poem? Why do you think these animals were chosen? Do you agree that children should act differently than animals with respect to fighting? What do you think the rising of angry passions means? Can you think of examples? What is wrong about losing your temper?

3. "Anger"

Pages: 40 BofV

Grade Levels: 4-9

Description: Poem - Compares a mild form of anger to the bee who stings when provoked but then flies away. This is contrasted to the snake who seems to carry a grudge and strikes without provocation.

213

Key Points: Mild temper is somewhat acceptable if truly provoked and gently expressed. Uncontrolled and sustained anger is never appropriate. It usually causes great harm to everyone including he who spews it forth.

Questions: How does the author describe the bee's anger as opposed to the snake's disposition? What may be some valid reasons for mild anger? What are appropriate ways to express it? Has anyone had a personal example? Who can think of an example of prolonged and strong anger? What often happens to a snake that has struck at someone? What are some of the things that can happen because someone has lost their temper?

4.   "The Poor Man and His Seeds"
Pages: 165 YP
Grade Levels: 4-9

Description: Tale - Describes how a poor farmer inadvertently drops a few of his sorely needed seeds. Rather than mourn his loss, he decides to recover his lost seeds. After much digging he uncovers a buried treasure.

Key Points: The poor farmer had every cause to grow upset over his misfortune. Instead, he channeled his energy to resolving his problem. The buried treasure came as an unexpected bonus.

Questions: Why were the lost seeds so important? What did the poor man choose to do? What came as a result of his efforts? Why do you think people have a tendency to lose their tempers when misfortune arises? What do temper tantrums accomplish? What rewards can you expect when you channel your energy to solving the problem that upset you?

5.   "Solitude"
Pages: 552-553 BofV, 244-245 YP
Grade Levels: 4-12

Description: Poem - Argues that those who focus their relationships on what is wrong about life will often walk alone. Suggests that we work out our problems discretely and maintain relationships with others.

Key Points: Those who have tendency to display inward turmoil (including temper displays) will turn off most people and reduce the likelihood of outside help.

Questions: What is typical of the actions that attract the companionship of others? What is typical of the actions that drive people away? Why do you think this is so? Who can think of an instance where a person turned you off because they were too negative or too upset about something? Why is it wise to maintain composure and a positive demeanor?

6. "How Robin Hood Met Little John"
Pages: 308-311 BofV
Grade Levels: 4-9
Description: Story - Describes the circumstances of Robin Hood's and Little John's first introduction to each other.
Key Points: Each man was ready to fight at the first provocation. While it eventually turned out fine, it was possible that one of these two (who later became devoted friends) might have received serious harm or even death as a result of their tempers.
Questions: What caused the two to fight? What clues do we have that one or both might have been seriously hurt? How did they eventually feel about each other?   Why was the fight unnecessary? Has anyone ever been involved in a conflict because one or the other lost his temper? What are some of the things that can occur when someone becomes too angry?

7. "Little Girls Wiser Than Men"
Pages: 318-319 BofV
Grade Levels: K-9
Description: Story - Describes how a minor spat between two little girls prompts a near brawl from their parents and relatives. All learn a lesson when it's noticed that the two little girls have made up despite the growing hostilities of the adults.
Key Points: This story illustrates the foolishness of many fights. Often we allow the spontaneity of the situation to cloud our judgment and trigger our anger.
Questions: What caused the two little girls' conflict? How did the adults react to the situation? What lesson did the adults learn from observing the little girls' resumption of play? What could have happened had the adults continued to carry on? Who can think of an instance where people joined an argument or fight without first learning the circumstances? Why is this a foolish course of action?

8. "The Gift of the Magi"
Pages: 166-170 BofV, 62-69 YP
Grade Levels: 7-12
Description: Story - Describes how a husband and wife sacrifice much to purchase a Christmas gift for each other. They find their sacrifices only serve to lessen the value of the gift they are to

215

receive. They are able to smile despite how poorly things worked out.

Key Points: Despite grounds for frustration and friction, the husband was able to keep his composure and find humor in the situation.

Questions: What did the wife sacrifice to buy the watch chain? What did the husband sacrifice to purchase the combs? How did they resolve their problem? Do you think this may have been frustrating? How could the couple have handled this unfortunate occurrence? What would angry words or bitter feelings have accomplished? Why is it wise to think of positive things when misfortune occurs?

9. "King Alfred and the Cakes"

Pages: 196-198 BofV, 94-96 YP

Grade Levels: K-12

Description: Story - Describes how King Alfred fails to fulfill his responsibility to watch over some cakes in the oven. He is scolded for his inattention by the woman of the house. Eventually the two work out their problem satisfactorily.

Key Points: The woodcutter's wife was quick to lose her temper and judge the King's actions without understanding all circumstances.

Questions: What did King Alfred fail to do? What caused him to be so inattentive? Do you think it was justified? What was the wife's response? What should she have done before making up her mind? What are some things that we often lose our temper over? Do our judgments always turn out to be the right ones when we judge in haste? How can we avoid losing our tempers?

10. "Cain and Abel"

Pages: 205-206 BofV

Grade Levels: K-12

Description: Story - Recounts world's first recorded murder--that of Cain killing Abel. Cain denies his crime, does not accept responsibility and is not repentant.

Key Points: Cain was angry with both his brother and the Lord. He chose to vent his anger rather than to seek understanding. Both Cain and his brother pay a dear price for Cain's loss of temper

Questions: What did Cain do to his brother? What reasons did the story give for Cain's act of murder? Do you think this murder was justified? What punishment did Cain receive? What could Cain have done otherwise? What are some of the reasons we lose our tempers? What bad things can happen when we lose our tempers?

11. "The Silent Couple"
Pages: 215-216 BofV
Grade Levels: K-12
Description: Tale - Describes the disastrous results of a recently married couple who allowed anger and stubbornness to control their actions.
Key Points: Our tempers can lead us to foolish acts. We often lose good judgment when we lose our tempers.
Questions: What contest was agreed to by the newly wedded couple? What happened as a result of the tempers and stubbornness? Do you think they acted wisely? Why would they follow through on such a foolish agreement? Can anyone think of an instance when someone acted foolishly because they lost their temper? How does one control temper? What should be done after one loses one's temper? What shouldn't be done?

217

TIMIDITY

1. "Our Lady's Juggler"

Pages: 782-787 BofV, 362-369 YP

Grade Levels: 7-12

Description: Story - Describes how a juggler chooses to become a monk in order to better serve the Mother Mary. After much despondency over his lack of skills, he finds happiness in finding that sharing his one talent of juggling is as acceptable as anything else he might offer.

Key Points: The juggler was too hung up on what he couldn't do to see what he could accomplish.

Questions: What was Barnaby's trade? How did he come to be a monk? Why was he so discouraged in his new calling? What did he finally come to understand? What are some of the limitations that people place on themselves? How does it make us feel when we view ourselves as inadequate? Do you think one success can lead to others?

2. "In Praise of the Strenuous Life"

Pages: 416-418 BofV

Grade Levels: 7-12

Description: Speech - Teddy Roosevelt speaks of both individuals' and nations' needs to lead the strenuous life. Whether one works for a livelihood or for the betterment of mankind makes little difference. He states that the key is that all must be actively engaged in some fruitful endeavor.

Key Points: What we do is not as important as the fact that we are doing something. Those that are timid should choose endeavors that build their courage and resolve to do more.

Questions: What did Roosevelt expect of the individual who is born into a life of ease or who finds himself in a position to have little need to work for a living? How does he feel about those too timid to try or take a stand on an issue? What approach might we take to build our courage to get involved? Why is it important to face life with courage?

3. "Kill Devil Hill"

Pages: 418-422 BofV, 154-160 YP

Grade Levels: 4-12

Description: Story - Describes the events at Kitty Hawk on the day the Wright brothers successfully flew their first airplane.

Key Points: The Wright brothers were never focused on the risks of their flying ventures. Instead, they used each mishap as a means to adjust their efforts.

Questions: How did many of the people of Kitty Hawk view the efforts of the Wright brothers? Do you think this might have been discouraging? Why did the brothers pick a windy day for their flight even though it might prove more dangerous? What can you always be assured of if you give up or never begin? Who can think of an instance where someone advised you to give something up because it was due to fail? How should you react?

4. "Sail On! Sail On!"

Pages: 565-566 BofV, 232-233 YP
Grade Levels: 4-12
Description: Poem - Describes the imagination, daring and determination of Christopher Columbus in discovering America.
Key Points: Columbus had no one to lean on for strength except his God and his own inner courage. Because he was fixed on a goal, he was able to overcome his fears and obstacles.
Questions: What were some of the complaints and concerns expressed by the mate? How did Columbus respond to these worries? Why is it hard to act without the support of others? How do you think Columbus was able to hold his course despite the lack of support? What good things can result from courage to act on what you feel is right?

5. "Try, Try Again"

Pages: 532 BofV
Grade Levels: K-6
Description: Poem - Describes the need to keep trying. It argues that persistence brings success which in turn develops courage.
Key Points: Timidity can be overcome by continually trying until success is achieved. This perseverance also leads to a greater courage. Success provides the seed for continued success.
Questions: What does the author ask of a person? What does the author promise to those who heed his advise? Do you agree? What are some things we are timid about doing? Why is it wise to ignore defeats and continue trying? What is the payback for this effort?

6. **"Androcles and the Lion"**
    Pages: 118-119 BofV
    Grade Levels: K-9
    Description: Fable - Describes how a runaway slave befriends a lion who in turn saves the slave from certain death.
    Key Points: Androcles didn't have to help the lion. His runaway status as well as the unpredictability of the beast would have been sufficient reason for him to keep his distance. His courage paid off in the end.
    Questions: Why was Androcles on the run? How did he help the lion? Would Androcles have been justified in avoiding the lion? How did the lion eventually return his kindness? What opportunities for courage do we have on a daily basis? What about instances when timidity seems justified? Why does it make sense to take a risk when the cause is just?

7. **"Truth Is Mighty and Will Prevail"**
    Pages: 615-616 BofV
    Grade Levels: K-12
    Description: Story - King Darius proclaims Zerubbabel winner of a contest where contestants choose the "strongest thing in the world." Zerubbabel chooses truth and is rewarded with a promise to have his people's temple rebuilt.
    Key Points: Zerubbabel chose an answer that was not flattering to the king. Because he chose wisely and acted through the exercise of his conscience, he impressed the king and won the reward. His actions took courage.
    Questions: What three choices were presented before the king? Why do you think the king was most impressed with Zerubbabel's choice? Do you think it required courage on Zerubbabel's part to speak his conscience? Why? Who can think of an instance when it might be difficult to speak one's mind? What is gained by such courage?

8. **"The Funeral Oration of Pericles"**
    Pages: 244-246 BofV
    Grade Levels: 7-12
    Description: Speech - Pericles (475 B.C.) delivers this oration to honor Athenians killed in battle. He describes the principles upon which their democracy was built.
    Key Points: We should be an example to many rather than imitators of others. This requires courage. Those who must first look to others before acting will never achieve their fullest potential.

220

Questions: What was the occasion for this speech? What was the message behind Pericles' first line. Do you think this practice was a factor in Athens' greatness? Who can think of an instance when someone was timid about moving forward and lost out to someone else? Where are areas in our day-to-day lives where bold action usually pays off?

9. "The Charge of the Light Brigade"
Pages: 220-222 BofV
Grade Levels: 7-12
Description: Poem - Describes a battle during the Crimean War (1854) between British cavalry and a Russian artillery line. Only 195 out of 673 survived. Demonstrates obedience, courage and self-sacrifice.
Key Points: Acting without complaints or hesitancies is sometimes required of soldiers and citizens. Often the benefits are indiscernible and take months and years before fruition. The courage ultimately pays off.
Questions: What was asked of the six hundred? What were the results of the charge? Why did they do this? Do we need to know all the immediate reasons for fulfilling an assignment? When do we act even though all the reasons for the action remain unknown?

10. "St. George and the Dragon"
Pages: 192-195 BofV, 96-100 YP
Grade Levels: K-9
Description: Story - Describes a knight (Sir George) on quest of duties that only a knight can perform. He finds a country about to be destroyed by a dragon, kills the dragon and is eventually made king.
Key Points: When we decide on a course, we must be prepared to accept the challenges that will confront us. Those with the courage to choose a noble course will eventually earn their reward.
Questions: Why were all of the people hiding within the walls of the city? Why was the king's daughter purposely trying to find the dragon? What did Sir George do to earn him the love and respect of the people? When did Sir George first commit himself to action? Why did this require courage? What early commitments can we make that will require courage but will always pay off in the end?

11. "The Ride of Collins Graves"

Pages: 173-175 BofV

Grade Levels: 7-12

Description: Poem - Describes the courage of a man who risked his life to warn others of onrushing flood waters.

12. "Great Men"

Pages: 418 BofV

Grade Levels: 4-9

Description: Poem - Describes how man's effort and not material wealth makes a nation great.

13. "Concord Hymn"

Pages: 713 BofV

Grade Levels: 4-12

Description: Poem - A tribute to the embattled farmers who fought the professional British troops at Concord during the initial stages of the Revolutionary War.

VANDALISM

1. "Second Inaugural Address"
Pages: 795-797 BofV
Grade Levels: 7-12
Description: Speech - Lincoln suggests that the Civil War may be God's way of serving justice for the acts of man. He makes special effort not to lay all of the blame on the South. He concludes with a promise to bring the nation together again.
Key Points: Lincoln seems compelled to point out the senselessness of the destruction that has beset the country. Destruction (vandalism) is often done in the name of a cause. Unfortunately, the senselessness of the destruction is often not evident until many years have passed.
Questions: Who can cite instances in the speech where Lincoln grieved over the fatalities and destruction caused by the war? Why do you think he acknowledged that both sides thought their cause was just? Did the South's sincerity make their actions right? What senseless destruction do we find in our world of today? What reasons might people cite for vandalizing something? Do you think these reasons make it right?

2. "Barbara Frietchie"
Pages: 720-721 BofV, 300-302 YP
Grade Levels: 7-12
Description: Poem - Describes Barbara Frietchie's loyalty and bravery when she boldly demands that her American flag not be defaced. She did this at the peril of her possessions and even her life.
Key Points: There are times when one person's courage helps us realize our need to respect the innate worth of certain things. When we lose respect for special things, we erode the underpinnings that hold our institutions together. It is easy to lose sight of our need to respect these things.
Questions: Why did everyone in Frederick hide their U.S. flags? How did Barbara Frietchie react to this cowardice? What did she say when the Confederate guns shot up her house? Are there things in our neighborhoods that are cherished by individuals just as much as Barbara Frietchie cherished her flag? Is it fair for another to vandalize or destroy just because they had nothing better to do or felt a need to vent their anger?

3. **"Thomas Jefferson and James Madison"**

Pages: 341-342 BofV

Grade Levels: 7-12

Description: Letters - Exchange of sentiments between two old friends who were bonded by a common experience and vision. Each expressed satisfaction in the service they rendered to future generations of Americans.

Key Points: Both Jefferson and Madison fashioned themselves as builders engaged in the construction of liberty. Each had the satisfaction in knowing they had constructed something that was enduring and good (Constitution, including the Bill of Rights). This satisfaction awaits anyone who builds something worthwhile. Those who destroy (vandalize) will never feel the same deep and enduring satisfaction.

Questions: What did these two men build that seemed to be the source of their friendship and feelings of accomplishment? Has anyone received a similar feeling of accomplishment and friendship? What caused this to be so? How might the feelings and friendships related to vandalism and destruction differ from that which is felt by those who build?

4. **"Childhood and Poetry"**

Pages: 339-340 BofV, 122-124 YP

Grade Levels: K-12

Description: Poem - Author describes an incident from childhood where he received a gift from someone he had never seen nor would see. He described the impact this act of kindness had on his life.

Key Points: There are builders and destroyers. The little boy who shared his toy sheep with a complete stranger was a builder of a better world. Taken in a similar vein, one who spends time picking up litter or mending a fence is a builder, while the individual who defaces property is a destroyer. Our world will reflect our percentage of builders and destroyers.

Questions: What act of kindness was described in the story? How did this kindness affect the author? What did the author mean when he said that all of humanity is somehow together? Can anyone describe how this story might have something to do with building up or tearing down of our physical surroundings? Would this be a second perspective on how all of humanity is somehow together? Why is it foolish to believe that vandalism only hurts or affects someone else?

5. "The Selfish Giant"

Pages: 292-295 BofV

Grade Levels: 4-9

Description: Tale - Describes how a giant learns a lesson about how kindness and consideration benefit everyone, including himself.

Key Points: Often we allow things to become run down (or destroy it ourselves) because we are selfish. The selfishness can take many forms, but it usually boils down to thinking only of ourselves and our own amusements. As in this story, the selfishness often comes back to hurt everyone, including ourselves.

Questions: What selfish act did the giant commit? What happened as a result of his sign? Who ended up suffering the most? How do we bring on harshness (winter, wind, frost) to our physical surroundings today? Who ultimately suffers when we damage our desks, bathrooms, lockers, etc? How can we collectively take care of what we have?

6. "Song of Life"

Pages: 142-143 BofV, 56-57 YP

Grade Levels: 7-12

Description: Poem - Describes three small acts of service and the far spread influence each act produced. Argues that little acts can become mighty with time.

Key Points: While little acts of service can grow to mighty contributions, so can little acts of vandalism grow to mighty acts of destruction.

Questions: What three small acts of service are described in the poem? Who can name some of the significant things that grew from these little acts? Can anyone think of places where little acts of vandalism add up to major messes? What happens that makes this so? How can you prevent these things from happening in your schools or neighborhoods?

7. "The Man Who Tossed Stones"

Pages: 113-114 YP

Grade Levels: 4-9

Description: Tale - Describes how a rich man eventually paid for his habit of cluttering the road with stones he had no use for. Now poor and desolate, the man stumbled on the very rocks he had carelessly discarded.

Key Points: The man channeled his disregard for others' welfare by cluttering areas that were not his own. He paid the price for his actions down the road. This often happens when neatness and appearance are limited to one's personal satisfaction. We often pay a personal price when we pay little heed to our environment.

Questions: What habit had the rich man practiced during his years of plenty? What does this say about his concern for others? What price did he ultimately pay? Who can think of instances where we show our disregard for everyone but ourselves? How might life pay us back? How is it that such things as litter and graffiti turn out to harm everyone in the long run?

VULGARITY

1. "America"

Pages: 718-719 BofV
Grade Levels: K-12
Description: Song - Outlines the essence of America.
Key Points: The words to this song are sublime in their power to communicate the greatness of our country. Contrast this language with the vulgar terms that have crept into our day to day language. Those who are wise will cultivate the higher expression of language.
Questions: What are some of the terms used to describe America? When you close your eyes and repeat these descriptive words, what do you see? Who can describe the difference between the use of these terms and the slang and vulgar words we often use? Which is the most impressive? Which will serve you best in your latter years?

2. "The Gettysburg Address"

Pages: 568-569 BofV
Grade Levels: 4-12
Description: Speech - Dedicates a burial site for many of the soldiers who died in defense of the nation. Lincoln eloquently states that his own words are inadequate when compared to the deeds of those who gave their lives in the battle. Concludes with a challenge to not let these men and their cause die in vain.
Key Points: While Lincoln states that his words will soon be forgotten, this is not what happens. The sublimity of his words and the simple eloquence of his thoughts are remembered and cherished by generations. Vulgarity is a poor substitute for spoken language in its highest form.
Questions: What is the setting for Lincoln's speech? Why do you think this speech is so well remembered? What sentences or thoughts impress you the most? Who can remember a speech that moved you to some emotion? Why do you think this is so? What do you think of those who have the ability to express themselves well? Why is correct speech an asset rather than a liability?

3. "Abraham Lincoln Offers Consolation"

Pages: 177 BofV
Grade Levels: 7-12
Description: Letter - President Lincoln expresses his heartfelt consolation over a mother's loss of her five sons to the cause of freedom.

Key Points:	The language in this letter is wonderful in its power to express deep and profound thought. It serves as a suitable contrast to vulgar language with all its limitations.
Questions:	Why did Lincoln compose the letter? What did Lincoln mean when he used the phrase, "and the solemn pride that must be yours to have laid so costly a sacrifice upon the altar of freedom?" What is it about these words that grabs one's attention? What is much of our language like today? What differences can you find between Lincoln's choice of words and those often used in conversation today? Which approach will serve you best when you must communicate in business or in similar critical situations?

4. "Diamonds and Toads"
Pages: 112-114 BofV
Grade Levels: 4-9

Description:	Tale - Describes the exploits of two sisters who are granted similar opportunities for service. One is kindhearted and is rewarded with treasures each time she speaks. The other is vain and self-centered, and toads and serpents spill out of her mouth each time she speaks.
Key Points:	The metaphor of diamonds symbolizing uplifting speech and toads and snakes representing vain and vulgar speech is well presented. Our speech conjures images that effect how others view us.
Questions:	How did the two sisters differ? What rewards for kindness came to the youngest? What rewards for vanity, laziness and vulgarity came to the eldest? Why do you think the fairy chose these particular rewards (or punishments)? How do you think vulgar speech is often viewed by others? Why is it wise to think and speak wholesome thoughts?

CONSIDERATIONS FOR FOLLOW-UP ACTIVITIES

NOTE: These follow-up activities are not prescriptive. They are offered as considerations only, in the hope that they might stimulate the creative thought processes of the teacher or parent. Obviously, such factors as setting, maturity levels and prevailing conditions must be factored in before a follow-up activity becomes a productive tool.

1. Students collectively draft a concise position statement (two or three sentences) on each virtue under consideration. The accumulation of these position statements can become the code of conduct for the class. Students might receive copy of finished code at the end of the year.

2. Design a service opportunity in school or community to provide opportunity to put virtues into practice.

3. Have students (anonymously) submit names of classmates or staff who are exemplary role models for the virtue. These names might be posted or recognized in some way.

4. Have students collect quotes that illustrate the positive aspect of the virtue. Post the quotes. May wish to provide incentives to encourage student participation.

5. Have students collect newspaper or magazine stories that illustrate the virtue. These contributions could be displayed on bulletin boards, compiled in a student-edited book or presented in some other appropriate way.

6. Use report card or similar document to offer positive comments on a student's efforts with respect to specific virtues.

7. Incorporate the virtue as a factor in determining candidates for recognition programs (i.e.; Student of the Month, Caught You Being Good).

8. Have students look for examples of the virtue in the regular curriculum. As examples are discovered, spend a few minutes of class time discussing the virtue in the context from which it has been found.

9. Design writing activities that illustrate the virtue. Various forms of poetry, short stories, fables, etc. are excellent mediums. Use the completed products as forums for further discussion.

10. Have students send out letters to students from other states or countries asking if they might write back on how they feel about a particular virtue or how presence or absence of the virtue is affecting their own classroom or school. Incentives can be added that reward such things as the longest reply, the most replies, the furthest distance reply, etc. The replies can be displayed or used in a variety of positive ways.

11. Design an assignment where students individually or collectively design a slogan that captures the essence of the virtue. Slogans can be committed to memory and used in some constructive way (i.e.; posted, printed and presented to parents, orally shared with other classes, etc.).

12. Have students compile a Hall of Fame that acknowledges famous people who owe their celebrity (at least in part) to their practice of the virtue. Have students submit names and then present their rationale for their choice. Allow class to discuss, debate or vote on final list of inductees.

13. Have students find examples of school rules, governing laws or practiced customs that have been developed due to the absence of a particular virtue. These examples can be discussed to illustrate how the individual practice of virtues would mean less rules and greater freedoms for all.

14. Have students find examples of advertisements that suggest behaviors that run counter to the virtue. Discuss what the advertisements are trying to accomplish and the ramifications involved.

15. Ask students for names of people who might come in to talk about the positive aspects of the virtue. Past graduates, parents, local celebrities and business employers can be good choices.

16. Set up pairings with younger grade students where your students can have discussions or give talks on the positive aspects of a virtue. (Note: Students might need some coaching on appropriate ways to share what they have learned.)

17. Set up situations where students can demonstrate the virtue by serving classmates or other students in the school (i.e.; tutoring, being a friend, etc.).

18. Have students write thank you notes to celebrities or individuals (i.e.; school or community people) who have demonstrated the virtue in some observable way. Students might explain in the note what impressed them about the individual's behavior.

19. Design an art assignment where the virtue is illustrated in some concrete or abstract form. Have students describe verbally or in writing their rationale for their art choice.

20. Have students select a career that is significantly interrelated to the virtue. Discuss reasons for choice to illustrate why the mastery of the virtue is tied in with successful performance of the job. Students might select a "career a day" or a "career a week" until the practical connections between the virtue and job success are thoroughly covered.

21. Allow students to individually or collectively write and perform short skits that illustrate the virtue in some meaningful and practical way. Skits can be performed for parents, other classes, etc.

22. Have students bring in examples of television shows or movies that send the wrong message about the virtue. Follow up with letters to the stations, sponsors, actors, companies, etc. that explain reasons for concern and suggestions for improvement.

23. Have students bring in paperback books that serve as good or bad examples of the virtue. These can serve as a mini-library of books available for student checkout. Have students devise and carry out the procedures and rules that govern the process. Develop a process where students can report on what they have read.

24. Have students clip out pictures from magazines or discarded books that illustrate the virtue in practice. These would serve as the basis for a collage that could be displayed in the room or hallway.

25. Brainstorm with class to identify the various ways the virtue is demonstrated in real life. Might follow up with discussions on specific examples or rank the various examples in order of importance.

> NOTE: The authors express their appreciation to the staff of the Center for the Advancement of Ethics and Character at Boston University for their compilation, "100 Ways to Promote Character Education." Many of the Follow-up Considerations listed above are adaptations from the Center's compilation.